Dyslexia

"Gavin Reid is a trusted friend and advisor to parents and teachers of children who learn 'outside the box'. In this extraordinarily comprehensive guidebook, he explains current research on why some children have difficulties and offers practical suggestions on how to help. This valuable resource should be essential reading for anyone concerned with children's learning."

Jane M. Healy, Educational Psychologist and author of 'Different Learners: Identifying, Preventing, and Treating Your Child's Learning Problems'

"There is no-one better placed than Gavin Reid to provide such a comprehensive, up-to-date and clear guide to dyslexia. He tackles the confusion and controversies that surround this area, and empowers parents to communicate as partners with teachers to achieve the best for each child. His approach is calm, considered and respectful, valuing the range of abilities and also acknowledging the emotional needs of young people with dyslexia. I would highly recommend this book to anyone who has a child who is, or who might be, dyslexic, and to all who are involved in teaching children and young people."

Jennie Guise, Chartered Psychologist, DysGuise Ltd, UK

"Informative, engaging and empowering... Gavin's new book is a must read for all educators and any parent who has a child who learns differently. Gavin's clear style, unique care, passion and expertise help provide the keys to unlocking the potential of our young people with dyslexia. With his insights and practical recommendations this book will be extremely beneficial in homes, schools and colleges worldwide."

Mandy Appleyard, Principal Teacher & Educational Consultant, Fun Track Learning Centre, Perth, Western Australia

"Gavin Reid's humane and informed approach is ever more evident in his second edition. His insights into the difficulties encountered by parents are highly accurate and very helpful as is his advice on how to counter them."

Craig Dobson, Head of Science, Thames High School, New Zealand

"Gavin Reid has produced a wonderfully written book offering a fresh perspective on dyslexia. A very useful guide, offering clear and concise information, together with invaluable insights, designed to inform and empower parents seeking help for their children. Most certainly a work that I would consider an important addition to all professional libraries."

Marcia Mann, Founding Fellow and Vice President, Academy of Orton – Gillingham Practitioners and Educators, New York

Dyslexia

A Complete Guide for Parents and Those Who Help Them

Second Edition

Gavin Reid

A John Wiley & Sons, Ltd., Publication

This second edition first published 2011
© 2011 John Wiley & Sons, Ltd.

Edition history: John Wiley & Sons, Ltd. (1e, 2004)

Wiley-Blackwell is an imprint of John Wiley & Sons, formed by the merger of Wiley's global Scientific, Technical and Medical business with Blackwell Publishing.

Registered Office
John Wiley & Sons Ltd, The Atrium, Southern Gate, Chichester, West Sussex, PO19 8SQ, United Kingdom

Editorial Offices
The Atrium, Southern Gate, Chichester, West Sussex, PO19 8SQ, UK
350 Main Street, Malden, MA 02148-5020, USA
9600 Garsington Road, Oxford, OX4 2DQ, UK

For details of our global editorial offices, for customer services, and for information about how to apply for permission to reuse the copyright material in this book please see our website at www.wiley.com/wiley-blackwell.

The right of Gavin Reid to be identified as the author of this work has been asserted in accordance with the UK Copyright, Designs and Patents Act 1988.

Wiley also publishes its books in a variety of electronic formats. Some content that appears in print may not be available in electronic books.

Designations used by companies to distinguish their products are often claimed as trademarks. All brand names and product names used in this book are trade names, service marks, trademarks or registered trademarks of their respective owners. The publisher is not associated with any product or vendor mentioned in this book. This publication is designed to provide accurate and authoritative information in regard to the subject matter covered. It is sold on the understanding that the publisher is not engaged in rendering professional services. If professional advice or other expert assistance is required, the services of a competent professional should be sought.

Library of Congress Cataloging-in-Publication Data

Reid, Gavin, 1950–
    Dyslexia : a complete guide for parents and those who help them / Gavin Reid. – 2nd ed.
        p. cm.
    Includes bibliographical references and index.
    ISBN 978-0-470-97374-5 (hardback) – ISBN 978-0-470-97373-8 (paper)
    1. Dyslexic children–Popular works.   2. Dyslexia–Popular works.   I. Title.
    RJ496.A5R45 2011   *616.85*   OCLC   7/21/11
    371.91'44–dc22
                      Rei
                                                              2011009314

A catalogue record for this book is available from the British Library.

This book is published in the following electronic formats: ePDFs 9781119970903; Wiley Online Library 9781119970897

Typeset in 12/14pt Times New Roman by Aptara Inc., New Delhi, India.
Printed in Malaysia by Ho Printing (M) Sdn Bhd

1   2011

Contents

About the author

Dr. Gavin Reid
Ph.D., M.A., M.App.Sci., M.Ed.,
B.Ed., AMBDA, Assoc. F.B.P.S.
E mail: gavinreid66@gmail.com;
www.drgavinreid.com

Gavin Reid is an educational psychologist based in Vancouver, Canada. He was also visiting professor at the University of British Columbia, in Vancouver, Canada and is currently a consultant on learning disabilities at the Center for Child Evaluation and Teaching (CCET) in Kuwait and a consultant with Global Educational Consultants, the Institute for Child Education and Psychology (Europe) and the Open University in the UK. He was a senior lecturer in the Department of Educational Studies, Moray House School of Education, University of Edinburgh from 1991 to 2007. He wrote and developed the first master's course on dyslexia in the UK in 1993, which became the basis for the Open University (OU) course 'Difficulties in Literacy Development'. He has been a consultant for the OU since 1999.

He is a co-founder and director to the Red Rose School for children with specific learning difficulties in St. Anne's on Sea, Lancashire and co-founder of the Lighthouse School in Cairo, Egypt. He has made over 800 conference and seminar presentations in more than 65 countries, including Norway, Denmark, Sweden, Germany, the United States, New Zealand, Australia, Hong Kong, Singapore, Iceland, Poland, Republic of Ireland, Slovakia, Croatia, Ljubljana, Estonia, Greece, Cyprus, Thailand, Austria, Slovenia, Malta, Israel, Egypt, Gambia, Canada, Dubai, Kuwait, Spain and Hungary.

Currently he has 25 books in print in the area of teacher education in the field of dyslexia, literacy, learning styles and motivation, and classroom management. Many of his books are used as course texts in courses throughout the UK and in many other countries. These include: *Dyslexia: A Practitioner's Handbook* (3rd edition, Wiley, 2009); *Dyslexia: A Complete Guide for Parents* (Wiley, 2004); *Dyslexia and Inclusion* (2005); *Motivating Learners in the Classroom: Ideas and Strategies* (2007) and *Learning Styles and Inclusion* (2005). He is co-author with Shannon Green of *100 Ideas for Supporting Pupils with Dyslexia and Dyslexia: A Teaching Assistants Handbook* (2007). A number of his books have been translated into Arabic, Polish, French, Italian and Greek. He is also the co-author of a computer-aided diagnostic assessment and profiling procedures (Special Needs Assessment Profile [SNAP]), which has received three national award commendations and was winner of the Special Needs Category at the NASEN/TES book awards in Birmingham, UK in March 2006.

He has been invited to be external examiner at 15 universities worldwide for PhD candidates and master's courses. He was a member of the British Dyslexia Association Teacher Training Accreditation Board from 1996 to 2007 and was overseas patron for the Learning and Behaviour Charitable Trust in New Zealand. He is the international consultant for the Canadian Academy of Therapeutic Tutors and advisor to the International Dyslexia Association board (BC Branch) and consultant to the parents' organization All Special Kids (ASK) in Geneva, Switzerland. He is also on the Editorial Board of two International Journals in Dyslexia and Literacy.

Gavin Reid uses his experiences as a teacher, educational psychologist, researcher, university lecturer and, most importantly, as a parent in his work.

Preface and Acknowledgments

May I extend a warm welcome to you as a reader of this second edition of *Dyslexia: A Complete Guide for Parents*. You will note I have also extended the title to include . . . *and Those who Help Them*. It is important that parents should not be seen as separate or isolated. Collaboration is the key and communication is the means. Parents and teachers need to work as informed partners and that is the thinking behind extending the title. I also feel that although this book is written for parents, many professionals will also benefit from reading it.

This second edition has developed many of the themes and ideas in the first edition (published in 2004). The overall theme of this book is to provide parents/carers and families with knowledge and understanding of dyslexia. The aim is to empower parents and to provide them with the confidence through knowledge and understanding to deal with the range of professionals they may encounter at different stages of their child's education. The book also considers post-school issues, such as college and the workplace, and provides insights into how the needs of people with dyslexia can be met beyond school. There is also a chapter on self-esteem and the emotional needs of young people with dyslexia. These factors are important in meeting learning needs.

The author lives and works in Canada and does a great deal of work in the US and Canada, but has a sound knowledge of the situation in the UK and Europe, as well as in Australia and NZ and the Middle East. It is anticipated that this knowledge will help to make the book applicable to international audiences.

There has been increased recognition of dyslexia in many countries over the years and the numbers being assessed as dyslexic are increasing, but often the accompanying support and interventions are not available. This can be confusing for parents and it is the aim of this book to clarify any confusion and to provide straightforward guidance. Parents can be confused by the vast range of programmes and interventions as well by as the different policies and procedures adopted by different countries and school districts.

I hope you will find this book comprehensive, as it is intended to cover almost all the areas that parents will want to know about, including research, assessment and teaching. The most recent references and research have been considered. It is also hoped that parents will be able to identify with the case studies and suggestions and relate these to their own situation. This book also aims to clarify and explain some of terms used, particularly the terms used in psychologists' reports.

There has been a considerable number of significant breakthroughs and advances in the field of dyslexia in recent years and it is important that parents are kept informed and understand the implications of these for the current and future education of their child.

I have been fortunate to have benefited from considerable support in writing this book. Parents' associations have been happy to contribute ideas and examples, centers of good practice such as the Red Rose School in Lancashire, UK run by my good friends Sionah and Colin Lannen, my wife Shannon Green, who contributed with ideas, suggestions and critical comment when necessary, and my wide international network of friends and supports in many countries, particularly Canada, the US, Scotland, England, Ireland, Australia, Kuwait, Switzerland, New Zealand, Cairo, Hong Kong and Singapore, as well as participants in the online course for parents that Shannon Green and I run through ICEPE (Europe) (see appendix).

I have been fortunate enough to give talks, workshops and seminars to parents' groups in over 50 countries and to teachers in over 65 countries. It is always heartening and gratifying to speak with parents. One can learn so much from them, and their sincerity, and sometimes anxieties, can be heartfelt. As a parent myself of a young person with special needs I can understand and empathize with these parents and it has always been my personal and professional aspiration to provide as much support to parents as possible, both locally nationally and internationally. I sincerely hope that this book contributes to that support.

Gavin Reid
Vancouver, Canada

Chapter 1

What is dyslexia?

Dyslexia is a term that most of you will have heard of and will have some idea of its features. Many professionals you deal with will claim they know what dyslexia is. Yet in reality there are many misunderstandings and misconceptions about dyslexia as well as a fair amount of controversy. This has a direct impact on parents, and particularly those parents finding out for the first time that they have a child who is dyslexic. In the United States and Canada we often use the term 'learning disability', an umbrella term, which also includes dyslexia. In the UK and Europe the term 'dyslexia' is used more openly — governments recognize it and legislation and educational policy take it into account. Similarly in New Zealand and in Australia, there have been considerable advances in the use of the term dyslexia in recent years. In the Middle East and Asia, both US and UK models are used and the term is also applied more openly there too. Dyslexia is an internationally accepted term and the condition affects children and adults in every country and in every culture irrespective of the language or the education system.

Dyslexia: A Complete Guide for Parents and Those Who Help Them, Second Edition. Gavin Reid.
© 2011 John Wiley & Sons, Ltd. Published 2011 by John Wiley & Sons, Ltd.

Every day more and more parents are told that their child is dyslexic and immediately alarm bells start to ring. They ask themselves, 'Could we have found out about this earlier? What are the social and emotional considerations? What are the educational implications, how might it affect exams, college and careers? What exactly is dyslexia? What can we do to help?'

Having been in the position of assessing and identifying many thousands of children with dyslexia, I am fully aware of the questions, anxieties, concerns and the hopes of parents. I am also aware that there has been good progress in acceptance and support for dyslexia. But there is still a great deal to be done and in many areas parents are left confused and concerned. I have also been in the position of being told by a professional that my son has severe special needs and although this is difficult to accept, one of the first feelings one experiences is that of relief — relief that your 'gut feeling' that something was not right was not just a figment of your imagination but was in fact correct. With this knowledge parents have a clearer idea of what they have to deal with, and at last can set about doing that. This last point is important because this book is not intended to be a catalog of despair, but rather a 'lifeline' and source of hope for many thousands of parents who may find themselves searching for answers and desperately seeking guidance and advice.

This opening chapter provides a straightforward account and description of dyslexia. It also touches on the overlap with other disabilities such as dyspraxia, dyscalculia and attention deficit hyperactivity disorder (ADHD). This potential overlap can be confusing and often prevents the most appropriate intervention from being put into place.

Shannon Green and I run an online course on dyslexia for parents which includes a discussion forum. It is interesting to receive communication from parents in different parts of the world regarding their concerns. In many cases I am struck by the similarities no matter where they. Consider this parent's experience:

> We have a nine-year-old boy and for three of his school years he displayed signs of dyslexia. This was only brought to our attention at the end of last year which was quite a shock as, if we had been told earlier, maybe I would have handled situations differently with homework and so on. It took until this year to have him assessed.

This is not unusual, many parents wait a long time for a formal diagnosis. Most education authorities operate what might be referred to as a 'wait to fail' model. That means the child needs to be have fallen quite far behind before an assessment takes place – essentially, the child has to have failed. This is a reactive model and one that can cause considerable problems, frustrations and a sense of hopelessness. Some education providers are now attempting to redress this situation by developing more proactive policies. For example, in the US the policy known as 'response to intervention', in theory at least, is intended to be proactive and identify children with difficulties at a young age before the difficulty becomes too entrenched. This policy, although theoretically commendable, is not without its critics.

There are other examples of early intervention and school-based assessment procedures in the US, Canada and UK which seem to be successful and will be discussed in chapter 3 (Crombie, Knight & Reid, 2004; Dyslexia Scotland, 2010).

So, what is dyslexia?

My view of dyslexia is that it is a difference in how children (and adults) process information. That is, how they take information in (input); how they understand it, memorize it and organize it in their mind (cognitive processing); and how they demonstrate they know this information (output). Children and young people with dyslexia can have differences (which can take the form of difficulties) at all of these stages – input, processing and output. Generally, these differences can be seen in relation to print, but other areas of learning can also be affected. That is why dyslexic difficulties can persist even when reading skills improve. Dyslexia can have an impact on all areas of learning. As children go through school they often use compensatory strategies to deal with challenges and can become quite adept at this.

Characteristics of dyslexia

Dyslexia relates to how information is processed

This means that dyslexia involves more than reading, but affects learning, including understanding and following oral instructions, as well as reading accurately and fluently and presenting written work.

Children with dyslexia can have difficulty learning through the auditory modality

The auditory modality refers to listening. This can be problematic as much of the teaching in school is through the auditory modality. It is important therefore to ensure that teaching and learning is multisensory – auditory, visual, kinesthetic (experiential) and tactile (through touch).

Reading, spelling and writing difficulties

Reading, spelling and writing difficulties are characteristic of dyslexia. This includes reading speed and writing speed.

Reading

The common view is that children with dyslexia have difficulties with sounds (phonemes) – that is, the smallest unit of sound in a word. They can have difficulty in distinguishing between similar sounds and sound combinations. They may also have difficulty in identifying where in a word a particular sound comes and recognizing the same sound in different words. This is referred to a phonological awareness and is often one of the early indicators of dyslexia. It can sometimes be noted in a difficulty with nursery rhymes.

Spelling

Although spelling and reading use different processes they are both features of dyslexia. Spelling can often take bizarre forms and even after many years of tuition some children still experience difficulties with the same word. They may have difficulty in remembering and applying spelling rules so the word 'easier', for example, may be spelt 'easyer'. They may also make visual and phonological errors. Spelling can be problematic but with specialized spellcheckers such as TextHelp™, spelling can usually be quite readily corrected.

Writing

Writing can be difficult on two counts. Handwriting can be a problem and this will be discussed later in relation to the possible overlap with dyspraxia. But it is strongly advised that the young person with dyslexia, as soon as possible, becomes proficient in the use of a word processor. There are many excellent computer programs available to help with this (see Appendix 2).

Some – in fact quite a number of children with dyslexia – can become quite expert and very creative in writing. But this can still be a problem as often they have difficulty in expressing what they mean. This can be frustrating and can result in under-accomplishment. With a clear structure for work this can be overcome. Indeed, many successful authors are dyslexic!

Dyslexia is individual

Children with dyslexia may have slightly different characteristics from each other. They may all have some common core difficulties, for example reading or spelling, but the actual characteristics and the nature of the difficulties can be different. It is important to view each child with dyslexia as an individual.

Children with dyslexia can have difficulty remembering information

Memory can be problematic. This can apply to working memory and short-term memory as well as long-term memory. This means that remembering oral instructions can be challenging, especially if a list of items is presented at the same time. The short-term, working memory can only hold a limited amount of information at any one time, and children and adults with dyslexia can have difficulty in remembering accurately even a limited amount, so it is best to provide one instruction at any one time.

Long-term memory relates to recalling information that has been learnt some time previously. Much of the success of retrieval of information learnt depends on how well the information is understood and organized at the time of learning. This will be followed up in some detail in later chapters.

Difficulty in organizing information

Whether we are aware of it or not, we always make some attempt to organize new information. We might group new items to be remembered into one familiar category. Organizing information is important if we are recalling a sequence of events, and children with dyslexia can have difficulty with this. This can also affect their performance in examinations unless some supports are in place.

Overlap

There may be an overlap between other learning difficulties such as dyspraxia (difficulty with coordination and movement), dysgraphia (difficulty with handwriting), dyscalculia (difficulty with numbers) and attention deficit hyperactivity disorder (ADHD; attention and focussing difficulties). Children with dyslexia can experience some elements of the other difficulties, but this would usually be secondary to the main difficulties relating to dyslexia.

Phonological difficulties

This is one of the main difficulties associated with dyslexia. These difficulties can be seen at various levels. Adams (1990) identified at least five levels of difficulty:

- knowledge of nursery rhymes, which involves only an ear for the sounds of words;
- awareness of rhyme and alliteration, which requires both sensitivity to the sounds and an ability to focus on certain sounds;
- blending of phonemes and splitting of syllables to identify phonemes — this demands an awareness that words can be sub-divided into smaller sounds;
- phoneme segmentation requires a thorough understanding that words can be analyzed into a series of phonemes;

- phoneme manipulation requires a child not only to understand and produce phonemes, but also to be able to manipulate them by addition, deletion or transposition.

It is important that intervention tackles phonological processing. It is much easier to find appropriate intervention for younger children as most reading programs deal with phonological processing and many books for very young readers emphasize the different sounds in words. But it can be challenging for older children as by the time they are teenagers they are usually more interested in the content of books even though they may have difficulty in reading them and phonics programs can be quite deskilling and perhaps demoralizing for them. In this case it is important to use an approach that relates to meaning as well as phonics.

Early indicators

There are a number of screening tests that can be used, but it is important to appreciate that these are not meant to be diagnostic — they can alert you to the possibility of dyslexia but a full assessment is necessary before you can be sure that your child has dyslexia.

Below are some areas that need to be considered in the early detection of dyslexia.

- **Communication and language**: Poor phonological skills and a lack of awareness of rhyme and rhythm can indicate that they may have later difficulties in learning to read and write.
- **Difficulty in listening to stories**: This can indicate that they have a difficulty with the auditory modality and following the sequence of a story, as well as attention and focusing difficulties.
- **Memory**: Children who are unable to remember more than two items of information, for example, may have a difficulty with working memory.
- **Sequence of events in a story:** This can be challenging for children with dyslexia as they may have difficulty in organizing information and placing it in an order of events.

- **Speech**: They may have some articulation problems, although this is not always the case.
- **Naming and ordering items in sequence**: Remembering the names of common items can be challenging. They may also show inconsistent performance in recalling names of objects (i.e., doing it correctly one day but not the next).
- **Physical development and movement**: This can be a feature of early identification Young children with dyslexia may have some fine or gross motor difficulties, but again this is not always the case. Coordination skills can be identified at this early stage through observation in general physical activities and in writing. Balance has been found to be an important ability for learning. Fawcett and Nicolson (2008) reported on their earlier research in which they indicated that children who are poor at balance tasks while doing something else are likely to encounter other learning problems. This can be done by asking the child to balance on one foot while reciting a rhyme.

You will have noted that identifying dyslexia is not straightforward as there are many combinations of difficulties that children with dyslexia may have. The chapter on assessment (see chapter 3) will show how these can be narrowed down to arrive at a diagnosis. It is important for parents to understand this as they will have to interpret the school and educational psychologist's reports.

Some general factors that can indicate dyslexia

Pre-school

Concern may be raised in a pre-school child if some of the following are present:

- forgetfulness;
- speech difficulty;
- reversal of letters;
- difficulty remembering letters of the alphabet;
- difficulty remembering the sequence of letters of the alphabet;
- a history of dyslexia in the family;

- coordination difficulties (e.g., bumping into furniture);
- tasks that require fine motor skills (e.g., tying shoelaces);
- slow at reacting to some tasks;
- reluctance to concentrate on a task for a reasonable period of time;
- confusing words that sound similar.

School age

- reluctance to go to school;
- not enjoying school;
- reluctance to read;
- difficulty learning words and letters;
- difficulty with phonics (sounds);
- poor memory;
- coordination difficulties;
- losing items;
- difficulty forming letters;
- difficulty copying;
- difficulty coloring;
- poor organization of materials.

After around two years at school

- hesitant at reading;
- poor word-attack skills;
- poor knowledge of the sounds and words continued;
- difficulty recognizing where in words particular sounds come from;
- spelling difficulty;
- substitution of words when reading (e.g., bus for car).

Middle school years

As above but also:

- behavior difficulties;
- frustration;
- abilities in subjects apart from reading.

Secondary/high school as above but also:

- slow to complete homework;
- misreading words;
- asking others for information;
- poor general knowledge;
- taking longer than others in most written tasks.

College/university difficulty in:

- remembering and organizing class timetable;
- keeping appointments;
- planning study time;
- performing in exams to the same level as in continuous assessment;
- planning essays and elaborating main points;
- reading and writing at the same rate as others.

The above lists are some of the indicators. People with dyslexia do not need to show all of these − even two or three can be sufficient in some cases and can justify a full assessment.

Definition of dyslexia

There are many definitions of dyslexia and most countries have their own; further, you will often find a number of definitions used within one a single country. Usually these definitions are statements that do not mean much to parents − or in fact to some educators! They are usually couched in professional terminology and they try to incorporate a broad description using as few words as possible. Here are some of the definitions.

The International Dyslexia Association (IDA)

Dyslexia is a specific learning disability that is neurological in origin. It is characterized by difficulties with accurate and/or fluent word recognition and by poor spelling and decoding abilities. These diffi-culties typically result from a deficit in the phonological component of language that is often unexpected in relation to other cognitive abil-ities and the provision of effective classroom instruction. Secondary consequences may include problems in reading comprehension and reduced reading experience that can impede the growth of vocabu-lary and background knowledge. (Adopted by the Board of Directors: 12 November 2002. IDA Fact sheet revised March 2008; accessed July 2010, http://www.interdys.org/FactSheets.htm)

The Canadian Learning Disabilities Association (January 2002)

Provides a lengthy definition on learning disabilities which incorporates dyslexia. It is in fact quite detailed and helpful.

Learning disabilities refers to a number of disorders that may affect the acquisition, organization, retention, understanding or use of verbal or nonverbal information. These disorders affect learning in individu-als who otherwise demonstrate at least average abilities essential for thinking and/or reasoning. As such, learning disabilities are distinct from global intellectual disabilities. Learning disabilities result from impairments in one or more processes related to perceiving, thinking, remembering or learning. These include, but are not limited to: lan-guage processing, phonological processing, visual spatial processing, processing speed, memory and attention, and executive functions (e.g. planning and decision-making).

Learning disabilities range in severity and may interfere with the acquisition and use of one or more of the following:

- Oral language (e.g., listening, speaking, understanding)
- Reading (e.g., decoding, phonetic knowledge, word recognition, comprehension)
- Written language (e.g., spelling and written expression)
- Mathematics (e.g., computation, problem solving)

Learning disabilities may also involve difficulties with organizational skills, social perception, social interaction and perspective taking.

Learning disabilities are life-long. The way in which they are expressed may vary over an individual's lifetime, depending on the interaction between the demands of the environment and the individual's strengths and needs. Learning disabilities are suggested by unexpected academic under-achievement or achievement that is maintained only by unusually high levels of effort and support.

Learning disabilities are due to genetic and/or neurological factors or injury that alters brain function in a manner that affects one or more processes related to learning. These disorders are not due primarily to hearing and/or vision problems, social-economic factors, cultural or linguistic differences, lack of motivation, inadequate or insufficient instruction, although these factors may further complicate the challenges faced by individuals with learning disabilities. Learning disabilities may co-exist with other disorders such as attentional, behavioral or emotional disorders, sensory impairments, or other medical conditions.

British Dyslexia Association (BDA)

Dyslexia is a specific learning difficulty which mainly affects the development of literacy and language related skills. It is likely to be present at birth and to be lifelong in its effects. It is characterised by difficulties with phonological processing, rapid naming, working memory, processing speed, and the automatic development of skills that may not match up to an individual's other cognitive abilities. It tends to be resistant to conventional teaching methods, but its effects can be mitigated by appropriately specific intervention, including the application of information technology and supportive counseling. (http://www.bdadyslexia.org.uk/whatisdyslexia.html; accessed November 2009)

Republic of Ireland

Dyslexia is manifested in a continuum of specific learning difficulties related to the acquisition of basic skills in reading, spelling and or writing such difficulties being unexpected in relation to an individual's other abilities and educational experiences. Dyslexia can be described at the neurological, cognitive and behavioral levels. It is typically characterised by inefficient information processing, including difficulties in phonological processing, working memory, rapid naming, and automaticity of basic skills. Difficulties in organisation, sequencing and motor skills may also be present. (Task Force on Dyslexia in Republic of Ireland, 2001, p. 28)

New Zealand

Dyslexia is a spectrum of specific learning difficulties and is evident when accurate and/or fluent reading and writing skills, particularly phonological awareness, develop incompletely or with great difficulty. This may include difficulties with one or more of reading, writing, spelling, numeracy, or musical notation. (Dyslexia, Ministry of Education, 2010, p. 3)

You will note that there are many similarities in these definitions from different countries. It might be a good idea to ask the school your child attends how they define dyslexia as this may have some bearing on the intervention that is to be used.

Having developed and taught a great many training programs for parents and for schools I have developed the definition below as a blueprint for a working definition of dyslexia:

Dyslexia is a processing difference, often characterized by difficulties in literacy acquisition affecting reading, writing and spelling. It can also have an impact on cognitive processes such as memory, speed of processing, time management, co-ordination and automaticity. There may be visual and/or phonological difficulties and there are usually some discrepancies in educational performances.

There will individual differences and individual variation and it is therefore important to consider learning styles and the learning and work context when planning intervention and accommodations (Reid, 2009).

The main points in this definition are:

- **Processing difference:** This can highlight the differences between children with dyslexia and between dyslexic children and other children.
- **Difficulties in literacy acquisition:** Without doubt this is one of the key areas of dyslexia as it is usually difficulties with reading that first alert the parent or the teacher.
- **Cognitive processes:** Cognition means learning and processing information and it is this that can be challenging for children with dyslexia. This refers to how information is processed and this affects memory, processing speed, the ability to retain and transfer information, to utilize prior learning and to develop automaticity in learning (being able to do something automatically and consistently).
- **Discrepancies in educational performances:** This is often one of the most obvious indicators of dyslexia. There can be a difference between the reasoning and the processing abilities. This means that students with dyslexia can solve problems and can reason, but often have difficulty in displaying this in written form. Discrepancies in different areas of performance within different areas of the curriculum can often be noted and often this is very obvious between written and oral work.
- **Individual differences:** It is important to recognize that students with dyslexia are individuals and their individual learning differences need to be respected. Not all students with dyslexia will have the same profile, although they may all meet the criteria for dyslexia.
- **Learning and work context:** Some learning and work contexts can highlight the person's dyslexic traits while others can minimize the impact of their dyslexia. For example, if a dyslexic person is attempting to locate information from a library they may have difficulty in accessing an index, finding the appropriate book and locating the information in that book. Without guidance this kind of task can be challenging for students with dyslexia. Other tasks such as those that involve some degree of creativity or visual processing may be easier. Getting the task and the environment right for learning is important and highly important for the person with dyslexia.

Four points seem to emerge from all the definitions shown above. These are:

1. Dyslexia is developmental – that means that it can become more obvious as the person has to tackle different kinds of tasks such as those involving reading and learning.
2. An understanding that the central characteristics of dyslexia relate to literacy.
3. An appreciation that different and special teaching and learning approaches are necessary.
4. An acknowledgement that there can be additional secondary factors associated with dyslexia.

Parents should ask educational authorities and school administrators how they meet the needs of children with dyslexia. It is important that in response to this request schools can comment on the following:

1. The need to provide a clear statement on dyslexia. Additionally in appendix 3 to this book there is information on DSM-IV and DSM-V. These refer to the Diagnostic Statistical Manual published by the American Psychological Association and is generally regarded as a leading authority for professionals seeking advice on definitions and characteristics of learning difficulties.
2. An indication of the precise identification criteria used for dyslexia in the school district.
3. An indication of how these criteria will be used, by whom and when.
4. A description of the kind of challenges the student with dyslexia will experience at different stages of schooling and in different areas of the curriculum, followed by an indication of the type of supports that will be implemented.
5. The need to provide parents with pointers to resources, books, programs, approaches and technology that can be used at home.
6. An indication of the role that parents will/can play in identification and support.
7. The implications for preparing the student for formal examinations and the type of additional supports and accommodations that can be made available to the student.

8. The implications for curricular choice and access and show how the school can accommodate to the student's learning needs.
9. The different levels of training the staff have in dyslexia.
10. The provision for the longer term, particularly the transition to post-school study and how the school can ensure that appropriate support and information is provided to students, parents and other relevant professionals (e.g., career advisors).

Parents can play a key role in ensuring that schools provide them with this type of information. In my experience most schools will be able to do this, but may not unless parents specifically ask for it.

Common characteristics of other related learning disorders

The International Dyslexia Association (IDA) has produced a series of informative fact sheets on their website (http://www.interdys. org/FactSheets.htm).

One of those sheets relates to the overlap between dyslexia and other learning difficulties. Some of the key points relating to this are shown below and will be developed in later chapters.

Dysgraphia (handwriting)

- Unsure of handedness.
- Poor or slow handwriting.
- Messy and unorganized papers.
- Difficulty copying.
- Poor fine motor skills.
- Difficulty remembering the kinesthetic movements to form letters correctly.

Dyscalculia (math)

- Difficulty counting accurately.

- May misread numbers.
- Difficulty memorizing and retrieving math facts.
- Difficulty copying math problems and organizing written work.
- Many calculation errors.
- Difficulty retaining math vocabulary and concepts.

Attention deficit hyperactivity disorder (ADHD; attention)

- Inattention.
- Variable attention.
- Distractibility.
- Impulsivity.
- Hyperactivity

Dyspraxia (motor skills)

- Difficulty planning and coordinating body movements.
- Difficulty coordinating facial muscles to produce sounds.

Executive function/organization

- Loses papers.
- Poor sense of time.
- Forgets homework.
- Messy desk.
- Overwhelmed by too much input.
- Works slowly.

It is important to recognize that many of these syndromes can overlap. This means that some children with dyslexia can have attention difficulties or movement and coordination difficulties. This is not always the case but we should be open to the possibility of overlap between the various syndromes. Obtaining a label is important, but it is also important to obtain an individual educational program for your child and find a school with sufficient resources to ensure the program is implemented. Obtaining the presenting difficulties and strengths is therefore just as important as the label. It is crucial to obtain a learning profile of your child based on a detailed assessment. This learning profile will provide guidance for intervention and it is important that this is obtained. It should be detailed enough to provide the range of challenges your child experiences and how these can be met in the learning environment. There should also be reference to the type of support you can provide at home.

Parents' challenges

This chapter has provided information on what dyslexia is and how it can be recognized by parents and educators in different countries. It is important that parents' needs are listened to and considered. Obtaining this very often stems from the assertiveness of parents themselves advocating for their right to be heard. It is important that this is carried out in an informed manner. Many parents tell me that they have been a catalyst for some of the initiatives carried out in schools for children with dyslexia. Parents therefore have an important role to play.

Consider this from a parent of a dyslexic child (summarized from a transcript of a video I made at a conference in Toronto, Canada). He discusses the impact on his daughter who is dyslexic of bullying at school. He described the situation when a basically happy young girl seemed to change and was coming home devastated. He indicated that one of his concerns regarded her self-esteem as that seemed to be affected quite a bit by the bullying. Both parents discussed the situation with their daughter and together they came up with a plan of action. They decided to ask the school if they could do a PowerPoint presentation on dyslexia with the aim of educating their daughter's peer group about what dyslexia is and the need to accept and acknowledge children's differences. The consensus was that the PowerPoint presentation was successful and had the desired impact on her peer group. This was an informed and successful response by the parents and their daughter to a potential crisis. For many parents, however, dealing with dyslexia can be a leap into uncertainty and anxiety. They can face conflicting advice and opinions, and often have to stick by their own instinct on what is best for their child.

During the research for this book I found that some of the priorities harbored by parents included the following:

- maintaining their child's self-esteem;
- helping their child start new work when he/she had not consolidated previous work;
- protecting the dignity of the child when dealing with professionals/therapists;
- helping in the child's personal organization;
- dealing with peer insensitivity;
- dealing with misconceptions of dyslexia.

These responses touch on some of the key areas, particularly the emotional aspect of dyslexia. They also touch on the misunderstandings and misconceptions that can exist on dyslexia. Some of the other key issues that parents have to deal with include the following:

- **Frustration:** Some parents can experience frustration and feel that their child's needs are not being met. This may highlight the gulf that can be sometimes be seen between home and school. This underlines the importance of effective and shared communication.
- **Trust:** Parents have to place their trust in the school system. They may or may not have some choice over the system they choose. Many have not. Some school may not recognize dyslexia and this can present a challenge and cause a great deal of anxiety. In this case parents may have to play a role in providing information on dyslexia to the school and to work with the school to provide information on dyslexia.
- **Understanding:** Knowledge and awareness of dyslexia vary from country to country and indeed within countries and school districts. Having spoken on dyslexia to parents' associations in many different countries this is becoming very apparent — almost without exception a scheduled and advertised talk to a parents' association will include many teachers in the audience. It is important that parents understand what dyslexia is, and this should be explained to them as soon as

their child is assessed. It is equally important that teachers are aware of the different dimensions of dyslexia.

- **Emotional aspects:** If a child is failing in literacy or finds some aspects of learning challenging, then he/she may be affected emotionally. It is important that this is addressed and preferably prevented.

There are a number of ways of helping to maintain or boost children's self-esteem, but one of the most obvious and most effective ways is to ensure that they achieve some success and receive genuine praise. In order for praise to be effective children have to be convinced that their achievements are worthy of the praise. When children feel a failure it is difficult to reverse these feelings and often they need to change their perceptions of themselves. This can be a lengthy process and ongoing support, praise and sensitive handling are necessary.

Summary

This chapter has provided some of the key characteristics of dyslexia and how these can be recognized. The chapter has also indicated the different definitions of dyslexia and how this may impact on you as a parent. Although parents harbor many challenges and anxieties there should also be a great deal of hope. The landscape is changing – many countries have policies on dyslexia and most recognize dyslexia as a discrete condition. There may be differences in priorities between some schools and parents and differences in the focus of intervention, but with effective communication parents and schools can form a significant and strong partnership and go a long way to supporting children with dyslexia develop the skills in literacy that they require to reach their potential.

Chapter 2

Finding out about dyslexia

The most frequent questions I am asked by parents, particularly after carrying out an assessment on their child, are 'Where can I find out about dyslexia? How do I know that the sources are reliable?' and, very frequently, 'What does the latest research on dyslexia indicate?' It is not surprising that parents want this information. It can complete the picture for them – they know about their own child and now they want to know what impact dyslexia may have on their child. It is important therefore to have an understanding of the research. You will be aware that research in dyslexia is frequently changing with new research directions now apparent. Nevertheless, having worked in the field for many years and having witnessed many new research projects, many of the key themes and research findings have stood the test of time. It is important to have a good understanding of these as this will provide you with confidence and understanding to evaluate these approaches and reach your own conclusions on the value of new research and how it may impact on your child and the education system.

This chapter will therefore look at the current research in dyslexia and provide you with insights into dyslexia from professional and

Dyslexia: A Complete Guide for Parents and Those Who Help Them, Second Edition. Gavin Reid.
© 2011 John Wiley & Sons, Ltd. Published 2011 by John Wiley & Sons, Ltd.

research perspectives. As a parent, this should help you decide what questions to ask schools and generally have a more informed understanding of dyslexia.

Causes of dyslexia

We find that many parents, quite rightly, want information about the causes of dyslexia. There is a great deal of work on the neurological and genetic relationship with dyslexia. The widespread use of magnetic resonance imagery (MRI) and functional MRI (fMRI) and other forms of brain imagery such as positron emission tomography (PET) allows scientists and neuropsychologists to observe the brain at work. This can show how particular parts of the brain function with different types of task. Guinevere Eden, a neuroscientist at Georgetown University, Washington, DC, indicates the importance of this by suggesting that much is happening in the developing brain (Guyer, 2010). She indicates that brain cells are growing and dividing, and structures are maturing. This results in connections being made and it is important to have some idea of how the connections are forming. fMRI can indicate this by providing researchers with pictures revealing which parts of the brain activate when a person carries out certain tasks. The image of the brain shows brightly colored hot spots which indicate exactly where the brain is processing specific types of information – sounds, sights, thoughts and actions.

Eden indicates that fMRI works by sensing changes in the natural magnetic properties of blood cells that carry oxygen. When brain cells are active and firing – when they are responding to visual or other stimuli – they use more energy and so need more oxygen. In response to the increased energy demands of the active brain cells, the blood flow increases near active areas of the brain. fMRI senses this increased blood flow and this is shown as a bright color (hot spot) in the image.

Genetic factors

Another new direction has been in the field of genetics. There has been a considerable amount of research activity focussing on the genetic basis of dyslexia.

- It has been estimated that the risk of a son being dyslexic if he has a dyslexic father is about 40%.
- Gilger (2008) suggests that different genetic regions can be responsible for different aspects of the reading and writing process such as: reading and verbal ability, single-word reading, spelling, phoneme awareness, phonological decoding, pseudo- as well as non-word reading and writing, IQ, and language skills, rapid naming and verbal short-term memory. Gilger warns though that one needs to be wary of studies that make sweeping generalizations based on genetic evidence.
- Many of the gene studies do indicate the presence of a possible site for 'dyslexic genes'; many of these are found in Chromosome 6. Significantly, they may be in the same region as the genes implicated in autoimmune diseases which have been reported to show a high level of association with dyslexia (Snowling, 2000).
- Familial risk is therefore a useful indicator of dyslexia and can be seen as early as pre-school.

Magnocellur visual system

- There are two types of cells found in the neural tracts between the retina and the visual cortex: *magnocells* are large cells that code information about contrast and movement; *parvocells* are smaller and code information about detail and color.
- Cooperation between these two systems enables us to perceive a stationary image when we move our eyes across a scene or a page of text. When reading, the eyes do not move smoothly across the page but in a series of very quick jumps (saccades) in order to fixate successive portions of the text.
- Stein (2008) provides evidence that the development of magnocellular neurones is impaired in children with dyslexia. Stein argues that the visual system provides the main input to the routes for reading and therefore the most important sense for reading is vision. He therefore suggests that the great variety of visual, phonological, kinesthetic, sequencing, memory and motor symptoms that are seen in different dyslexics may arise from differences in the particular magnocellular systems that are most affected by the particular mix that each individual dyslexic inherits.

- Stein (2002) has also highlighted convergence difficulties and binocular instability as factors that could affect the stability of the visual stimuli when reading. In terms of intervention, even simple procedures such as the use of colored overlays can, in some cases, make a difference.
- Kriss and Evans (2005) found that 45% of dyslexic children read 5% faster with an overlay, compared with 25% of non-dyslexic control children; when a more conservative criterion of 8% increase in reading speed with an overlay was applied, these figures dropped to 34% and 22%, respectively.
- Everatt (2002), in a comprehensive review of visual aspects relating to dyslexia, suggests that the visual representation processes, the magnocellular system, factors associated with visual sensitivity and colored filters, and eye movement coordination can each account for the visual difficulties experienced by people with dyslexia. It should be noted that not all those diagnosed as dyslexic present visual deficits, and indeed some people who are not dyslexic present evidence of visual deficits.

Cerebellar deficit hypothesis

- Fawcett and Nicolson (2008) argue that the cerebellar deficit hypothesis may provide a single coherent explanation of the three main difficulties in dyslexia – reading, writing and spelling.
- They also suggest the cerebellar deficit hypothesis provides an explanation for the overlapping factors between dyslexia and the other developmental disorders.
- One of the functions of the cerebellum is in the precise timing of procedures (e.g., several motor movements) that accomplish some sort of behavioural response or task performance. This timing of sequences may play a critical role in making task accomplishment or behavioral skills automatic.
- Indeed, a critical aspect of learning a skill may be to make its accomplishment automatic. This means that the skill can be carried out without the individual giving it too much thought – and resources can be used to undertake other behaviors or processes simultaneously.

For most adults and children, the ability to walk, talk and possibly read and write may be partially or completely automatic.

- Consequently, Fawcett and Nicolson (2008) put forward the hypothesis that dyslexic children would have difficulty in automatizing any skill (cognitive or motor). This has implications for teaching and learning in that there will be a significant need for over-learning to be practiced with children with dyslexia.

Hemispheric symmetry

- According to Geschwind and Galaburda (1985) the difficulties in processing information experienced by people with dyslexia is due to structural differences between the hemispheres, and this likely develops in the prenatal period. This view has received considerable support from subsequent studies.
- Knight and Hynd (2002) are of the opinion that the principal findings to emerge from these studies suggest that misplaced cells may be present in some areas of the brain, particularly the outer layer of cortex, which is usually cell-free. According to Galaburda and Rosen (2001) these misplaced cells can be found predominantly in the left hemisphere in areas associated with language and these areas can be associated with dyslexia.

Phonological processing

- There is substantial evidence that the acquisition of phonological skills is crucial for successful reading and that difficulties in acquiring phonological skills is the cause of dyslexia.
- Early phonological training improves word literacy, a major distinguishing factor between dyslexics and non-dyslexics from early literacy learning to adulthood (Snowling, 2000; Vellutino, Fletcher, Snowling & Scanlon, 2004). Children who find it difficult to distinguish sounds within verbally presented words would be predicted to have problems learning the alphabetic principle that letters represent sounds. These would be the children who are most likely to be dyslexic based on the phonological deficit hypothesis.

Phonological awareness and multisensory programs

In educational settings there has been considerable activity in the study of phonological awareness in relation to dyslexia. There are many multisensory language approaches that focus on phonological teaching approaches. One that has had the biggest impact is the Orton-Gillingham (OG) approach. The IDA suggests that many programs today incorporate methods and principles first described in the foundational work seen in the OG approach, as well as other practises supported by research (IDA factsheet, Multisensory Structured Language Teaching, 2009). The OG approach is very popular in the US, Canada, the Middle East and Asia. Other programs that are popular, particularly in the UK, include Sound Linkage (Hatcher, 1994), the Phonological Awareness Training Program (Wilson, 1993), the Hickey Multisensory Teaching System (Combley, 2001) and THRASS (http://www.thrass.co.uk), as well as individual programs such as Letterland (http://www.letterlandcanada.com) and Toe by Toe.

Wise et al. (1999) conducted a large-scale study using different forms of 'remediation' and found that the actual type of phonological awareness training was less important than the need to embed that training within a well-structured and balanced approach to reading. Adams (1990) argues that combining phonological and 'whole language' approaches to reading should not be seen as incompatible. Indeed, it is now well accepted that poor readers rely on context more than good readers. Language experience is therefore as vital to the dyslexic child as is a structured phonological awareness program. A high priority may be on language experience, print exposure and comprehension activities.

Glue ear

Peer (2009) has developed a strong argument emphasizing the need to acknowledge glue ear syndrome as an influential causal factor in dyslexia. She suggests that hearing loss during the first two years of life may result in a delay in emerging receptive or expressive language, or both. Peer argues that glue ear is a chronic condition for many children, meaning that they experience significant hearing loss over a lengthy period of time. This may also lead to a lack of concentration as well as an inability to process the fine sounds that are necessary for auditory perception and speed of processing, which is key to language learning. Furthermore it does seem to be prevalent when investigating numbers of children affected by repetitive bouts of the condition.

Additional language learning

It is quite widely recognized that children with dyslexia often find learning a foreign language challenging. Dal (2008) provides an indication of the areas that are important for foreign language learning. These are:

1. phonological processing (poor grasp of sound, lack of awareness of individual sounds within words);
2. memory (working memory might be limited, there may be inaccurate representations in long-term memory);
3. auditory discrimination (uncertainty of the sound which has been heard, difficulty in discriminating between similar sounds, difficulty in knowing where a spoken word ends and a new word begins);
4. sequencing (getting things in order, e.g., letter order in words);
5. speed of processing information (tendency to be slower in responding to incoming information);
6. visual discrimination/recognition (poor ability to differentiate between similar-looking words).

Many of these areas can be demanding for children with dyslexia.

Dal suggests that the problems dyslexic students experience in learning a foreign language are closely related to written and oral skills in their mother tongue. He further suggests that although most language teachers and schools acknowledge that dyslexic students might have difficulties learning a foreign language, the policy of inclusion means that little special provision is made for them in language classes and that many language teachers are unsure of how best to teach them.

Alternative intervention and research

One of the areas that may have far-reaching considerations is what is known as 'alternative therapies' (meaning not commonly used in the mainstream). These tend to be popular, innovative and often have media appeal and in some cases extravagant claims of success. That is not to say they are not helpful – some of the evidence, in fact, seems to support the benefits of some alternative interventions.

It is important that new and alternative interventions are evaluated and that the research is seen to be rigorous and robust. Fawcett and Reid (2009) suggest that the gold standard in experimental design for evaluating interventions is the double-blind placebo-controlled study. It is taken from the medical field where it is widely used to evaluate the effectiveness of new drugs and whether or not they have harmful side-effects. A double-blind approach means that neither the experimenter, the child, the teacher nor the family know which approach the child is receiving, either the therapy which the study is testing or whether they have been given an alternative (the placebo). It is important to make sure that studies are double-blind to overcome any tendency for performance to improve simply because the child or the experimenter expects this or wants it to happen. In some studies, a crossover technique is used. This means that half the children receive the placebo in the first set of trials. This is held to be ethically sound, because no one is deprived of an intervention thought to be beneficial. A stringent and well-controlled system would mean that the trial supervisor was not aware of who received the placebo and who received treatment. This approach is relatively easy within a medical setting, but is less easy to adhere to in an experimental educational setting. There has been considerable debate on whether or not the approaches typically used in the education system, for both traditional and alternative interventions, have been sufficiently researched. Improvements made using a specific method may reflect the commitment of the teacher rather than the effectiveness of the intervention.

Some alternative approaches that are currently popular include the following.

Dietary approaches

There has been considerable popular coverage on the use of food additives and much anecdotal evidence to support the view that these may have an adverse affect on learning. Richardson (2001) suggests that there is a wide spectrum of conditions in which deficiencies of highly unsaturated fatty acids appear to have some influence. Further, Richardson argues that fatty acids can have an extremely important influence on dyslexia, dyspraxia and ADHD. She argues that the truly essential fatty acids (EFA), which cannot be synthesized by the body, must be provided in the diet. These are linoleic acid (omega 6 series) and alpha-linoleic acid (omega 3 series). She suggests that the longer chain highly unsaturated fatty acids (HUFA) that the brain needs can normally be synthesized from EFAs, but this conversion process can be severely affected and limited by dietary and lifestyle factors. Some of the dietary factors which can block the conversion of EFA to HUFA include excess saturated fats, hydrogenated fats found in processed foods, deficiencies in vitamins and minerals, as well as excessive consumption of coffee and alcohol, and smoking. Richardson and her colleagues (Cyhlarova et al., 2007) show that reading performance in both dyslexics and controls is linked to higher total omega 3 concentration, and that for dyslexic subjects was negatively related to omega 6 concentration, suggesting that it is the balance between the two which is relevant to dyslexia.

Dietary approaches have popular appeal as well as the effect of other environmental influences on children's learning. This latter point has been taken up in detail by Sue Palmer in *Toxic Childhood* (2006). Essentially, focussing on environmental influences and a healthy diet are beneficial and may make the conditions for learning more effective. It should be considered however that this is no substitute for effective intervention. It may enhance the success of an intervention but it is not a substitute for it.

Movement approaches

Blythe and Goddard (2000) and Goddard Blythe (2005) developed a series of exercises that emerged from their longstanding work at the Institute of Neuro Developmental Physiological Psychology (INPP). According to Blythe the term NDD (Neuro Developmental Delay) describes the omission or arrest of a stage of early development. Blythe established INPP to investigate the links between physical development and problems with reading, writing, spelling, coordination, behavior and emotional functioning in both children and adults. It is based on the view that every normal, full-term baby is born with a set of primitive or survival reflexes that are inhibited or controlled by higher centers in the brain during the first year of life. If these are not inhibited at the correct time, they remain active in the body and can interfere with balance, motor control, eye functioning, eye–hand coordination and perceptual skills and this can result in behavioral symptoms (e.g., frustration, hyperactivity and hypersensitivity) and failure to match performance to ability. Blythe and Goddard Blythe suggest that symptoms such as difficulty learning to ride a bicycle, mixed laterality (preferred foot, hand, ear, eye, etc.) above the age of eight years and a range of literacy difficulties can be accounted for by NDD.

Goddard Blythe (2005) investigated the extent of this in a study of 810 children with special educational needs in order to assess whether neurological dysfunction was a significant factor underlying academic achievement. The progress of 339 children aged 4–5 years of age was tracked through the school year to see whether children with higher scores on the INPP Developmental Test Battery (indications of neurological dysfunction) performed less well academically at the end of the school year and 235 children aged 8–10 years undertook a specific program of developmental exercises (The INPP Schools' Developmental Exercise Program) for 10 minutes a day under teacher supervision over the course of one academic year. The results showed that the children who participated in the daily INPP exercises made significantly greater improvement on measures for neurological dysfunction, balance and coordination when compared to a control group. Children who had scores of more than 25% on tests for neurological dysfunction and whose reading age was less than their chronological age at the outset also showed small but significantly greater progress in reading than children who did not take part in the program.

Brain Gym

Brain Gym (educational kinesiology) is an example of an alternative approach that has become mainstream. It is based on the work of Dennison (1981), Dennison and Hargrove (1986), Dennison and Dennison (2000) and Hannaford (1995, 1997) on the importance of dominance and laterality. The influence of dominance patterns on learning has been influential in classrooms, especially with children with specific learning difficulties. Information provided on the website gives a broad range of academic studies, many of them published in the Brain Gym journal.

Meares-Irlen Syndrome

Meares-Irlen Syndrome refers to the presence of a visual defect that can be related to difficulties with light source, glare, wave length and black and white contrast. A number of areas of difficulty are implicated in this:

- eye strain;
- poor visual resolution;
- reduced span of focus;
- impaired depth perception;
- poor sustained focus.

The assessment procedures are usually carried out though a screening process by people who have undergone courses to become screeners. Some optometrists also carry out such screening. During the screening the individual is asked a series of questions after being shown pages containing different patterns, musical notes, geometric figures and words. Observations are then made on how he/she responds. For example, observations will be made on the length of concentration span, whether the figures jump, run off the page, merge and if vision is blurred when concentrating on complex visual images. The color of any lenses that are prescribed are usually determined by the responses to these factors as well as some additional and more sophisticated laboratory procedures.

Helveston (2001) suggests that much of the supporting evidence for the success of visual treatments is anecdotal. At the same time the treatment has been very popular and many recipients have claimed it has been successful. Arnold Wilkins, a scientist with the Medical Research Council (Wilkins, 2003), clearly supports the notion of visual stress and produced a sophisticated screening device, the Intuitive Colorimeter, which measures the degree of therapeutic tint. Wilkins has performed a number of controlled scientific studies to examine the effectiveness of the use of tinted glasses following assessment using the Intuitive Colorimeter (Scott et al., 2002; Wilkins et al., 1996).

Fast ForWord

This program was designed to train children in recognizing the sounds which prove most difficult for them. In order to help them, the sounds they hear are drawn out by 50%.

The program starts at an easy level with slowed down onset and, as the children progress, the onsets become faster and faster. Children are asked to complete around 10 hours' practice a week in 20-minute sessions for 6−8 weeks, which leads to significant improvements in their ability on the games and also on the Tallal test (Fawcett & Reid, 2009).

This intervention, although popular, is still seen as being outwith the mainstream at the moment. It has been popular with parents' groups (All Special Kids [ASK], Geneva, personal correspondence, 2010).

Dyslexia is a global concern

Dyslexia is also an area where significant collaborative studies have taken place. Many of these have involved joint initiates with researchers from different countries and continents. International organizations such as the International Dyslexia Association (www. interdys.org), the Learning Disabilities Association of America (LDA) (http://www.ldanatl.org), British Dyslexia Association (www.bdadyslexia.org.uk), research organizations such as International Academy for Research in Learning Disabilities (www.iarld.com) and reading researchers such as those from the Society for the Scientific Study of Reading SSS-R (www.triplesr.org) have all been instrumental in international collaborative initiatives.

Dyslexia-friendly

It is important for parents to be aware of the drive towards making all schools dyslexia-friendly. This campaign initially emerged in the UK but the term now has an international currency. Dyslexia-friendly is essentially learner-friendly so it can amount to good practice in teaching. It suggests that teachers and schools need to incorporate dyslexia-friendly approaches into teaching strategies and learning materials. There is evidence that making schools dyslexia-friendly can make a substantial difference. Coffield, Riddick, Barmby and O'Neill (2008) showed that the development of 'dyslexia-friendly standards' for all schools within a local authority provided a useful tool for developing effective in class intervention. Those teachers who were using dyslexia-friendly approaches in their classrooms tended to focus more on making sure that tasks were introduced and explained clearly and on providing support materials to help pupils write their own answers rather than looking at ways to assist pupils with the writing process itself.

In the Coffield et al. study (2008) there appears to be some very positive outcomes from asking the students for their views. The majority of students were able to identify some aspects of classroom practice that they found beneficial. These included:

- teachers reading aloud information to the whole class;
- the provision of cue cards and other support materials;
- the use of readers and scribes in examinations; and
- the possibility of working with a partner.

It is important that parents are able to ask schools if they have dyslexia-friendly procedures in place.

Implementing dyslexia-friendly approaches

There are now many good examples of schools implementing these approaches and they are being incorporated into different curricular areas. They are also being integrated into new technology and ICT innovations. For example, the ICT company iansyst Ltd (www.iansyst.com) offers top accolades in the form of prestigious awards to teachers using technology in a dyslexia-friendly manner. The 2009 Best Practice Award was won by specialist teacher Hilery Williams. It featured collaborative and technology-based learning where six schools linked up online to watch a talk by a well-known children's author. During the online link-up classes from each school took turns to perform an extract from the author's book using puppets they had made themselves. Each performance presented different interpretations and ideas about the book, allowing the children to learn from each other.

Williams indicated that she is currently working with a group of children using resources researched from the internet; the children have jointly mind-mapped a discussion around a YouTube video. She said this will ultimately lead to a multimedia presentation and made accessible to schools. These children will then be able to coach classmates and teachers to help them use technologies effectively.

I think it is so important to focus on what learners can do, not where they have difficulties. It is essential that educators are able to create a positive environment for dyslexic children. In this respect, assistive technologies can liberate the teacher just as much as the pupil – they really are a fundamental part of creating a dyslexia-friendly culture. (Press release, Dyslexia-Friendly Best Practice Awards has a winner! http://www.iansyst.co.uk)

Five theories

To summarize this chapter five views of dyslexia are presented. They have been mentioned in some way in this chapter but it may be useful for parents to see them categorized in this way.

1. **Phonological deficit hypothesis:** This relates to the difficulties with sounds and relating the sounds to the visual symbol and where in the word the sound comes. There will also be sound confusion and auditory discrimination difficulties. Children with phonological difficulties will also have a difficulty with rhyming.
2. **Double deficit hypothesis:** This relates to the work of Wolf (1996). The two deficits are phonological awareness and naming speed. This means that people with dyslexia take longer to name objects and this can also be related to word-finding difficulty.
3. **Magnocellular deficit hypothesis:** This relates to visual processing and visual tracking in particular. According to Stein (2008), the great variety of visual, phonological, kinesthetic, sequencing, memory and motor symptoms that are seen in different degrees in dyslexic profiles may arise from differences in the particular magnocellular systems that are most affected by the particular mix that each individual dyslexic inherits.
4. **Dyslexia automatization deficit:** This refers to the difficulty with automaticity that learners with dyslexia often experience. In practice this means that they will take longer to assimilate new information to the point of mastery. They usually need longer to do this and a considerable amount of over-learning.
5. **Cerebellar deficit hypothesis:** This refers to the work involving the role of the cerebellum in learning. Fawcett and Nicolson contend that this is highly important and has implications for learners with dyslexia.

Irrespective of the impact of the research on parents it is important that sound advice is taken before spending money on new approaches. It is crucial to find out if the approach has been well researched and if so, by whom and how. Communication with the school is also important in this respect.

Comment

The aim of this chapter has been to provide parents with insights into the wide range of research in dyslexia but importantly not to close any doors. It is important that parents seek out the information they need for their own situation. Hopefully the information in this chapter can guide them with this, but it is important to remember that the field of dyslexia is always changing with new products and new directions. It is important therefore that parents do not necessarily need to know all that is out there, but more importantly they need to how to assess and evaluate the value to them and their child of any new or existing approach.

Chapter 3

Finding out if my child is dyslexic

This is one of the most important chapters in this book. Too many children are *too* late in being identified. Yet it is well known that early intervention is crucial and that early identification is necessary for effective intervention to take place. Parents need to ensure that if they suspect their child is not performing as well as he/she should, then a full and formal assessment should take place as soon as possible. This should be available through the school, but in almost every country – the US, Canada and Europe, New Zealand and Australia and in the Middle East – there are long waiting lists to obtain an assessment from the school psychologist. Many parents opt to go to an independent psychologist and this will be worthwhile if it results in a diagnosis that can accelerate the provision of support for your child. Often schools are instrumental in raising concern and in arranging an assessment, but this is not always the case. It is important that parents know what a full assessment involves, how to obtain one and what one should look for in selecting an assessor and in understanding the assessment report.

Dyslexia: A Complete Guide for Parents and Those Who Help Them, Second Edition. Gavin Reid.
© 2011 John Wiley & Sons, Ltd. Published 2011 by John Wiley & Sons, Ltd.

This chapter indicates the key points and issues in identification and assessment and this will include interpreting teacher and psychologist reports and how parents can play a part in this process.

The importance of an assessment

Once parents, or teachers, have recognized that the child may have some, or all, of the characteristics of dyslexia it is important to obtain a full and comprehensive assessment. One of the questions parents often ask is how early an assessment should take place. This is quite difficult to decide because some of the characteristics of dyslexia can be noted in the normal development of young children. But if the child has not made the expected progress throughout the first year of school, then at that point a formal assessment should be considered. The assessment can identify some possible reasons for the lack of progress as well as locate areas of strength and weakness and a diagnosis if appropriate. An assessment should also lead to a set of recommendations and the results may suggest a further specialist assessment, such as that from an optometrist, speech or occupational therapist. But there should be a clear way forward in terms of intervention as a result of the assessment.

Some professionals hold the view that it is inadvisable for a formal assessment for dyslexia to take place while the child is still very young. While one must be cautious when assessing a very young child due to the possibility of misdiagnosis or unnecessary and premature labeling, the advantages of early assessment and obtaining a comprehensive profile of the child's cognitive and learning strengths and weaknesses can outweigh any possible disadvantages. Parents too may feel that a formal assessment is not the best path to follow. Consider this comment from a parent who was undecided about which path to follow:

> The school has been pushing for assessments since 1st grade. However, I resisted since the results weren't going to change the remediation plan; I feared a label in a private international school might decrease the chances to get into another school; and I worried my kid's confidence would be affected by earlier testing. However, now we are about to start the assessments next week.

There are two important issues here. The first is that there is a view that an assessment may not make a difference to the intervention. I would dispute that and suggest that it should and it may be necessary to put some pressure on the school to ensure that it does. It is also important that when an assessment is requested parents ensure at this stage suggestions for intervention will be made and, more importantly, the school will consider them. The other point is that one should not necessarily equate assessment with a label. An assessment can be informative and can provide a label that can inform practice. If a label is not provided the assessment can still inform practice, the assessment can still inform practice. Additionally, it is important to consider the impact of a label and this will need to be discussed in full if the parents feel it is an issue. In the case mentioned above the parent felt that other schools might discriminate against her child because of the label dyslexia. This is unusual. Schools should not be in this position and it is unlikely for any school to have no children at all with dyslexia. It is more likely and more common to find at least one child with dyslexia in almost every class. The main concern is that delayed assessment may result in delayed intervention.

The research in dyslexia and early intervention (Crombie, Knight & Reid, 2004) indicates the advantages of early identification and suggests that early intervention will be more successful if a clear profile of the child's difficulties and strengths is available.

Lyon Reid (1998), in discussing the situation in the US, made the following comment:

> We have learned that for 90% to 95% of poor readers, prevention and early intervention programs that combine instruction in phoneme awareness, phonics, fluency development, and reading comprehension strategies, provided by well trained teachers, can increase reading skills to average reading levels. However, we have also learned that if we delay intervention until nine-years-of-age, (the time that most children with reading difficulties receive services), approximately 75% of the children will continue to have difficulties learning to read throughout high school.

This emphasizes the importance of early identification and the recognition of appropriate early intervention. Many schools and school districts do have well-developed policies for the early years and in the US the 'response to intervention' policy can be useful if implemented and evaluated appropriately. But often children with dyslexia will require additional considerations to those given to most children in the early years and more intensive input, such as that described by Lyon Reid. It is important that schools link up with parents as early as possible to ensure that early identification can take place and that parents play a key role in this.

Who assesses?

If you, or your child's teacher, suspect that there is a possibility of dyslexia, then it is important to obtain a full assessment. The procedures for obtaining this vary from country to country, and even within a country this can vary considerably. Educational psychologists are the group of professionals that can provide a full diagnosis and accompanying learning profile from which recommendations for teaching and learning can be made. In some countries specialist teachers who have undergone recognized courses in dyslexia often undertake some form of assessment, but it should be noted that in many countries there can be a requirement that an assessment by an educational psychologist is carried out before any special provision, diagnosis or special arrangements can made.

It is also important to ensure that the psychologist is registered in the state, province or the country you live in. You can obtain a list of registered psychologists from the website. Each jurisdiction will have a list of registered psychologists, or you can ask the school for one. The school may be able to give you the names of psychologists they have used previously. As an example, if you live in British Columbia, a list of registered psychologists can be obtained from the BC College of Psychologists (http://www.collegeofpsychologists.bc.ca/verify.php). There are Colleges of Psychologists in other Canadian provinces such as Ontario (http://www.cpo.on.ca) and Saskatchewan (http://www.skcp.ca). In California there is the California Association of Licensed Educational Psychologists (CALEP) (http://www.calep.com/Members.html). In some locations the governing body for psychologists can be a Health Association. For example, in Texas there is the Health

Professions Council (http://www.hpc.state.tx.us) which coordinates regulatory efforts among the various health care licensing boards represented on the HPC, and this includes psychologists. The mission statement of the HPC in Texas indicates that each board and agency of the HPC will strive to share ideas, resources and functions to provide efficient and effective services to the citizens of Texas.

This type of initiative has also been taken up in the UK. The Health Professions Council (http://hpc-portal.co.uk/online-register) will provide a list of registered psychologists. In the UK the title 'educational psychologist' or 'registered psychologist' is protected. This means it is a criminal offense if someone in the UK uses a protected title if they are not registered with the UK Health Professions Council. These regulations and regulatory bodies are there to serve parents and clients and ensure that clients are obtaining what they are seeking in the way of an assessment.

Teacher assessment

Teacher assessments are also very important, but ideally teachers and professionals should be working together in a collaborative manner as each will have something useful to contribute to the assessment. The message here is that everyone – psychologist, teacher, parent and other professionals, when appropriate, such as occupational therapists, speech and language therapists and medical personnel – may have a role to play in an assessment. An innovative approach to this can be seen in the groundbreaking work being carried out in Scotland, with an online toolkit coordinated by Dyslexia Scotland (Dyslexia Voice, March 2010). It is important for parents to be aware of this as the toolkit will be used by teachers and can help to go a long way in ensuring that dyslexia is recognized in schools and that individual children are identified. The toolkit was launched as part of the Scottish Teacher Education Committee Framework for Inclusion and can be viewed at www.frameworkforinclusion.org/assessingdyslexia. It received a good review in the *Times Education Supplement* (27 August 2010). The review indicated that feedback from teachers had been overwhelmingly positive and that it represented a very comprehensive and practical toolkit. Sir Jackie Stewart, at the launch of the initiative in June 2010, suggested that it was a groundbreaking initiative which would help teachers to work together and bring about early recognition in all areas of Scotland (http://www.frameworkforinclusion.org/ AssessingDyslexia/launch/ scenario.php?ID=3&status=).

The working group who developed the toolkit appreciated that many teachers feel unprepared for assessing dyslexia and the toolkit adopted a three-tier approach to deal with this. The first tier is that which helps all teachers at least recognize the signs of dyslexia. The second tier is for teachers who have done additional training in dyslexia and are in a position to help and advise others. The third tier is for those who have some experience and competence in assessment, including the use of standardized assessment procedures. The working group recognized that there is no one test that can fully assess for dyslexia and that teachers need to access a range of assessment materials. This type of resource can be an invaluable support for parents and provide a degree of reassurance that at least there are moves in the right direction to ensure that every child at risk of dyslexia is identified. Margaret Crombie, who led the working group, suggested that the toolkit sits well in the Framework for Inclusion initiatives in Scotland and it is in fact hosted on their wesite:

http://www.frameworkforinclusion.org/AssessingDyslexia/launch/ scenario.php?ID=4&status=1.

Educational psychologists

Educational psychologists are usually highly qualified professionals in psychology and education who have an understanding of the cognitive processes involved in learning. For that reason they are permitted to use cognitive tests, such as tests that measure intelligence. These are usually referred to as closed tests. The benefit of this in the case of dyslexia is that it can eliminate any other reason for lack of progress in attainments, such as low IQ. If the IQ does come out as low, then the educational priorities will be different from a child who has a higher IQ who is perhaps not performing to their ability. At the same time it needs to be appreciated that an IQ score is not a benchmark for success but is in fact an aggregate of a range of scores from language and non-verbal tests (see appendix 1). It can help to identify strengths and weaknesses and educational priorities. For example, the child with a low IQ may need to focus on language comprehension, while in the case of a child with dyslexia with a higher IQ, reading accuracy or fluency may need to be prioritized. It should however be noted that the IQ test, because of its focus on language, can discriminate against children with dyslexia and the IQ score may not reveal their real potential.

The IQ test usually used by the educational psychologist is the Wechsler Intelligence Scale for Children (4th edition) (WISC-IV) (for adults the equivalent test is the Wechsler Adult Intelligence Scale [WAIS III]). These tests can be supplemented by others, such as the Wechsler Individual Achievement Test (WIAT-III) and this test can correlate with the dimensions of WISC. The educational psychologist has therefore got a battery of tests at her/his disposal (see list of tests used by educational psychologists in appendix 1). In many countries the educational psychologist provides a diagnosis, though this is always best acquired through collaboration with the school.

An assessment by an educational psychologist is usually carried out if the school, or the parents, suspect that the child is not making the progress that would be expected given his/her abilities in other areas. It can also be carried out privately (see earlier in the chapter).

Specialist teacher

Although this varies from country in country some schools have trained and experienced specialist teachers who can carry out a school-based assessment. For example, in the UK the British Psychological Society (BPS) has approved a course of training in psychometrics for specialist teachers that allows them to use some of the tests available. In the US, Canada and in Australia it is more customary for school psychologists to carry out these tests.

An assessment conducted by a specialist teacher will provide diagnostic information on the child's level of reading, spelling, writing and number work. Reasons for any lack of progress should be offered and recommendations on teaching programs and strategies should be made, including what parents can do at home.

The class teacher

The class teacher is best placed to obtain first-hand and detailed knowledge of the child's difficulties and strengths as well as the learning preferences and learning style of the child. Some class teachers also have knowledge of dyslexia, although this can vary considerably. It is encouraging to note that in the US the International Dyslexia Association annual conference attracts an audience in excess of 3,000 and a large proportion of these are classroom teachers. As a parent you will also have a good knowledge of your child and his/her learning pattern and specific difficulties and strengths. It is important to provide this information to the teacher. This further underlines the importance of good communication with the school.

Baroness Mary Warnock (Came & Reid, 2007) suggested that the role of the teacher in the assessment process is crucial and that every teacher in every school has the responsibility for noticing a child's problems, assessing precisely what he/she can and cannot do, and then providing support, or seeing that it is provided by someone else. She further suggests that if this were done early enough, in many cases the difficulties could be overcome. She goes on to say that a child frustrated by an inability to learn, or do something that others seem able to do, will find him/herself in trouble as he/she will fall behind contemporaries academically so that school becomes a misery. These points indicate the importance of teachers taking ownership of assessment as early as possible and that early identification is crucial to prevent the spiral of failure that so often accompanies the school performances of students with literacy difficulties.

Curriculum focus assessment

It is also important that an assessment takes account of the child's performances within different areas of the curriculum. It may provide an explanation as to why a child is having difficulty in one area of the curriculum and perhaps not in another. For example, why may the child be experiencing difficulty in English, but not history, geography or science? These are questions that would need to be investigated, and this investigation is as important as individual cognitive and other child-focussed assessments. For example, in history, children need to be able to decode, contextualize and analyze a range of types of texts, such as diaries, letters, recorded oral testimony, press journalism, posters, leaflets, official documentation such as Acts of Parliament and government reports, all of which can be challenging for children with dyslexia. The assessment should also identify particular strategies or resources that can help to access the curriculum for a particular child, and for that reason it is important to focus part of the assessment on the actual curriculum. This can be achieved through curriculum-focused teaching approaches that may have strands and targets built in to the teaching process.

Emotional factors

A full assessment should facilitate the planning of appropriate intervention that will help to prevent the child with dyslexia from becoming overwhelmed by learned helplessness. This occurs when the child begins almost to give up learning and can sometimes be seen even in quite young children with dyslexia.

Preventing such failure or dealing with it as early as possible can help to maintain the child's self-esteem. Every effort should be made to ensure that the difficulties displayed by the child and the underlying problems do not detract from the development of skills in learning and in access to the curriculum. At the same time, feedback to the child needs to be handled very carefully.

Reid and Kirk (2001) discuss the cycle of 'disaffection, defiance and depression' and provide evidence from a number of studies to suggest that people with dyslexia, and in particular teenagers, are particularly vulnerable and that the whole aspect of self-esteem needs to be carefully considered and managed. This point is supported by Hales (2009) and Hunter (2009), who suggest the vulnerable period of transfer from primary to secondary is one that needs careful attention.

According to Hales not being accepted by a 'group' can lead to lowering of self-esteem so it is important that parents keep an eye on the child's emotional well-being. There is research to show that problems with reading can result in a negative self-concept and this can have an influence on actual attainment and result in feelings of inadequacy

(Riddick, 1995; Riddick & Lumsdon, 2002). Tunmer and Chapman (1997) found that pupils aged 5–7 who were having problems with reading were also developing a 'negative self-concept' where reading was concerned. They suggested that this had a negative influence on the individuals' 'actual attainment' and progress within the academic setting.

Role of parents in the assessment

Most schools now accept (or at least they should) that parents have a key role to play in the assessment process. Some in fact emphasize the key role parents of children with dyslexia can play in collaboration with schools.

Parental participation in the assessment

Pre-assessment

Before an assessment takes place parents need to ensure that the school is informed of the following:

1. Early pre-school development.
2. The age at which key milestones were reached (e.g., when the child started talking and walking).
3. Any reasons why the parents feel that their child may have dyslexia.
4. Any other reason for possible difficulty in learning, such as problems at birth.
5. Home factors such as behavior, interest in learning and things they find motivating.

The assessment

A formal assessment can be a daunting process for both the child and the parents. It is important that any stress attached to this is minimized. The child should be prepared for the assessment. The actual word 'assessment', however, need not be used as this in itself may induce stress. There are a number of ways of indicating to the child what will happen without using the word 'assessment'. This will minimize any anxiety. Essentially the tester is engaging in a range of activities with the child to find out how he/she learns and what can be done to help to improve learning. This views assessment as a positive activity, which of course it should be.

The parent(s) should try to be available immediately after the assessment to get some initial feedback and to reassure their child on his/her performance. Parents also need, if possible, to speak with the tester before the assessment in order to find out how long the procedure will take and what kind of information he/she is looking for in the assessment.

The person conducting the assessment will need some background information from the parents particularly relating to any concerns they may have about the development and the behaviors/characteristics of their child. It is helpful to provide some details on how the child behaves at home in terms of his/her social skills, learning pattern and motivation. Much of this information of course varies with the age of the child, or young adult, who is to be tested.

Feedback from the assessment

Feedback following the assessment is extremely important and should ideally involve the class teacher, member of school management team, the parents and, if appropriate, the child. The parents, however, usually want some immediate informal feedback from the assessor. It is also important to give the child some informal feedback as soon as possible after the assessment depending on the age of the child. The feedback to parents should include the following:

1. Details of the tests administered and the reasons why particular tests were used.
2. The child's test behavior, motivation, whether he/she was interested in the test materials, whether the child managed to maintain interest throughout the assessment.

3. The results – how they compare to the norm (average); if possible you can ask to see a graph or some other visually displayed profile.
4. The implications of the results – this is important as the results should provide information on a diagnosis, and importantly recommendations for intervention or further assessment.
5. Follow-up assessment and details of any monitoring of progress that will be carried out. This is important and arrangements and time sequence for monitoring of progress should be indicated. It is important as a parent you are reassured that the assessment is not the end of the process, but in many cases the beginning. Details of short-, medium- and long-term monitoring should be indicated, although this can best be negotiated with the school.

Understanding assessment reports

The formal reports on assessment can vary considerably from psychologist to psychologist. Each can have a different style but there are some common and crucial elements that all reports should have.

1. **Biographical details**: This is for the record as the report will very likely become an official school document. It is important that it has details such as date of birth, school history and date of assessment and the dates and brief details of any previous assessment.
2. **Background information**: This includes reasons for the assessment and the challenges that the child experiences at school or at home. This section will also provide details of previous assessments.
3. **Tests used**: This provides a list of the tests used. It can be divided into cognitive assessment (tests that look at reasoning and processing of information) and achievement tests, which includes the tests that look at performances in attainments such as reading and spelling and math. (See appendix 2 for details of the WISC-IV and some other tests.)
4. **Results:** The report should include a section reporting on the results. This may be interspersed throughout the report, but all the test scores should be displayed and the average (mean) should also be indicated as well as the range. This can help parents see at a glance where their child performed in relation to the average for his/her age range.

Table 3.1 Wechsler Intelligence Scale for Children (WISC-IV)

Indices	Composite score	Percentile rank	95% Confidence interval	Qualitative description
Verbal comprehension	119	90	111−125	High average
Perceptual reasoning	112	79	103−119	High average
Working memory	88	21	81−97	Low average
Processing speed	97	42	88−106	Average

These may also be in terms of percentiles and this is an accurate form of reporting on results. The average for a percentile would be 50 percentile, above average over 75 and below average under 25. You can see in Table 3.1 the range of percentiles scored by this child. His verbal comprehension was in the top 10% of the population for his age range while his working memory was in the lower 21% of children in his age range.

It is also not uncommon to have the type of discrepancies noted here where the reasoning scores (verbal comprehension and perceptual reasoning) are higher than the processing scores (working memory and processing speed).

5. **Discussion**: This will include comment on the results. This should indicate the implications of the strengths as well as the weaknesses. It is this discussion which has often to be explained personally to parents and to teachers. This will indicate whether or not dyslexia has been diagnosed and the criteria that have been used. Most countries take the lead from the *Diagnostic Statistical Manual* (4th edition) (DSM-IV, 1994; DSM-V is to be published in 2013). This indicates the criteria for diagnosis. In practice most states, provinces and educational authorities have contextualized this for their own use in their own area. Some, however, can refer directly to DSM-IV for the criteria they use (see appendix 3 for some information of on DSM-IV and V criteria).

6. **Key points**: These can be helpful for parents as they will know this is the most important information. An example of this from a recent assessment I conducted is shown below:

Key points in the assessment

Cognitive
Ali* scored comfortably in the average range overall in the cognitive assessment.

His working memory was in the low average range.

His visual/perceptual scores are all consistently above average.

His reasoning scores are significantly higher than his processing scores.

There is a significant discrepancy between his verbal abilities and his written language.

Attainments
Ali scored in the low average range in the single-word reading test.
He also had difficulty in decoding unknown words.

His spelling was in the low average range.

His listening comprehension was in the average range.

His mathematical scores were just on the average range.

He scored in the below average range for phonological awareness.

His phonological memory was also in the below average range.

His reading comprehension – both silent and oral reading – was in the average range.

His reading fluency was below average and represented his weakest area in the reading tests.

His writing is quite inconsistent and he was unable to utilize his full vocabulary in the piece of written work he completed for this assessment.

The assessment results – both the cognitive assessment and the pattern of attainments – indicate that Ali is dyslexic.

*Not his real name.

It should be remembered that there will be different dyslexic profiles and that not all children with dyslexia will have Ali's profile. There are however some classic characteristics in the profile above, such as the difficulties with decoding and with reading fluency. It can also be noted that working memory was also low. Processing speed quite often comes out low too but this can usually be seen in low reading fluency scores.

7. **Recommendations or areas of priority for intervention**: This is an important part of the report and will be discussed fully in chapter 4. But it is important that a report should contain some indication of the areas for intervention. Below are some examples taken from a report on a 10-year-old boy who has been diagnosed as dyslexic.

Areas for intervention

1. Decoding skills
2. Developing sight words
3. Self-monitoring of comprehension
4. Expressive writing skills, including grammar and sentence conventions
5. Reading accuracy and spelling
6. Developing inferential language skills
7. Developing word processing skills

It is important to recognize that not all children assessed and diagnosed as dyslexic will need the same supports and their priorities can be different. There are, however, some factors parents should be aware of and the core supports that may be necessary. This very likely will include the development of decoding skills. This is sometimes called word attack skills and refers to the ability to take a new word and break it down into its constituent sounds (phonemes) and blend these together to make a word. There are a considerable number of sub-skills linked to this process. Dyslexic children can experience challenges accessing many of the sub-skills of reading. As we will see in chapter 4 it is also important to ensure that reading fluency and reading comprehension are prioritized as well as learning and study skills. You will also note that word processing skills are also mentioned in the priorities and this is an important area for children with dyslexia. Being proficient in word processing can be highly advantageous to the young person with dyslexia. Word processing a document can help with planning, organization, spelling and general presentation. It is important that children with dyslexia can do this as young as possible.

Spelling

The pattern of spelling can be diagnostic and quite revealing. It is important therefore that a diagnostic spelling test is used. Some of the errors children make can be quite characteristic of dyslexia. Some examples are shown below. Often these errors may not be corrected using a conventional spellchecker and specialized spellcheckers such as TextHelp™ need to be used. You will note some of these difficulties in the extract below.

Benjamin* has significant difficulties in spelling. This was noted in the WIAT-III spelling test and also when he was engaged in free writing exercises. In the WIAT spelling subtest Benjamin had considerable difficulties with words with double consonants for example the double 'o' as in 'book', the double 'e' sound as in geese and the double 't' rule as in words such as 'sitting'. He also omitted letters quite frequently, including final sounds in words. He had difficulties with spelling rules and in general his spelling is significantly discrepant in relation to his overall language abilities and indeed his reading. His spelling pattern is characteristic of the significant difficulties he displays in written expression in general.

*Not his real name.

Written expression

Young people with dyslexia often have difficulty with expressive writing. They can be quite creative but may have difficulty in putting their thoughts into words. This can often alert parents (and teachers) that something is not quite right. It can be frustrating to experience this type of difficulty when they have great ideas but difficulty in putting them into words. This will be discussed in chapter 4 but it can feature in the characteristics for identification and assessment. You can note this in the box below.

In the WIAT-III his written expression score was in the below average range. He had difficulty in generating words in a set time that conformed to certain features, such as words that describe something round. He also had difficulty in copying sentences and creating compound sentences from two simple sentences. In the story writing component of the WIAT-III he also experienced considerable difficulty and was unable to write more than one sentence in the time allocated. To provide more information on this area the Test of Written Language (TOWL-4) was used. This test focusses on written language and a number of written tasks are given including a piece of writing in which Benjamin had to describe a picture that was provided. The picture was a stimulating one that described a calamitous event. The written piece was then scored for story composition and contextual writing conventions (grammar, syntax, etc.). In both these scales Benjamin scored in the low/below average range. He was unable to utilize his full vocabulary and comprehension abilities in the written work. Spelling and punctuation subtests were also given within the test. In both of these Benjamin scored significantly below average.

This can be an area of concern for parents as often the ability of children is assessed through written work. How to deal with this will be discussed in chapter 4, but essentially they need a structure and framework to ensure that they develop the points in a logical order. Often providing the person with dyslexia with key words can be helpful too.

The spectrum of difficulties

Parents can sometimes be confused by the complexity of labels and the overlap between different labels. Weedon, Reid and Long (2010) have developed a special needs assessment profile (SNAP) which can help teachers and parents identify the key features in a child's profile and show how the syndromes may overlap (see www.snapassessment.com). The important point is that parents are involved in the gathering of information for the SNAP profile. There is also feedback specially designed for parents, as well as a website of information on what can be done in terms of school intervention and at home to help the young person deal with the challenges identified in the profile.

Summary

This chapter has provided insights in the assessment process. It has focused on the role of the educational psychologist in assessment and indicated how they can diagnose dyslexia and the role parents can play in this process. Parents have an important role to play in assessment generally and are often the first to notice that their child is not performing as he/she should. It is important that parents and the school communicate effectively so that the assessment – whether obtained through the school or privately – can be implemented as early and as effectively as possible.

Chapter 4

Learning to read and why it is difficult for children with dyslexia

Introduction

Learning to read is one of the most important skills that are developed in the early stages of education. It is very disheartening for parents when they discover, usually quite early on in the process, that their child is having difficulty reading. Often there is no shortage of advice – some of it conflicting. They may hear the comment 'just wait – it is still early', some people may suggest a different kind of reading material that they have had good experiences with and others may recommend some reading programs and approaches that are commercially available. Much of this advice can be sound, but it can also be confusing. Parents still have to decide the best approach for their child.

The purpose of this chapter and the next one is to provide straight-forward advice on the development of reading skills and why for some children these can be difficult to acquire. Reading can be a complex process and there are different stages to the acquisition of reading skills.

Dyslexia: A Complete Guide for Parents and Those Who Help Them, Second Edition. Gavin Reid.
© 2011 John Wiley & Sons, Ltd. Published 2011 by John Wiley & Sons, Ltd.

The key points in the reading process are shown below. It is important to recognize that reading involves the following:

- recognition of all the sounds in the alphabet (44 in the English alphabet);
- recognition of all the letters in the alphabet;
- knowledge that individual letters and groups of letters make the sounds in words;
- the need to be able to blend words together to make sounds and words;
- the need to develop sight words so that words can be read automatically; this is what is needed for reading fluency;
- the need to be able to break new words down into smaller units – letters/sounds in order to read the word;
- the need to be able to understand the words in text;
- eventually, the need to be able to 'read between the lines' and understand the inferences the author is making (inferential reading).

The key skills are:

- auditory (recognizing the sounds);
- visual (remembering the letters shapes and sight word recognition);
- comprehension (understanding the text).

The acquisition of these skills can develop spontaneously for some, but most children need to be taught them. Children with dyslexia however, even after many sessions of teaching, may still have difficulty in acquiring them. This can be frustrating for them and of course for their parents.

Factors to consider

Looking in more detail at the factors above, the specific aspects that are important in the acquisition of literacy and the difficulties that can be experienced by children with dyslexia are shown in Table 4.1.

There is substantial evidence that phonological awareness is crucial to the development of reading skills (Mahfoudi & Haynes, 2008;

Table 4.1 Specific aspects important in the acquisition of literacy

Word attack skill	Description
Letter recognition	Recognizing the shape of the letter
Segmentation	Being able to break the word down into syllables and units
Blending	Joining the sounds and the syllables together to make the word
Phonemic awareness	Awareness of the sounds that combinations of letters make
Grapheme–phoneme correspondence	Being able to associate the sounds with the visual formation of the letter
Automaticity	Reading fluently because each word does not have to be actively decoded.

Vellutino et al., 2004). Phonological awareness is an umbrella term that includes awareness and manipulation of speech at the word, syllable and phoneme levels. Mahfoudhi and Haynes (2008; quoting the National Reading Panel, 2000) in the US argue that explicit, structured phonics instruction – teaching the rules that link speech information with letters and letter patterns – improves word recognition skills and contributes to spelling, reading fluency and reading comprehension in children with dyslexia (National Reading Panel, 2000).

There is a great deal of research that indicates that children's prior knowledge in their understanding of new knowledge is a key factor in literacy development (Keene & Zimmerman, 2007; Wray, 2009). It is important that this prior knowledge needs to be brought to the forefront of the learner's mind (i.e., made explicit), if it is to be utilized effectively. This means that pre-reading discussion is important as this can clarify the concepts and the ideas, as well as the key words, in the text that the child may well have difficulty in decoding.

The reading process

Ehri (2002) suggests that, initially, to become skilled readers children need to acquire knowledge of the alphabet system and that this

Table 4.2 Other factors involved in reading

Skill	Description
Print concepts	Knowledge about phrases, sentences and the overview of the geography of the book (front, back, author, etc.)
Language concepts	Understanding of the groups and categories of objects (e.g., concept of animals and being aware that different animals, such as cats and dogs, belong in that group)
Prior knowledge	Achieved through pre-reading discussion to build up a background of knowledge on the book or text that is to be read
Vocabulary knowledge	Understanding of the meaning of the words in a text
Text interest level	The level of interest of the book (e.g., books aimed at eight year olds may not hold the interest of a teenager, even though the teenager's reading age is at the eight-year-old level)
Text difficulty	For the reader, the number of difficult and new words in the text

process presents some difficulty to struggling readers. Ehri suggests that learning to read involves two basic processes:

1. One process involves learning to decipher the print (i.e., learning to transform letter sequences into familiar words).
2. The other involves comprehending the meaning of the print. When children attain reading skills, they learn to perform both these processes in a way that allows their attention to focus on the meaning of the text while the mechanics of reading, including deciphering, operate unobtrusively and out of awareness.

Ehri suggests that children acquire listening comprehension skills in the course of learning to speak. She also argues that decoding print is not a natural process in the same way as speech. The brain is specialized for processing spoken language, but not written language. Many of the visual and auditory aspects of reading do not develop spontaneously in children with dyslexia. These skills need to be taught, and usually in an explicit, sensitive and structured manner.

Stages of reading development

Frith (1995) identifies the following developmental stages in the acquisition of reading skills.

Logographic stage

The child makes use of visual recognition of overall word patterns, which means he or she is able to recognize words as units. This may not necessarily mean the child can reproduce these words accurately (this would be an alphabetic skill), so the child can easily misspell words they are able to read.

Alphabetic stage

The child tackles the sound/symbol correspondence between the letter and the sound. Ehri suggests that the alphabetic stage can be divided into four phases that capture the changes that occur in the development of sight word reading: pre-alphabetic, partial alphabetic, full alphabetic and consolidated alphabetic. Each phase is labeled to reflect the predominant type of connection that links the written form of sight words to their pronunciations and meanings in memory. Therefore, during the pre-alphabetic phase beginners remember how to read sight words by forming connections between selected visual attributes of words and their pronunciations or meanings. This phase is called pre-alphabetic because letter–sound relations are not involved in the connections.

When pre-alphabetic readers read print in their environment, such as stop signs and fast food restaurant signs, they do this according to Ehri by remembering visual cues accompanying the print rather than the written words themselves.

The next phase is the partial alphabetic phase. Here beginners remember how to read sight words by forming partial alphabetic connections between only some of the letters in written words and sounds detected in their pronunciations. Because first and final letters are especially important, these are often the cues that are remembered.

During the next phase, the full alphabetic phase, beginners remember how to read sight words by forming complete grapho-phonemic connections. This is possible because readers know how the major graphemes symbolize phonemes. In applying this knowledge to form connections for sight words, spellings become fully bonded to pronunciations in memory. The final phase according to Ehri is the full alphabetic phase when readers are able to decode words by transforming graphemes into phonemes, and they are able to retain sight words in memory by connecting graphemes to phonemes.

Orthographic stage

The child possesses and comprehends knowledge of the letter–sound relationship as well as structure and meaning. This means that as well as being aware of rules the child can use cues and context.

Difficulties for the child with dyslexia

It has been argued that children with dyslexia can find the alphabetic stage difficult because the sound–symbol correspondence rests to a great extent on skills in phonics. Before children, therefore, acquire a competent understanding of the relationship between letter units (graphemes) and sound units (phonemes) they need a degree of phonological awareness (Snowling, 2000). Frith (2002) puts forward the view that writing and the desire to write helps to enhance the alphabetic stage of reading because spelling is linked more directly to the alphabetic principle and letter–sound relationships. This view is also supported by Bradley and Bryant (1991), who found that beginner readers in the process of acquiring the skills of the alphabetic stage use visual strategies for reading, but phonological strategies for spelling. In their study children read correctly words that were visually distinctive such as 'school' and 'light', but failed to read simpler words like 'bun' and 'sit'. Yet these children tended to spell correctly words they had failed to read (bun, sit) and spell incorrectly words they had read by focusing on the visual patterns (school, light).

Snowling (2000) suggests that children also find difficulty reading words that have inconsistent orthographic patterns, but that are pronounced in the same way (such as their and there). Irregular words can also be challenging and can be easily mispronounced (e.g., 'island' would be pronounced 'is-land').

Connectionist models

The connectionist model is popular for understanding literacy acquisition. It is suggested that children learn to read through the reciprocal association between knowledge of letter strings and phonemes and the development of the ability to connect letters and strings of letters to the phonemes that make up the sound units in language. This model suggests that children access all their cognitive capacities (skills) at their disposal to do this. The connectionist approach also implies that regular words will be accessed more easily than irregular words as the former will conform to a pattern that the child will learn over time and exposure to print, whereas irregular words are unpredictable and do not conform to a pattern.

English, unlike some other languages such as German, Spanish and Italian, has a considerable number of irregular patterns that contradict a pattern that the child may have learnt. For this reason regular words are more easily learnt than irregular words, and, additionally, because knowledge of irregular patterns places cognitive demands on memory and familiarity with phonological representations, these can be quite challenging for dyslexic children. One of the difficulties with models such as the connectionist model is that they may explain the processes involved in reading, but they do not inform about the conscious reading strategies readers may adopt. Nevertheless, this model does place some importance on over-learning as it implies that the connections become stronger with associations, and the more associations that are made the stronger the connections will be. According to Snowling (2000) these connections form a knowledge base that can be drawn upon when the child is faced with a new word.

Methods of teaching reading

The most popular methods teachers use in the teaching of reading include:

- phonic or phonically based;
- look-and-say – reading through sight word recognition;
- language experience – using context, background knowledge and language understanding.

Phonic model

The phonic method highlights the importance of phonology and the sounds of letters and letter combinations. There are a number of structured phonic programs that teach children to distinguish the 44 phonemes (sound units) of English, by using a variety of strategies. These strategies may include color-coding and marks to indicate short or long sounds. Although phonic programs are structured, and structure is beneficial for children with dyslexia, there are also difficulties associated with them. The most important include the possibility that:

- they may increase the burden on children's short- and long-term memory by increasing what the child needs to remember;
- there are still words that need to be taught as sight vocabulary because they do not fall into the 'sound blending' category (e.g., 'one' and 'many').

Phonic methods can help children who have an obvious difficulty in mastering and remembering sound blends and vowels and have difficulty in synthesizing them to make a word. At the same time they present learning that may seem to be out of context. Some difficulty may be identified in merging the two components (i.e., knowledge of sound and knowledge of language) to facilitate a meaningful reading experience.

Chall and Popp (1996) emphasize the need to teach phonics and argue that if taught well, it is highly meaningful – through phonics children can get close to the sound of a word and through that to the meaning of the word. They suggest a systematic phonics approach from pre-school with related activities set within a total reading program. This was also the finding of the US government report on reading (2000) and the UK Rose Report (2006).

Look-and-say model

Look-and-say methods emphasize exposure to print. The view is that children will become familiar with words and build up a sight vocabulary with increased exposure to print. The emphasis is therefore on words rather than speech sounds. This type of method therefore requires attractive books that become progressively more demanding. The use of flashcards and pictures can be used in the initial stages. The method, however, assumes a good memory for shapes of letters and words as well as the ability to master many of the irregularities of spelling and sound–symbol correspondence. This, of course, may be difficult for children with dyslexia, particularly since their memory may be weak and can rapidly become overloaded. Some elements of the phonic approaches can accompany most look-and-say methods. Indeed, Chall and Popp (1996) suggest that a good phonics program needs to pay attention to sight recognition and that fluent reading depends on both automatic sight recognition and the application of phonic knowledge.

Language experience models

Language experience methods focus on the use of language, both oral and written, as an aid to learning to read through various modes of language enrichment. This helps the reader develop important language concepts and schemata, which in turn help to bring meaning to print. Although the child may have a decoding problem, the experience gained in language can help to compensate for this and bring some meaning to the text. This model engages the child in the process of going from thought to speech and then to encoding in print and from print to reading.

Developing reading skills

There is considerable evidence to suggest that pre-reading activities can significantly assist the development of the reading process. Such activities as well as developing pre-reading skills help to develop essential skills in reading comprehension. Reading is interactive, as it combines the reader's background experience and previous knowledge with the 'new' text to be read. This interaction provides the reader with meaning and interpretation. Reading, therefore, is an interaction of previous knowledge involving the use of semantic and syntactic cues and accuracy in the decoding of print. It is important that in teaching reading these aspects are considered. It is likely that the child with dyslexia will find this interactive process difficult as his/her efforts and cognitive capacities are directed to either mechanically decoding the print or obtaining the meaning from print. But the simultaneous interaction of these processes is not easily accomplished.

Teaching reading – the debate

Although it is mainly teachers and educators that are involved in the debate over methodology, it is important that parents have at least an awareness of some of the issues that relate to the controversy in the methods of teaching reading.

The teaching of reading and the field of literacy have been subject to longstanding debate. Theories and methods have been reviewed, revised and recycled. Literacy is one of the areas that appear vulnerable to political initiatives and educational trends. It has become a heated subject of debate, particularly following revelations of dismal and disappointing attainment scores in national and international surveys. The issue of reading standards can be a national concern and lead to national debate. Much of the debate surrounds the differences in approaches between whole language and phonics approaches.

Whole language

This is based on the view that emerged from the work of Goodman (1976; Smith 1973, 1985), which suggests that skillful readers do not process individual letters, spelling–sound translations are irrelevant for reading and it is therefore not necessary to teach spellings and sounds. This view suggests that the teaching of phonics should not be emphasized because children have to learn phonic rules by themselves and can only do this through *experience* in reading. Phonics teaching, therefore, according to this view can result in an overemphasis on the technical decoding skills and as a result the meaning of the text will be lost.

There are considerable arguments against this (Adams, 1990; Rose, 2007; Turner, 1991). These center on the need for children to read words and acquire automaticity in the technical sub-skills of skills of reading before they can obtain meaning from a text. Adams (1990), in fact, argues that automaticity develops from actually reading words and not by ignoring or guessing them.

This view is supported by researchers and educationalists in other countries. Adamik-Já szò (1995) describes the Hungarian experience as based on reading programmes focussing on the oral language development of the child. This indicates that phonemic awareness is a prerequisite of reading instruction. Studies by Johnston et al. (1995) comparing the book experience approach in New Zealand with a systematic phonics approach in Scotland showed that children in the phonics program were significantly better at reading non-words and had significantly superior reading comprehension.

Ehri (1995, 2002) suggests that a weakness in the whole-language approach is the absence of systematic phonics instruction in the early stages. Attention is not paid to the need for young children to master the alphabetic system through learning letter shapes and names, sounds and letter correspondences, and blending sounds into words. Many children do not acquire these skills merely through exposure to print.

Bottom-up view of reading

This is essentially the phonics approach. Tunmer and Greaney (2008) argue that providing struggling readers with explicit and systematic instruction in word analysis skills outside the context of reading text is crucial. They suggest that this would ensure that children with reading difficulties recognize the importance of focussing on word-level cues as the most useful source of information in identifying words. They also maintain that this helps them overcome a tendency to rely on sentence context cues to identify unfamiliar words in text rather than using context to supplement word-level information.

Tunmer and Chapman (2004) argued that, as a consequence of the difficulties experienced by children with dyslexia in phonological awareness and knowledge of print, they may take longer than usual to acquire the 'self-improving' alphabetic coding skills necessary for achieving progress in reading. This is because the process of phonologically decoding a specific printed word a few times eventually cements the word's orthographic (visual) representation in lexical (sight word) memory. According to Tunmer and Chapman, phonological decoding can become a self-teaching mechanism that enables beginning readers to develop sight-word knowledge.

Top-down view of reading

The view described above is not without counter-argument and many argue that the emphasis should be on top-down approaches. For example, Stainthorp (1995) reports on a study that suggests that whole language strategies can modify performance in reading. She accepts, however, that the beneficial effects of context are partly dependent upon children having developed some decoding skills and the skills required for decoding should not be left to chance.

The key theoretical assumption of whole language is that reading acquisition is primarily a process in which children learn to use multiple cues (syntactic, semantic, visual, graphophonic) in identifying unfamiliar words in text, with text-based cues generally being used to generate hypotheses about the text yet to be encountered and letter-sound cues being used mostly for confirmation and self-correction (Shankweiler & Fowler, 2004) of the text (Snow & Juel, 2005).

The major shortcoming of this instructional philosophy is that it stresses the importance of using information from many sources in identifying unfamiliar words without recognizing that skills and strategies involving phonological information are of *primary* importance in the early and fundamental stages of literacy development. Research has established that making use of letter—sound relationships to identify unknown words is the basic mechanism for acquiring sight-word (i.e., word-specific) knowledge, including knowledge of irregularly spelled words (Adams, 1990; Ehri, 2005; Tunmer & Chapman, 2006).

A balanced approach and literacy standards

Clearly, a balanced approach is necessary when looking at the teaching of reading. Both the phonic method and the whole-language movement have many commendable aspects – both should be utilized in relation to the needs of the individual reader.

Welch and Freebody (2002) suggest that there are some general aspects to reading debates across national and international contexts. These include concern about literacy standards, and particularly declining standards and the increase in demands for literacy competencies for effective civil, social and cultural functioning in our society have perhaps created the misleading impression of a decline in literacy standards. It should however be noted that children with dyslexic difficulties usually have considerable difficulty in phonological awareness and, as a result, in acquiring alphabetic and phonic knowledge. This needs to be considered in the development of a balanced program for dyslexic children.

Dealing with reading difficulties

Games and activities

There are many activities that can be utilized to support a structured phonics program. Among the most appropriate of these is the use of games and structured activities to reinforce a particular teaching point. Many of these games and activities can be developed by the teacher, although there are some excellent examples available commercially. The website www.academyone.ca has examples of a number of games for English and math and how you can create these games yourself. The example shown, 'phonics challenge', is a word game that teaches children how to blend three sounds together to make a word. The voice reads the letter sounds and the word, and the child picks out the letters on the phonics keyboard. The keys make the sound of the letter (http://www.academyone.ca/primaryenglish.html; see also www.crossboweducation.com and THRASS – the handwriting, reading and spelling system – http://www.thrass.com).

Activities can include syllable segmentation games such as clapping names, rhyming skills games such as nursery rhymes and alliteration games such as games using pairs of objects with the same sound.

The use of context

Other strategies that can be used are those that rely on the use of context. Readers can utilize two principal types of context:

1. **Syntactic context**: The grammatical structure of sentences and clues from prefixes, punctuation, word endings and word order.
2. **Semantic context:** The meaning of words and the meaningful relations between words.

Syntactic context helps the reader predict the written word. If the child is reading only key words, he or she will not be able to draw on syntactic context for meaning. Extensive use of comprehension-monitoring strategies and self-correction to ensure they have understood what they have read is also important. Using inferences and even accurate guessing can be a powerful aid to dealing with the written word. It is important, therefore, that learners develop skills in using inferences and identifying the main theme and points in a particular story.

Context, therefore, as a reading strategy can be important and is evident in the following ways:

- within the sentence – before and after the word being read;
- within the text – before and after the sentence being read;
- within the reader – entire store of knowledge and experience.

To utilize fully the benefits of contextual reading it is also important for the reader to have a stock of sight words so that the context can be accurately obtained. For example, it has been argued by the proponents of the language experience approach that, instead of helping children build up a stock of sight words in order to read, perhaps teaching should be directed to helping children read in order to build up a stock of sight words. This would mean that sight words can be built up gradually within the context of reading itself. It is interesting to note that the 220 words on the Dolch list (the most commonly used words) make up around 75% of the words in primary reading materials (Chall & Popp, 1996). A classic dilemma is exemplified here between encouraging, indeed insisting on, reading accuracy of all the words and accepting the accurate reading of keywords that should be sufficient through the use of semantic cues for comprehension acquisition.

Dyslexia and reading in different languages

There is good evidence that dyslexia can vary across different languages (Everatt & Elbeheri, 2008). One of the key factors that can account for this variability is the differences in the orthographic features of different languages. Everatt and Elbeheri indicate that in some orthographies (languages) there is close to a one-to-one correspondence between the written symbol (grapheme) and the basic sound (or phoneme). In other orthographies, this correspondence is less transparent. A letter may represent several sounds, and a particular sound may be represented by different letters, depending on the context within which the letter or sound is presented. They indicate that the English orthography is the best example of a less than transparent relationship between letters and sounds; there are many English words that may be considered irregular or exceptions because there is not a direct relationship between the grapheme and phoneme.

German, in contrast, is relatively transparent for both reading and spelling (Zeigler & Goswami, 2005). Similarly, Hungarian has a highly transparent orthography (Smythe et al., 2004), which means that the Hungarian child should be able to pronounce written words relatively accurately simply from sounding out the individual letters or letter combinations within a word, leading to good word decoding accuracy levels and potentially increasing written-word learning.

The difference in how dyslexia can be noted in different languages can have implications for assessment. Much of the assessment procedures for dyslexia are based on identifying difficulties in phonological awareness and phonological processing. The work based on Arabic orthography suggests that literacy learning difficulties may be best predicted on the basis of assessment procedures that include measures of phonological processing, including phonological awareness (Elbeheri & Everatt, 2008). Irrespective of the orthography it seems that measures of phonological processing seem to present the best tools for predicting literacy weaknesses and identifying the underlying problems associated with dyslexia.

Concluding comments

This chapter has looked at the factors associated with reading and the different processes and models of reading. The teaching of reading is not straightforward and it can be confusing for parents to recognize if the approach being used by the school is the most appropriate one for their child. This is a crucial factor and this chapter has only looked at reading as a process, but it is important to place this in the context of your own child's interests, areas of difficulties and the supports available. The research clearly highlights the importance of phonic approaches and it is important that parents should be aware of strategies that can develop phonological approaches. At the same time parents should be aware of other methodologies that can be used for children with dyslexia. The need to develop reading comprehension, sight-word recognition, reading fluency and inferential reading are all important. The key, as indicated in this chapter, is that reading methodology should promote a balanced approach and very importantly needs to take account of the specific and individual challenges experienced by the child.

Chapter 5

Supporting my child with dyslexia

This chapter looks at strategies that parents can use at home and how they can link with schools as well as the factors that can influence the choice of the most appropriate school.

Strategies for reading

Decoding, sight words and reading fluency

These are three important aspects of reading. *Decoding* helps the reader break down words into smaller units, *sight words* help to build up automatic word reading and *fluency* helps with comprehension of the text. You will have noted in chapter 4 that decoding refers to the ability to break words down into the small units (phonemes) and blend them together to make words. Once a new word is learnt the child will eventually develop automaticity in that word and will be able to read it by sight (sight words). This means, of course, that he/she will *not* need to

Dyslexia: A Complete Guide for Parents and Those Who Help Them, Second Edition. Gavin Reid.
© 2011 John Wiley & Sons, Ltd. Published 2011 by John Wiley & Sons, Ltd.

break down (decode) the word every time they come across it. This is how children develop reading fluency. The challenge is that children with dyslexia often experience difficulty in acquiring automaticity. Often the same word has to be used repeatedly and over-learnt before they can acquire automaticity. As a result if they have to actively decode many words in a piece of text it will take longer for them to read it. The process of reading using sight words is faster than the decoding process. The key therefore is to try to help the child with dyslexia develop automaticity in word recognition. But they also need to know how to decode. The skills of decoding which requires knowledge of the sounds and the sound combinations as well as the letters are important as children with dyslexia will need to use these skills to break down words as they are reading. Reading fluency is important as it is connected to reading comprehension, and lack of fluency in reading can have an adverse effect on text understanding.

It is important therefore that children with dyslexia are taught decoding strategies as well as sight words and provided with strategies for reading fluency and comprehension. This chapter looks at each of those aspects in turn.

Decoding strategies

The ability to decode depends on the child's phonological awareness. This is the ability to be aware of sounds in words. The fact is that the 26 letters in the English alphabet can make at least 44 different sound combinations and it can be challenging for children with dyslexia to develop the letter–sound correspondence because there are many different combinations. The beginning stage of this is phonological awareness; the awareness of sounds and being aware of sounds that rhyme can be good practice for this. Nursery rhymes therefore do have an important part to play in this process. There is research to show that phonological awareness is challenging for children with dyslexia and is an important precursor to accurate and fluent reading (National Reading Panel, 2000).

Phonological processing involves phoneme identification and manipulation of phonemes when decoding words. This is the initial step in developing an understanding of the use of phonemes. Spoken language can be broken down in many different ways, including sentences into words and words into syllables (e.g., in the word simple, /sim/ and /ple/), onset and rime (e.g., in the word broom, /br/ and /oom/), and individual phonemes (e.g., in the word hamper, /h/, /a/, /m/, /p/, /er/). Manipulating phonemes is also important and this includes deleting, adding or substituting syllables or sounds (e.g., say can; say it without the /k/; say can with /m/ instead of /k/). These areas are usually challenging for children with dyslexia.

Word attack skills

Activities for developing word attack skills include:

- rhyming activities and rhyming games;
- blending and segmenting of words into onset and rime, that is the beginning of the word (onset) and the remainder of the word (rime);
- games involving blending, segmenting and deleting phonemes, word games and games such as Scrabble can also be good;
- exercises to help with the recognition of alliterations, sound patterns and rhyme within words;
- practice at identifying initial and final sounds in words; and
- practice at blending longer words.

Pre-reading discussion

It is important to engage in pre-reading discussion with the child before he/she reads the text. This means that if your child is about to make a start on homework that involves reading, you should discuss the background to the text with him/her before the text is attempted. There is a body of research that suggests that pre-reading discussion is one of the best predictors of a successful outcome in a reading activity.

Some questions that can provide a framework for pre-reading discussion are shown below. It can be more effective if the parent first reads the passage to the child, or perhaps use paired reading (see appendix 2), and then suggest some questions the child should ask him/herself as the passage is being read.

A possible framework for pre-reading questions

Some of the questions that can be asked in framing pre-reading questions include:

- Who are the main characters?
- How do you know they are the main characters?
- What do you know about the characters?
- What are they doing?
- Where is the passage (book) set?
- Can you describe the scene?
- What happens in the story?
- How does it end?
- Do you think it was as good ending, why/why not?

This type of activity will provide the reader with a sequence for the narrative and the key characters in the story, but it will also help the reader form opinions on the text. It is through forming opinions that a higher level of comprehension will develop.

Pre-reading discussion should be engaged in whether or not the child is a competent reader. The child may be lagging in decoding (skills in reading accuracy), but it is important that he/she does not lose ground in language comprehension. Usually children with dyslexia will have skills in comprehension.

If the child is about to tackle a book, it may also be helpful to obtain a video of the book. This will help to provide a visual image of the scene and an overall context for the main characters and the events.

Certainly this type of activity to enhance language comprehension will take place in school, but parents need to be aware of this to reinforce it at home.

Critical literacy

Critical literacy is how the reader responds to the text. That is essentially the level of understanding achieved from the text. We all know that a book can be understood at different levels and that different interpretations can be placed on what the author is saying. Many suggest that critical literacy can be placed at the highest stage of the literacy hierarchy. Eames (2002) suggests that critical literacy involves constructing meaning from text and that such meanings are achieved during interaction of reader and text, during discussion of text and when listening and responding to others. This has important implications for children with dyslexia and particularly young adults who may not have efficient decoding skills. Wray (2006) acknowledges that critical literacy is not a new concept and can be recognized as critical language awareness, critical social literacy and critically aware literacy. He argues however that there are some common threads running through the different approaches to critical literacy. One of the crucial factors rests on the assumption that being literate is not sufficient. He argues that to fully engage in critical literacy one needs to encourage children to investigate, question and challenge what the book is saying. This is important for children with dyslexia and particularly for parents. Often after an assessment parents ask me how they can help at home. I usually give a list of suggestions but also emphasize that reading is more than just acquiring the technical skills of print – it is more than cracking the code. Reading involves critical literacy and being aware of the implications of what the author is suggesting and perhaps why this is the case. Often these higher-order reading skills are lost to children with dyslexia as so much of their tuition time is taken up merely acquiring the skills of reading.

Consistency with school

It is important that parents know how reading is taught in school. There are a number of activities that parents can do at home that can help to develop the reading skills of their dyslexic child. It can however be more productive if parents use this time with their child to reinforce the reading activities that are taking place in school. For example, if the child is being taught specific sounds or spelling rules, then these can be followed up at home by parents. Generally speaking however any kind of literacy activity will be useful for the child. It is important however to ensure that the child does not become switched off from reading because of the demands it places on him/her. The role of the parents therefore is to help to instill an interest in reading, perhaps through discussion, reading to the child or reading together. These can minimize the demands of the reading task for the dyslexic child and make it more of a fun activity.

Reading practice

Practice in reading is important. The reading material does not need to be established works of literature, but can be anything that is going to interest the child. Newspapers and magazines can be just as useful as a source of reading material, and perhaps more motivating than some books. The key point is that practice is essential. It is through practice that reading can become part of the child's routine. It is important to try to establish this. The 'hi-lo' readers can be excellent – these are characterized by the high interest and low vocabulary level of the book and are ideal for children with dyslexia (see appendix 4).

Games

Games can be an excellent way of reinforcing reading. Although there are a number of commercially produced games (see appendix 4) parents can utilize popular game-type activities, even board games, or games such as Scrabble. These can help the child become more familiar with words and with reading in general.

Literacy programs in practice

As a parent you will be aware that many commercial reading programs available. These can be expensive and you do not want to waste precious time or money on an approach that may not be suitable for your child. Schools can provide advice on this and it is beneficial to link with the school as it is important that the teaching of reading at home and at school should be in harmony and complementary. An excellent source of advice are parents' groups and voluntary associations. In the US the International Dyslexia Association (IDA) has prepared a matrix of programs (Table 5.1) that can be accessed by parents so

Table 5.1 IDA matrix of programs

The International Dyslexia Association has produced a short matrix of
multisensory structured language programs indicating the type of
program delivery, the level of phonic instruction how each program deals
with fluency, comprehension, written expression and text construction
and the level of training needed.

The programs included in the matrix are: OG (www.OrtonAcademy.org),
Alphabetic Phonics (www.ALTAread.org), Association Method
(www.usm.edu/dubard), Language! (www.SoprisWest.com),
Lexia-Herman Method (www.Hermanmethod.com), Lindamood–Bell,
www.Lindamoodbell.com), Project Read, www.Projectread.com),
Slingerland, www.Slingerland.org), Sonday System
(www.SondaySystem.com), Sounds in Syllables, Spalding Method
(www.Spalding.org), Starting Over, Wilson Fundations and Wilson
Reading (www.wilsonlanguage.com).

they can decide themselves if a particular program is suitable for their child. Other countries have similar web advice and associations such as the British Dyslexia Association (BDA), the European Dyslexia (EDA), SPELD in New Zealand and Australia, the LDA in Canada, the Canadian Academy of Therapeutic Tutors (CATT) and Dyslexia International (http://www.dyslexia-international.org).

You may also want to consider the criteria set by the National Institute of Child Health and Human Development (NICHD, 2000; http://www.ed.gov/inits/americareads/nichd.html) that when teaching children who have a difficult time learning to read, explicit, systematic instruction is most effective in teaching reading. This instruction should:

- teach phonemic awareness (e.g., tell me the sounds in the word 'sat') at an early age (kindergarten);
- teach the common sound–spelling relationships in words;
- teach children how to say the sounds in the words;
- use text that is a composed of words that use sound–spelling correspondences that children have learned;
- use interesting stories to develop vocabulary and language comprehension; and

- the most effective classroom method for early reading instruction involves a combination of explicit instruction in word-recognition skills and reading-comprehension strategies with opportunities to apply and practice these skills in literature.

Orton–Gillingham

Programs based on this approach have become a central focus for multisensory teaching for children with dyslexia. The programs offer a structured, phonic-based approach that incorporates the total language experience and focuses on the letter sounds and the blending of these sounds into syllables and words. The approach rests heavily on the interaction of visual, auditory and kinaesthetic aspects of language.

Recent studies by NICHD in the US have concluded that the best strategy for preventing and correcting reading problems is explicit, systematic instruction that emphasizes:

- early letter knowledge;
- phonemic awareness;
- instruction in letter–sound correspondence and spelling generalizations;
- opportunity and encouragement to use spelling–sound knowledge in reading and writing;
- daily sessions for supported and independent reading with attention to fluency and comprehension;
- active exploration of concepts provided in written text.

According to the Canadian Academy of Therapeutic Tutors, the Orton–Gillingham approach meets all these criteria (http://www.ogtutors.com).

Orton–Gillingham lessons, according to Henry (1996, 2003), always incorporate card drills, spelling and reading, and usually include activities such as:

- **Card drills**: This involves the use of commercial or teacher-made cards containing the common letter patterns to strengthen the visual modality: phonemes (sounds) for auditory and kinesthetic

reinforcement and syllables and whole words to help develop blending skills.
- **Word lists and phrases**.
- **Oral reading selection**: This involves the teacher first reading the
  passage, then the student;
- Spelling of phonetic and non-phonetic words.
- **Handwriting**: Attention being placed on pencil grip, writing posture
  and letter formation. This would also include tracing, copying and
  practice, and making cursive connections such as *br*, *bl*.
- **Composition**: Encouragement to develop writing sentences, paragraphs and short stories.

Henry (2003) also maintains that lessons take place as a 'dynamic
discussion session with the teacher acting as facilitator as well as in-
structor' (p. xiv).

Issues to consider

The range of individualized programs for children with dyslexia is im-
pressive, and some of the principles of the programs and the approaches
advocated by their authors, such as 'multi-sensory', 'structured' and
'cumulative' approaches, can provide useful pointers in the development of support materials for dyslexic children. It is also worth considering the comments made by the National Reading Panel in the US
in their report 'Teaching Children to Read: An evidence-based assessment of the scientific research literature on reading and its implications
for reading instruction' (US Government, 2000). Of particular interest
is the panel's insistence on using evidence-based criteria to evaluate
interventions. They believe that the highest standard of evidence for
claims of success of a reading program is the experimental study, in
which it is shown that treatment can make such changes and effect such
outcomes. They suggested that when it is not feasible to do a random-
ized experiment, a quasi-experimental study should be conducted as
this type of study provides a standard of evidence that, while not as
high, is acceptable, depending on the study design.
Similarly in the UK the Independent Review of the Teaching of
Early Reading (Rose Report, 2006) strongly advocated high quality,

systematic phonic work that should be taught discretely. The knowledge, skills and understanding that constitute high quality phonic work should be taught as the principal approach in learning to decode (read) and encode (write/spell) print.

Phonic work, the report suggested, should be set within a broad and rich language curriculum that takes full account of developing the four interdependent strands of language: speaking, listening, reading and writing and enlarging children's stock of words.

Spelling

Spelling can be a frustrating and long-term difficulty for children with dyslexia. Accurate spelling requires good short- and long-term memory skills, skills in sequencing letters in the correct order, accurate listening to pick up the sounds in words (auditory perception) and the ability to remember spelling rules and the groups of letters that make up specific sounds such as 'ch' and 'sh'. These can be challenging for children with dyslexia. Moreover, once a child starts habitually misspelling a word it becomes almost ingrained and they misspell that word automatically. It is difficult to unlearn once the child has reached this stage. It is better to deal with spelling difficulties as early as possible.

When a child is writing a piece of information, the writing process, that is the content and the language expression, may take precedence over spelling. The child is too 'busy' concentrating on what he/she is writing to think about correct spelling. It is important therefore that time and opportunities are used for proof reading. Even proof reading or checking over one's own work can be difficult, but the extra few minutes spent can pay dividends, especially for dyslexic students in secondary school. It is best to proof read once for meaning and again for accuracy of spelling.

It is also a good idea for children or young adults with dyslexia to develop their own notebook of words that they usually misspell. They will then know which words to concentrate on when checking spelling.

The use of a word processor with a good spellchecker is of great benefit. Some spellcheckers may not identify some of the errors made by dyslexic children because the spelling does not resemble the actual word closely enough. Specially designed spellcheckers such as

TextHelp™ are superb because they can identify dyslexic spelling errors.

TextHelp™

TextHelp is particularly useful for assisting with essay writing. It has a read-back facility and a spellchecker that includes a dyslexic spellcheck option which searches for common dyslexic errors. Additionally, Text Help has a word prediction feature that can predict a word from the context of the sentence giving up to 10 options from a dropdown menu. Often dyslexic students have a word-finding difficulty and this feature can therefore be very useful. This software also has a Word Wizard which provides the user with a definition of any word; options regarding homophones; an outline of a phonic map; and a talking help file.

Look, cover, write and check

This procedure is used to help develop spelling accuracy. it involves a number of stages that the child can utilize to spell accurately. First, the child looks at the word so that he/she will have a visual image of it, then the word is covered and the child writes it and finally checks if it has been spelt accurately.

This process can promote visual learning of words. Additionally, even if the word is not spelt correctly, the child will have the opportunity to self-correct and this in itself can help develop accuracy.

Writing

Writing, particularly creative writing, can be very frustrating for children with dyslexia. It is also frustrating for parents who know that their child is capable of performing to a higher level. Usually there is a discrepancy between the child's written performance and his/her knowledge of the subject. Children with dyslexia do not usually perform to their best in written work. This is unfortunate and frustrating.

Certainly parents can help to encourage their child to write and word processing can help this process considerably, but some additional support is also necessary. Children with dyslexia need structure and cues to help develop their writing and to generate ideas. Structure words that may be used include:

- When
- Where
- People
- Sound
- Color
- Background

These words can prompt ideas and generate a fuller piece of work.

Another method of helping with writing that is used in schools and can be used by parents is writing frames, which can help with aspects of creative writing. This can include providing key words, a beginning sentence, a framework for the plot and perhaps a final sentence. Writing frames can be used as a guide which parents may find useful if the child becomes frustrated in a writing exercise.

One of the key factors in relation to writing is confidence. Unfortunately, children with dyslexia may not have much confidence in writing or indeed in learning. Boosting the self-esteem of the child with dyslexia is therefore very important.

Working at home with your child

It is important that undue pressure is not put on the child at home. This is easier said than done as sometimes homework can take the child with dyslexia twice as long to complete as non-dyslexic children. It is not fair on the child that school work should absorb their leisure time. If it does, it would be wise for the parents to talk to the teacher and some consideration may be given to this issue by the school.

Essentially home can be a refuge for children with dyslexia. It is important therefore that the child does not experience additional pressures from well-meaning, but anxious parents. This can be difficult as parents, rightly, want the best for their child and achievements at school are important to secure a place on college and university courses as well as work in an increasingly competitive employment market.

Guidance to parents on the issue of working at home includes:

- Consider what would be an adequate amount of time to spend on homework and ensure that your child is not spending more time than he/she should.
- Discuss any issues arising from the length of time spent on homework with the school.
- Discuss the homework with your child before he/she starts it – a parent can help the child establish exactly what has to be done and the materials that are needed.
- Ensure that the homework is carried out in an environment that suits your child's learning style. If they need background music, then allow this as it may help them to concentrate.
- Discuss the homework with your child when it is completed and discuss the comments made by the teacher on the homework.
- Ensure there is a balance in your child's out-of-school time between school work and free time.
- Extra tuition can sometimes be helpful, but it is important that any tuition independent of the school should link with school work, otherwise it could be counter-productive.
- Remember that some television programs can be educational, so do not restrict this although clearly television should be used in moderation. Similarly learning through the internet can be very educational, but it is only one means of obtaining information. Television and learning through the internet can become a family activity with at least two members of the family involved.
- Try to ensure that the child sees learning as fun. The internet can help to achieve that and children with dyslexia often prefer exploratory and investigative learning to remembering information and facts.

Secondary school subjects

It is important to take note of some of the challenges children with dyslexia face in the range of subjects in secondary school.

Table 5.2   Reading strategies

Strategy	Function
Talk	Discussion is crucial for most children with dyslexia. It is an active form of learning and can also help you monitor your child's understanding.
Drama	Some learners can develop comprehension more effectively through active participation. This uses the kinesthetic (experiential) modality and this type of learning can be essential for some learners. Encouraging drama activities can be very beneficial.
Drawing	Visual representation can also be essential for many learners with dyslexia – some children can only learn visually so even the most basic of information may have to be presented visually.
Listening	All children need to develop listening skills. For some this can be challenging so it is important that listening is given high priority, but it is equally important that listening should be only for short periods of time and interspersed with other activities.
Role play	Can be excellent tool for developing imagination. It helps to facilitate children's creativity and furthermore can make learning individual. Additionally, role play uses the kinesthetic modality and this experiential type of learning can benefit many learners with dyslexia.
Feelings	It is important to recognize that learning involves the whole person – the emotional aspects of learning are important. It is crucial to identify any anxieties your child may be experiencing around the learning process.

(from www.icepe.eu course for parents; Reid, 2010)

Math

- **Symbols:** Understanding and remembering symbols to many children with dyslexia represents learning a new language. It is important that time is taken to allow students with dyslexia to get to know symbols even basic ones such as multiply and divide.

Strategy

You need to encourage the teacher to allow more time and ensure your child achieves mastery before moving on to the next step.

- **Quantity:** Much of math is about understanding and using quantities and solving problems based on the relationships between quantities. This can be demanding for students with dyslexia.

Strategy

Ensure over-learning takes place so that children can immediately recognize the different quantities, practice putting them in rank order with the biggest first and then reversing this placing the smallest first (you may want to make up games based on this).

- **Organization:** Children with dyslexia often get muddled when doing math problems because their working is spread all over the page. They often take more steps to solve a problem than other children so will need space for this. Many mistakes are made because the page is crowded.

Strategy

It will be time well spent at the beginning of a task to ensure your child has enough space on the page for the work they are doing and it might be useful to help them organize the page. Perhaps some work such as additions can be done at the side of the page clear of the main problem.

- **Rules and sequences:** There are many rules and sequences in math and remembering these can place a burden on the child with dyslexia.

It is important the rules are consolidated in long-term memory, but to remember these effectively it is best if learning takes place in context.

Strategy

It might be a good idea to have a separate notebook for the rules your child has to remember. They can refer to these as they are being used. It is only through using the rules in context that they will be consolidated in long-term memory. Practice placing procedures in sequence and number and color code each sequence. You could use a traffic light sequence, i.e., red, amber and green for one, two and three.

- **Poor recognition of shapes:** This can be a problem for children with dyslexia. Some have good visual spatial skills but many have not, especially if the shapes are not meaningful for the child.

Strategy

It might be a good idea to have a notebook for 'shapes only' that are used in math such as polygon and hexagon. This can be a small notebook they can carry about with them that will have the common shapes which they can use as a reference. This is also a good way to build up automaticity. It might also be a good idea to put the number of sides the shape has next to each shape.

- **Reading and vocabulary:** Often children with dyslexia find math difficult because of the reading that is associated with math problems. Often math problems require copying numbers and copying as well as reading can prove problematic. When copying they may also lose their place on the page.

Strategy

Try to help your child simplify the vocabulary in math problems – it might be an idea to go over the sum or problem with them before they start to tackle it to ensure it has been copied correctly and the instructions have been understood. It may also be useful to use some form of concrete aid as a marker to ensure they do not lose the place on the book.

- **Reversals of numbers and confusions of letters and words:** This can be quite common especially with younger children. They may also confuse letters and words that look and sound similar.

Strategy

Help your child to trace over the numbers themselves. This will strengthen their kinesthetic memory.

- **Confusion of directional and place words:** Words such as left from right, up and down, back and front, before and after.

Strategy

Try to use color coding for this with a key for the child to see which color represents which word.

- **Attention and concentration:** Math can demand intensive attention over a period of time. This in itself can be demanding for children with dyslexia.

Strategy

Try to break the task down into small units or chunks. Try to make the breaks quite natural so the flow of the problem is not disrupted too much. It might be important here also to know your child's learning style, especially the best environment conditions such as working in silence or with background noise.

- **Frustration and anxiety:** It is easy for the child with dyslexia to become frustrated with math. Frustration can also produce fatigue and a feeling of 'learned helplessness'. They may then become anxious at the very thought of doing math and this in itself becomes a hurdle to overcome. It is best to try to prevent this from happening.

Strategy

Try to make math a game and use visuals as much as possible. It might also be worthwhile spending time with the child in a sort of 'paired math' where the first few problems are tackled together and then the adult gradually lets the child take the lead. Again, it needs to be remembered that math may be tiring for the child. Short tasks and frequent breaks may prevent fatigue.

- **Poor visual tracking and visual acuity:** This can be a problem because some children with dyslexia have visual difficulties and may miss lines or misread numbers.

Strategy

Use color paper instead of white – this can be less of a contrast and easier on the eyes than the contrast between black print and white paper. Transparent color rulers are also useful.

Learning styles in math

Math is a very challenging subject for students with dyslexia so it is important that they are aware of their learning preferences as this will help them access challenging materials more easily. This can also help you at home when working with your child.

Steve Chinn (2004) identified two types of math learning style: the inchworm and grasshopper.

The inchworm is the student who takes one piece of information at a time and places a heavy emphasis on sequence and procedure. The grasshopper is less likely to rely on sequence and tends to be a more random and perhaps more unpredictable processor of information. Many students with dyslexia tend to be grasshoppers. The result is that often they are unsure how they arrived at the answer and may find it more difficult to retrace their steps.

It is important therefore to help grasshoppers organize their work into a sequence and to help them identify the steps they are using. It is also important to support them in using their learning style more efficiently. That does not mean one has to try to change the style but help them use their style efficiently. For example, the grasshopper style is the most vulnerable in math because it is random and math is a precise and often sequential subject which requires strict adherence to processes and rules. The grasshopper learner therefore requires a structure to prevent them from going too far astray. On the other hand, the inchworm may take a long time to complete the problem as they may go through a very sequential and laborious route. Again this may be improved by checking to see if some of the steps can be omitted or shortened.

Additional language learning

It is quite widely recognized that dyslexic children often suffer from problems learning a foreign language. Dal (2008) provides some areas which are important for foreign language learning:

1. phonological processing (poor grasp of sound, lack of awareness of individual sounds within words);

2. memory (working memory might be limited, there may be inaccurate representations in long-term memory);
3. auditory discrimination (uncertainty of the sound which has been heard, difficulty in discrimination between similar sounds, difficulty in knowing where a spoken word ends and a new word begins);
4. sequencing (getting things in order, e.g., letter order in words);
5. speed of processing information (tendency to be slower in responding to incoming information);
6. visual discrimination/recognition (poor ability to differentiate between similar looking words).

Many of these particular areas can be demanding for children with dyslexia.

In a multinational survey conducted in primary schools in Austria, Denmark and Iceland, Dal, Arnbak and Brandstätter (2005) aimed to identify what schools could do to help dyslexic students participate in language classes, what language teachers do to help dyslexic students in language classes, what specific tools are used to help dyslexic students and what the language teachers see as the main problems of the dyslexic students learning a foreign language. The results of the survey indicate that, in general, the schools' policy is to include dyslexic students in foreign language but it was noteworthy that there was a huge variation within schools in each country and there was a discrepancy between the countries in the study. According to Dal the results suggest a need to make the problems of the dyslexic students in foreign language classes much more transparent in the official policy of the schools.

Dal (2008) suggests that the problems dyslexic students experience in learning a foreign language are closely related to written and oral skills in their mother tongue and that although most language teachers and schools acknowledge that dyslexic students might have difficulties learning a foreign language, the policy of inclusion means that little special provision is made for them in language classes and many language teachers are unsure on how to best teach them.

Examinations – reasonable accommodations

It is important for parents to be aware of what might be considered as reasonable accommodations for exams. This can vary from country to country but a good example is that from Ireland (see http://www.dyslexia.ie/examaccommodations.htm).

Accommodations include:

1. reader;
2. tape recorder;
3. word processor;
4. exemption from spelling and grammatical components in language subjects (waiver).

It is important that whatever accommodations are felt to be appropriate that the student him/herself has opportunities well before the examination to try them out. Discussion of the accommodations that can be used should be started at least two years before the exam. This will allow the student ample time to practice using the accommodation as efficiently as possible.

Summary

This chapter has provided some pointers for supporting your child at home and assisting you in your communication with schools. It is important to communicate with the school, but this needs to be a two-way process and parents have to feel comfortable with the school and at ease in their discussions with school personnel. The pointers indicated in this chapter about what can make a school effective for children with dyslexia need to be considered. It is also important to consider the individual needs of your child. Remember that you know your child best and you are likely the most tuned in to his/her needs. It is also important to communicate with your child and have open discussions on any anxieties and concerns and come to a consensus on the best way forward. Of course, with young children parents have to take this responsibility themselves but it is important to consider the emotional needs of your child irrespective of their age. Emotional strength can go a long way to help any child meet and deal with the challenges of dyslexia they are likely to encounter at every stage of schooling.

Chapter 6

Overlapping difficulties: Dyscalculia

Introduction

Although dyslexia is mainly related to literacy you may become aware of overlapping difficulties between dyslexia and other learning disabilities such as dyspraxia (movement and coordination) dyscalculia (number work) and ADHD (attention difficulties). Kaplan et al. (2001) challenged the view of focussing on specific syndromes and labels and suggested that there are no pure diagnostic categories of developmental disorders, but rather 'semi-random' clusters of symptoms related to motor coordination, learning and processing factors. For example, out of a study measuring 162 children for dyspraxia, reading difficulties and ADHD, 53 children obtained scores which classified them for 'pure' cases, 47 children did not meet the criteria for any of the three conditions and 62 were classified as overlapping in each of the three categories. Kaplan et al. suggested that overlap is the rule rather than the exception.

Dyslexia: A Complete Guide for Parents and Those Who Help Them, Second Edition. Gavin Reid.
© 2011 John Wiley & Sons, Ltd. Published 2011 by John Wiley & Sons, Ltd.

Labels are, however, helpful and essential. They can provide direction to parents and to schools and eventually can help the students themselves develop self-knowledge and personal strategies to help with their own learning. Nevertheless the label is only the starting point and attention needs to be paid to the specific characteristics of the child's profile. It is important that a full assessment is obtained to provide an accurate picture of the child's strengths and difficulties and, as was indicted in chapter 3, this can also provide a label if appropriate.

Dyscalculia

According to research undertaken at University College London (Butterworth, 2003) some children beginning school will have been born with deficits that could impact on their ability to deal with all or part of the curriculum, including numeracy. It is believed that 4% of children are severely dyslexic and a further 6% are affected at the mild—moderate level. It is also believed that about 40% of these will experience significant difficulty with mathematics. There is therefore concern that a large number of the population will have considerable difficulties with the processing of mathematics to a level which may affect their performances in the curriculum.

Difficulties such as this are usually termed dyscalculia and it is suggested that students with dyscalculia are troubled by even the simplest numerical tasks: for example, selecting the larger of two numbers, counting the number of objects in a display or activating the meanings of numerals.

Factors associated with dyscalculia

Students:

- may have an impaired sense of number size — this may affect tasks involving estimating numbers in a collection and comparing numbers;

- can usually learn the sequence of counting words, but may have difficulty navigating back and forth, especially in twos, threes or more;
- may find it especially difficult to translate between number words, where powers of ten are expressed by new names (ten, hundred, thousand) and numerals (where powers of ten are expressed by the same numerals but in terms of place value);
- may find reading and writing numbers problematic especially numbers over 1,000;
- may find learning and recalling number facts difficult — they often lack confidence even when they produce the correct answer; they also fail to use rules and procedures to build on known facts, e.g., they may know that $5 + 3 = 8$, but not realize that $3 + 5 = 8$ or that $5 + 4 = 9$;
- may have a lack of an intuitive grasp of number magnitudes makes checking calculations especially difficult;
- may have difficulty in understanding which type of arithmetical operation to use;
- may have trouble with money;
- may have exaggerated difficulties with intensive numbers – i.e., those involving x per y, either explicitly or implicitly – such as speed (miles per hour), temperature (energy per unit of mass), averages and proportional measures;
- may have spatial problems, which affects understanding of position and direction;
- will usually have difficulty in handling data, including graphs, charts and diagrams.

Chinn (2004) has done a great deal of work on dyscalculia, learning styles, thinking styles and dyslexia. He suggests there are several consequences of thinking styles for learners with dyscalculia as they may have what he calls a grasshopper learning style, a style that takes in the whole picture rather than a step-by-step, inchworm approach. The grasshopper would very likely be the right brain learner, who learns in a random, global style and needs to see the whole rather than the individual parts, while the inchworm needs to see the individual parts first and prefers a structured approach.

According to Chinn and Everatt (2009) there are combinations of the factors that may lead to mathematics learning difficulties and to dyscalculia. These include the following:

- An extreme grasshopper (see above), who may be reluctant to note and document his/her 'working' so it is difficult to note where the errors have occurred. An extreme and inaccurate grasshopper, probably impulsive, will fail.
- An inchworm can be a very slow processor when undertaking mathematics problems. As a result he/she may fail because of the length of time taken. It is necessary therefore to ensure that additional time is provided for students who have dyscalculia difficulties.
- An inchworm with poor short-term memory will fail in mental mathematics and be slow in written work.
- An inchworm with poor long-term mathematical memory for basic facts and procedures will fail as the memory demands that mathematics makes as they progress through school exceed their capabilities.
- Over-reliance on counting strategies, a poor understanding of place value and procedural errors will create mathematics learning difficulties.
- Poor retrieval of basic facts without compensatory strategies could create mathematics learning difficulties, especially in rigid teaching environments.
- High anxiety may prevent a learner from engaging in mathematics activities.
- Poor presentation skills and not using the paper appropriately.
- An inability to see the patterns and generalizations and develop concepts – this can also account for extra time being needed.

Chinn (2009) suggests children with dyscalculia have difficulty with the following:

- remembering basic addition facts;
- the ability to make one-to-one correspondence when counting;
- 'seeing' that four objects are 4 without counting (or 3, if a young child);
- counting backwards instead of forwards;

- fluently counting less familiar sequences, such as 1, 3, 5, 7, 9, 11 . . . or 14, 24, 34, 44, 54, 64 . . .
- can only access the 2 ×, 5 × and 10 × facts;
- may be able to learn multiplication facts, but will forget them overnight;
- have difficulty in writing numbers which include zeros, such as 'three hundred and four' or 'four thousand and twenty-one';
- write 51 for fifteen or 61 for sixteen;
- have difficulty estimating;
- usually weak at mental arithmetic;
- forget the question asked in mental arithmetic;
- have poor organization of written work, for example, columns of numbers are not lined up;
- have poor skills with money, for example, they are unable to calculate change from a purchase;
- are very anxious about doing *any* mathematics;
- do not 'see' that 7 + 5 is the same as 5 + 7 or that 7 × 3 is the same as 3 × 7;
- rush to get any task completed, or avoid the task by not starting it.

This list is not exhaustive. But it does give you some ideas and pointers when you are working out if your child has dyscalculic difficulties as well as dyslexia.

Supporting your child with dyscalculia

It is important that parents are able to understand the challenges that their child may experience in math even though they may not be able to provide practical help. This depends on the age of the child; it is likely that most parents will be able to support young children who are doing basic math, but as the problems become more complex and specific many parents may not be able to provide the practical support needed. While this can be a problem it is worth emphasizing that even without the technical 'know-how' it is still possible for parents to support their child with dyscalculia.

Table 6.1 Suggestions for strategies

What to look out for	How to help
Problems with reading the questions in mathematics. This can cause great distress and may lead to a lack of self-esteem.	Offer support to read the question. Read the question in chunks. Be aware of the higher readability levels of mathematic texts so you will need to encourage re-reading.
Hesitancy limits their spontaneity to participate in mathematic activities.	Read with a highlighter pen and offer support to find the relevant mathematical words, numbers and number words in the question.
Comprehension difficulties when reading new or unfamiliar words are a barrier to grasping the underlying concepts.	Build up a word wall of the vocabulary for each topic. Highlight the number words in one color, the calculation vocabulary in another color and the final step of the problem in a third color.
Repeated re-reading is needed to understand the meaning.	Use the chunking and highlighting technique. Identify the calculation steps and write out each calculation in numbers and symbols.
If questions are long, the first part may be forgotten. The readability level of mathematical vocabulary is often higher than the child's reading ability.	Allow the child extra time and ensure that he/she is not under pressure to read and respond quickly. Teach the child to use the chunking technique. Number the steps to solving the problem and write the calculation needed at each step.
May lose their place when reading a long question and miss out vital words.	Track down the lines of text using a ruler or bookmark card. Try using a colored overlay or colored ruler.
Children with directional problems concentrating on a left-to-right reading flow may not see vertical tables in a piece of text.	Tables in questions can be printed in different colored text or get your child to highlight this.

(*Continued*)

Table 6.1 (*Continued*)

Reading a large number is difficult, as it has to be split up into thousands and millions by counting in threes from the right. Then it has to be read correctly from the left. Children who struggle with right and left find this hard.	Teach the technique for reading a large number by chunking the figures from the right in threes. Use a place value chart to help with this.
May not see the decimal point and so have problems with place value.	Use color coding to teach place value with arrow cards. Use a large red decimal point and make it very obvious.

(Adapted from Henderson & Came, 2003).

- Gather as much information about the task as possible and ensure that your child has all the information needed to do it.
- Ensure your child has all the resources that are necessary for the task. It is worth ensuring that he/she has the right kind of calculator. Most computers have different types of calculators, for example the laptop I am working on at the moment shows a selection including standard, scientific, statistics, digit grouping, unit conversion and date conversion. There is also a prototype for working out fuel economy and mortgage repayments and interest rates.
- Start with what the child already knows and link this information to the problem being tackled. Your child may be surprised with how much he/she actually knows and with some discussion of the steps may well be able to tackle what seemed like an insurmountable problem.
- Try to help your child work out the rules and the logic of the problem. This is why pre-task discussion is important as he/she may have done a problem like this before but may only realize that after discussion.
- Together, you can work through a step-by-step solution to the problem. Get the child to write down the steps taken – this is important in case they make a mistake as they can retrace their steps to see where the mistake occurred. The actual practice of writing down the

steps can be important too and this can help to embed the process in memory.

- Identify concepts and rules – this is important and you can work together to identify some of the key ideas and rules. You can divide the page into concepts – ideas and examples. This can help with the transfer of learning and help with problems they may encounter later.
- Identify the math vocabulary used and ensure your child knows it. It is a good idea to compile a list of the words and their meaning in a notebook (Table 6.2). It may also be a good idea to use visuals in order to personalize it.

Coventry, Pringle, Rifkind and Weedon (2001) examined the demands that mathematics can present for students with dyslexia. They suggest that mathematical thinking exists as a distinctive entity partly because it explores areas of thought beyond the easy control of words. Weedon (1992) suggests that math involves ideas and relationships that cannot easily be put into words. These abstract concepts and ideas can be difficult for students with dyslexia because, as Coventry et al.

Table 6.2 Subject-specific vocabulary

History	Geography	Chemistry	Biology
Revolution	Terrain	Compound	Stem
Epoch	Climate	State	Physiological
Dynasty	Environment	Experiment	Cell mutation
English	**Mathematics**	**Art**	**Physical Education**
Metaphor	Calculate	Easel	Words used in specific
Literature	Fraction	Texture	sports such as: line
Syntax	Formulae	Sketch	judge, putt, ace, offside,
	Perimeter		substitute, dugout, free
			kick, etc.
	Modern		
Music	**languages**		
Score	Accent		
Sheet	Culture		
Orchestra	Customs		
Notes	Parts of speech		

suggest, it requires organization and access to knowledge, rules, techniques, skills and concepts. Often the rules that play an important part in maths have to be rote-learned.

Other skills which may be difficult to access for students with dyslexia are the spatial skills which are needed to help understand shape, symmetry, size and quantity, and linear skills which are needed to help understand sequence, order and the representations found in the number system. These aspects can prove demanding for dyslexic students and in addition they still have the literacy and other difficulties associated with dyslexia, such as working memory, speed of processing and automaticity. These can all have some implications for mathematics.

As indicated above, the technical language of mathematics may be difficult for students with dyslexia and dyscalculia. A student may understand the meaning of words such as 'difference', 'evaluate', 'odd', 'mean' and 'product', but then find that they have a quite different meaning in the context of mathematics. Ideas and concepts such as linear and sequential processing can be demanding because children and young people with dyslexia often have some difficulty with order, organization and sequencing, but in mathematical problems logic and sequence are often crucial. Precision is also necessary for mathematics, and accuracy and detail can often be demanding for dyslexic people as they tend to be more global and random in their thinking (Chinn, 2001; Reid, 2009).

Long-term memory and information retrieval can be problematic for students with dyslexia when they are tackling math problems. Much of this is due to the lack of organization at the cognitive level which is the initial stage of learning. If learning is not organized at this crucial stage, then retrieval will be difficult at later stage. Students with dyslexia may therefore have some difficulty with effective storage as well as accessing and retrieving information. It is for that reason that learning styles in mathematics is important (Chinn, 2001). Assisting your child to utilize a preferred learning style can help effective storage, retrieval and access to information.

Working memory can present some difficulties also because working memory implies that students need to hold information in their short-term store, which could be a fraction of a second, and process that information into meaningful stimuli. This is very important in mathematics as mental operations are necessary to do this, and this can be demanding for students with dyslexia, especially if information has to be held, even for a short time, in the student's head. It also emphasizes the importance of writing the 'working' and the steps of a mathematical problem clearly so that the student can retrace his/her steps when necessary.

Mathematics can therefore present a difficulty for students with dyslexia because of the sequential processes usually necessary for calculations, the burden such calculations usually impose on short-term/working memory and the language aspects associated with descriptions of mathematical problems.

Chinn (2001) suggests that learning style is an important factor in assisting the student deal more effectively with mathematical problems. He urges teachers to view learning styles, certainly from the mathematics view, with more flexibility and that it can be modified and adapted with teaching. Chinn suggests that much of the individuality associated with learning styles can be managed in a classroom setting. He does acknowledge however that teachers need to recognize the differences in strategies and in presentation preferences selected by different learners. Some learners therefore prefer oral instruction, while others need visual input, some will need concrete materials, and others find them unnecessary.

The Dunn and Dunn (1994) learning styles environmental model (Reid, 2009, 2006) is also applicable to the learning environment in mathematics – and indeed in all secondary subjects. Therefore, some children will prefer to sit formally at a desk while others will feel more comfortable in a relaxed position. The environment must be right for the individual. Although this may present difficulties in a class of 30 students, the student should still be provided with the opportunity to experiment with his/her style as much of the work may be done at home.

Chinn (2001) describes some of the learning styles that have been associated with mathematics. Bath, Chinn and Knox (1986) describe cognitive style in math by using the characteristics of inchworms and grasshoppers. The inchworm focusses on parts and detail of a mathematical problem, the grasshopper views the problem holistically, so while the inchworm is oriented towards a problem-solving approach and examines the processes needed to solve the problem, the grasshopper is answer-oriented and very likely use a flexible range of methods. The inchworm prefers to use paper and pen, the grasshopper rarely documents the method used.

Marolda and Davidson (2000) also described the characteristics of mathematics. They describe these as Mathematics Learning Style I and Mathematics Learning Style II. The former is highly reliant on verbal skills and prefers the 'how' to 'why', while the latter prefers perceptual stimuli and often reinterprets abstract situations visually or pictorially and prefers the 'why' to the 'how'. Similarly, Sharma (1989) describes two learning personalities: the qualitative style, which is characterized by sequential processing (parts to whole) and is procedurally oriented; and the quantitative method, which is characterized by visual processing (whole to parts). This type of student will generally approach problems holistically, may be good at identifying patterns and is more comfortable with mathematical concepts and ideas. An extreme difficulty in mathematics may be termed dyscalculia. This is appropriate if the student has difficulty with number concepts, as well as the difficulties in literacy and the other difficulties associated with dyslexia, described earlier in this book. There may therefore be some overlap between dyslexia and dyscalculia, but the use of the term dyscalculia suggests that the student has pronounced difficulties with mathematical concepts.

Nevertheless it is important for parents and teachers to be aware of the challenges presented by mathematics and the specific and additional challenges often faced by children with dyslexia.

Chapter 7

Overlapping difficulties: Dyspraxia and dysgraphia

Dyspraxia

Several terms are often used interchangeably with dyspraxia; in fact, the terms developmental coordination disorder (DCD) and dyspraxia are both seen as 'blanket' terms. Many other terms have been used to describe this condition. These include motor coordination problems, motor impairment, movement difficulties and clumsy, as well as developmental dyspraxia. The term 'developmental coordination disorder' (DCD) has become more influential in highlighting this area, with leading researchers using it (e.g., Wright & Sugden, 1996) and it appears in the American Psychiatric Association's (APA) *Manual for Mental Disorders* (DSM-IV, 1994).

The essential feature of DCD is described as 'a marked impairment in the development of motor co-ordination' (criterion A). The diagnosis is made only if this impairment significantly interferes with academic achievement or activities of daily living (criterion B). The prevalence of DCD has been estimated as high as 6% for children in the age range

---

Dyslexia: A Complete Guide for Parents and Those Who Help Them, Second Edition. Gavin Reid.
© 2011 John Wiley & Sons, Ltd. Published 2011 by John Wiley & Sons, Ltd.

of 5–11 years (DSM-IV). The problem affects more boys than girls in a ratio of 3–4:1 (Sugden, 2008).

Two set of conditions are involved: general difficulties with movement and coordination. Additionally, fine motor difficulties can be noted, particularly in children with handwriting problems. This is called dysgraphia and can overlap with dyslexia.

What is dyspraxia?

A very simple analysis of the term itself – dys = difficulty, and praxis = the ability to move efficiently and effectively in different environments. This informs us that dyspraxia is primarily a difficulty in achieving the motor milestones at the correct time and the implications are that carrying out many of the activities fundamental to living and learning will be delayed and difficult.

McIntyre (2001) suggests that understanding dyspraxia is more complex than the initial description suggests. There are two main interacting aspects to be considered. These are:

1. the thinking, planning, organizing and sequencing or the intellectual side of moving, which also involves remembering how to do things and using that information as a basis for progress; and
2. being able to carry out the movement itself. This is the physical or the 'doing' side and efficiency depends on the child having enough strength/muscle tone, balance, coordination and control, body and spatial awareness. When these are used correctly, movement is rhythmic and fluent.

McIntyre maintains that both of these factors contribute to children having a 'sense of self'. The importance of having a positive sense of self has been recognized for some time as being important for success in learning. But also important is a physical sense of self because that represents the basis of knowing what to do and how to do it, and this capacity in turn allows children to show what they have learned. Children with dyspraxia have difficulty with both.

Table 7.1 Movement skills and planning skills

Movement skills	Planning skills
Balancing: being able to sustain an upright posture and recover poise.	Knowing what to do; where to go, i.e., using environmental cues.
Coordinating different body parts to effect balance. Knowing where these parts are in relation to one another, i.e., body awareness. Appreciating body boundary, i.e., where the body ends and the outside world begins.	Remembering/reflecting and building on previous similar experiences in the memory store to inform the new one.
Controlling the pace/timing of movement so that a rhythm emerges.	Sequencing the order of actions, i.e., knowing what comes first then next.
Using the correct amount of strength, speed and space to organize an efficient movement pattern.	Using immediate feedback from one attempt to improve the next.

In Table 7.1 the movement skills represent the actual activity and the planning skills represent the control which the student needs over the activity. Often students with dyspraxia do not have this control.

Lack of a clear sense of the body's boundary gives children a disjointed sense of how to coordinate their body parts in the space around them and this affects the rhythm and fluency (success) of the movement. This applies not just to games and movement activities in school, but to all the activities of daily living:

- using a knife and fork;
- getting dressed;
- carrying a schoolbag;
- using scissors;
- using two hands doing different things;
- using a compass;
- sitting down (feeling where the seat is without looking).

Critical periods

It is important for parents to realize that there are periods of development that can be seen to be very critical. Generally this is in the first 4–7 years as at that time there is a lot of activity in the brain. It is using more glucose than at any other time in its life. That is the reason why early years of education are so important.

Terms

As indicated earlier, the terms developmental coordination disorder (DCD) and dyspraxia are 'blanket' terms to describe a child who may be termed as 'clumsy' and may not understand what needs to be done or be able to plan, leading to uncontrolled or uncoordinated movement. Like the other syndromes it can be seen as lying on a continuum from mild to severe and can affect fine-motor activities, such as pencil grip, and gross-motor activities, such as movement and balance. Portwood (2001) describes DCD as 'motor difficulties caused by perceptual problems, especially visual–motor and kinesthetic–motor difficulties'.

The definition of dyspraxia provided by the Dyspraxia Trust in England is 'impairment or immaturity in the organisation of movement which leads to associated problems with language, perception and thought' (Dyspraxia Trust, 2001). The processing difficulties described above appear to relate to skills that are necessary for a range of learning tasks and will affect attention, memory and reading.

Dyspraxia is an assortment of difficulties and, as with dyslexia, no two children will necessarily be the same. Again like dyslexia this can cause confusion for parents and they may question why two children with the same label can have different profiles. This emphasizes that the important information is not so much the label but the presenting characteristics.

DAMP

Some researchers and practitioners, mainly in Scandinavia, call the condition which we have called dyspraxia DAMP – Disorder of Attention,

Movement and Perception. This term highlights the area of perception or how children take environmental cues through their senses, for this is the first part of the learning process and as such is vitally important.

The incidence of dyspraxia

The Dyspraxia Foundation (2008) suggest that 6–10% of all children have some degree of dyspraxia. Numbers of children presenting with all different kinds of learning differences are increasing. It is believed there has been an 80% increase since 2001. So there will be children affected by dyspraxia in every classroom. Boys outnumber girls in the ration 4–5:1, but when girls do have dyspraxia they seem to be more severely affected.

Some further characteristics of dyspraxia

Children with dyspraxia may:

- move in an uncoordinated manner;
- bump into things because they misjudge the space between them;
- begin a task then forget what comes next;
- make the same mistakes over and over again;
- have difficulty articulating clearly;
- find it impossible to undertake tasks such as doing up zips and buttons;
- make two hands work together at the midline of the body.

Checklist for motor development

Some of the following can be indicators of motor difficulties:

- lack of coordination;
- trouble judging the force needed to throw a ball;
- difficulty with control and direction when throwing a ball;
- poor balance;

- poor posture and muscle tone;
- problems with running and jumping;
- difficulty with handwriting and scissor skills;
- low self-esteem;
- difficulty with the order of garments when dressing;
- difficulty organizing work, loses and drops things;
- forgets the right school books, leaves homework at home, also has difficulty organizing time;
- cannot tell directions, gets lost easily – may have difficulty finding way around the school;
- planning and layout of work may be poor;
- spacing of words and the size of the letters may vary from day to day;
- may have difficulty remembering an image when it is removed, for example copying from the board.

Overcoming barriers

As indicated throughout this book it is important to identify the barriers that your child is experiencing. In terms of dyspraxia and movement difficulties these barriers can be readily identified. Once identified it is important to establish a step-by-step process to overcome the barrier. This applies to all barriers, whether in literacy, language, numeracy or movement and coordination. Three key factors are practice, motivation and support. As Figure 7.1 shows, the barrier may seem quite a hurdle and perhaps even an insurmountable one. But the rider in this illustration had to encounter many barriers and obstacles to get to this level and that process does not happen overnight. It is good for children with dyspraxia, dyscalculia or dyslexia to have an aim – and they can aim high. The key is to identify the steps that can help to achieve that aim. Each step must be rewarding, measurable and achievable so it can take them on towards their main goal.

In the case of dyspraxia it is a good idea to ask if a formal assessment has or can take place. The Movement Assessment Battery is one example of a structured and detailed formal assessment which can inform practice. This can help to identify the steps to be taken in reaching the desired goal.

Figure 7.1 Overcoming barriers practice, motivation, support

Movement Assessment Battery

The Movement Assessment Battery (Henderson & Sugden, 1992) has seven key factors. These are:

1. ball skills;
2. static balance, manipulation of fine objects, rhythm;
3. dynamic balance;
4. fine manipulation;
5. avoiding objects of persons;
6. knowledge of body scheme and directional awareness;
7. self-care skills.

This test is concerned with identifying impairments in motor function such as manual dexterity, ball skills and balance. It also looks at emotional and motivational challenges.

Other factors which need to be considered in identifying needs in relation to dyspraxia are:

- eye–hand coordination;
- position in space;
- copying;
- visual and spatial relationships;
- laterality;
- self-esteem.

To recap:

- practice in standing, walking, marching;
- games that involve standing still for a short period of time;
- structured and clear movements from standing position such as point-ing to your toes and looking over your shoulder;
- standing on toes is a good exercise and this can progress to hopping and jumping;
- wobble board balancing – in twos is a good team exercise and one that can help to develop understanding of another person's needs and control. In this exercise the two children have to work together so it does demand a degree of cooperation;
- bench steps – this type of exercise can be easily practiced at home using household steps or the stairs in your house. This is good for developing coordination.

Dysgraphia

Introduction

You will have noted that dyspraxia can include children with fine motor difficulties as well as difficulties in movement and coordination. Those children who also have fine motor difficulties will find writing and sometimes keyboard skills challenging. This means that some children with dyspraxia also have dysgraphia. Of course it is not uncommon for children with dyslexia to have difficulties with handwriting and there can be an overlap between dyslexia and dysgraphia.

The importance of handwriting

Handwriting is important to communication. Even though computers can now replace handwriting for many of the main communication functions, handwriting is still required for many day-to-day purposes. Children who have severe difficulties in this area are therefore at a considerable disadvantage in the school system and in their lives outside the school. Learning to spell is aided by the motor patterns of letters becoming reinforced as the child learns to write them. Writing is a social skill in most cultures so it is important that any children who have difficulties in this area have these difficulties investigated and plans made to bring their handwriting to an acceptable level of legibility.

Writing difficulties are the most regularly reported problems in children who have DCD. According to Smits-Engelsman and Van Galen, 'the common feature of dysgraphic children is that even with the proper amount of instruction and practice, they fail to make sufficient progress in the acquisition of the fine motor task of handwriting' (1997, p. 165). Dysgraphia is characterized by illegible handwriting with letters wrongly sized or spaced incorrectly. Words are frequently misspelled even though the child may be able to read the word correctly. The first signs of dysgraphia generally appear when the child starts to write his/her name at nursery stage. Often there is overlap with other syndromes such as dyslexia, DCD and ADHD even at this early stage. This is only to be expected as dysgraphic difficulties relate to motor skills as well as to processing skills. Children need to learn both the thinking skills to enable them to communicate on paper and the motor and spatial skills to enable them to set out their work in a legible form.

Signs of dysgraphia include:

- poor pencil grip;
- too much/little pressure on pencil;
- poor letter formation and spacing between words despite practice;
- inconsistencies in style — mix of cursive and print in the same word, with a mix of upper- and lower-case lettering;
- unfinished words or letters;
- words omitted;
- awkward seating position when writing;

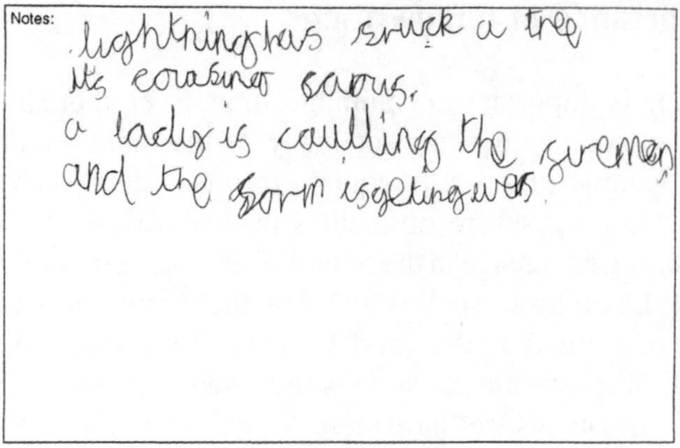

Notes:
lightning has struck a tree
its coming down.
a lady is caulling the firemen
and the form is getting wet

Figure 7.2 Characteristics of dysgraphia

- difficulty writing numbers and copying geometric shapes;
- difficulty with practical tasks, like using scissors;
- difficulty understanding and/or giving directions.

Figure 7.2 shows several dysgraphic characteristics. The inconsistency in letter formation and handwriting style is very obvious. What is not obvious is that this child has an IQ of 120 which places him in the above average category. In a situation like this a two-tier intervention is necessary. One is a well-structured, handwriting programme. The key is that this should be conducted *daily*. Second, it is important that the child is able to access a word processor as young as possible. This is crucial and a good word processing program to help develop keyboard skills is important.

Strategies for dysgraphia

Encouraging cursive writing

This is generally easier as the writing will start to flow more easily if the child does not have to think where to begin and end the letters. Each letter begins on the line. It will however require to be taught, showing the student how joins are made and ensuring the correct letter formation pattern.

Encourage correct pencil grip

There are many grips and specially shaped pencils and pens on the market — sometimes a triangular pencil is easier to hold correctly but there are many aids to help with this.

Teach the child how to sit well

An appropriate seating position is important. This will depend on whether the child is right- or left-handed. If the child's difficulties are severe, a sloping board may help.

Always encourage a multisensory approach

Get the child to see what they are writing (a good model letter or word), say what they are writing (at first to establish letter shape, for example saying, 'up, down and round' and then the letter sound or name; later spelling out the word), hear the sound of their own voice saying the procedure, write it (air writing, tracing in sand or other media that feel good to the child).

Accommodations

Parents should try to ensure these are in place if they feel they are appropriate for their child:

Scribe

In this case the child will use his/her own idea(s), and another person will do the writing. It is important that this does not affect the child's self-esteem and it is a good idea to speak to your child first and try it out before deciding if it should be used for examinations.

Additional time

This can be in the form of allowing the child to start the work ahead of the rest of the class. This may provide him/her with the opportunity to get through the tasks of writing without undue pressure. Parents may want to request and perhaps the child can get the work ahead of the class and start it at home and then finish it off at school.

Using paper with lines

This helps keep writing on the line.

Using graph paper or boxes

Is helpful for number work.

Templates

So the child does not have to spend time planning work. This is particularly important for any student with spatial dysgraphia.

Mind maps as tools for planning

Young people can brainstorm their ideas and then sort them by numbering them into a logical sequence.

Break down the tasks of writing into manageable stages

This can involve drawing the mind map, drafting, editing and proofreading. For a longer piece of work, this should be done on a computer to make the task easier.

A set of notes for classwork

This avoids the need to take notes while the child is listening as it may be a near impossibility for the young person to produce legible notes. Automaticity is something that students with spatial learning difficulties find very hard. Alternatively, the young person can be allowed to record the lesson so that separate notes are not required. Audio notetakers are an efficient way of doing this and organizing recordings for older students.

Mark for content and not presentation or spelling

Ensure that you praise the child for good attempts however.

Provide a framework to help with writing

This can provide a format and make it easier and quicker to write. This can certainly be done in school but it can also be encouraged at home by parents.

An example of writing stages:

- must contain two ideas;
- must mention four people;
- must say where, when, why and how;
- must say what happened;
- must say how it ended.

Case study

> I am 13. I have dysgraphia. I first found out I had this disability when I was 9. The reason it was discovered was because I was seeing a counselor for my behavioral problems. I was never able to finish my homework and then I got punishment which was actually more written work and I could not do that either. I was eventually tested and it was discovered that I had dysgraphia and also some dyspraxia problems.
>
> My disability affects my handwriting and also my balance. It causes me to fall over at least once a day, frequently ruining my clothes. In school I find it difficult copying from the whiteboard and often fall behind with my written tasks. My friends don't really understand, so don't help me and I hate to ask for help because I feel it is embarrassing. (Reproduced with permission from MacIntyre, personal correspondence, 2009)

You can see in the example above how important it is to ensure that the school is aware of the difficulties and particularly how important it is to ensure that attention is paid to self-esteem.

Handwriting checklist

Jones (2005) provides useful pointers for observing handwriting difficulties (Table 7.2).

Resources for dysgraphia

Computer software

There are many stockists using similar programs in both US and UK as well as in Canada, New Zealand and Australia. Some examples are shown below but you should contact the local stockist in your country.

- **Dragon** and **MacSpeech Dictate** (speech recognition software for PC and Mac).
- **Audio Notetaker** enables notes to be made through audio recording. The program helps annotation and organization of notes and audio files. Recordings of notes can be edited and exported to Mac.

Jones (2005) also provides the following list to help students with dysgraphia.

- handhugger pens/pencils
- chunky crayons/colored pencils
- ultra-pencil grips
- ridged comfort grips
- ridged ruler
- selection raised line paper
- plastic lower case letters
- left-handed ruler
- angle board
- plastic lower case letters
- selection of pencil grips
  - tri-glo grip
  - comfort grip
  - stubbi grip
  - triangular grip

Table 7.2 Handwriting difficulties

Observations	Yes	Consider
Does the child seem unsure which hand to hold the pencil in?		Hand dominance
Is the pencil held in an abnormal grip?		Grip
Does the child sit appropriately on a chair when writing?		Posture
Does the child slump forward onto the table when writing?		Posture
Does the child position the paper awkwardly when writing?		Paper position
Does the child lift their wrist off the paper when writing?		Grip
Is too much pressure applied through the pencil?		Grip
Is too little pressure applied through the pencil?		Grip
Are letters formed appropriately?		Letter formation
Are reversed or inverted letters evident?		Letter formation
Does the child commence writing at the left side of the page?		Left to right
Does the writing slope downwards across a page rather than follow a horizontal direction?		Letter formation
Are inadequate spaces left between words?		Spacing
Are the sizes of letters erratic?		Size of letters
Are letters incompletely formed, i.e., the cross bar is missing from the 't'?		Letter formation
Does the child's writing contain an erratic mixture of upper- and lower-case lettering?		Letter formation
Do you struggle to identify distinct ascenders and descenders in the child's writing?		Size of letters
Does the child struggle to join letters appropriately?		Joins
Does writing appear slow and laboured?		Speed
Is the speed of writing slow?		Speed

- handwriting whiteboard
- handwriting demonstration sheet
- copycat handwriting practice sheets
- eye–hand integrated cards
- tracing/coloring books/maze
- Berol handhugger pens

Summary of overlapping difficulties

This chapter and chapter 6 have highlighted the overlap between dyslexia and the others difficulties, such as dyspraxia, dysgraphia and dyscalculia. Although these are discrete and separate syndromes it can be noted that a number of children with dyslexia will also show some of the characteristics of these syndromes. These two chapters have provided a range of strategies that parents and teachers can use. Parents need this type of guidance and it is important that the information is shared between school and home.

There was also some discussion about the use of labels and although it is generally agreed that a label is useful, it will not in itself provide the information that parents require. They need to obtain a full profile on their child and the specific characteristics relating to their abilities and their performances. This will be followed up in the next chapter on attention difficulties, which is another potential overlapping difficulty.

Chapter 8

Attention difficulties

This chapter continues the theme of chapter 7 by looking at overlapping difficulties that can be related to dyslexia, this time focussing on attention difficulties and the syndromes known as ADHD and ADD. There has been considerable debate regarding the syndromes relating to attention disorders and there are a number of perspectives, particularly the medical, educational and social, which can present conflicting information that can be confusing to parents. The American Psychiatric Association's *Diagnostic and Statistical Manual of Mental Disorders* (DSM-IV; APA, 2000) provides criteria for diagnosis of ADHD (see appendix 3 for information on DSM-V). The key factors relate to inattentiveness, hyperactivity and impulsivity. Parents will already have realized that these factors can in some cases be noted in some of the behaviors shown by their dyslexic child. Some of the comments relating to these factors include 'often runs about or climbs excessively' and 'often interrupts or intrudes on others'. You can easily recognize these activities in some children with dyslexia. It is no surprise therefore that there can be an overlap between dyslexia and attention difficulties.

Dyslexia: A Complete Guide for Parents and Those Who Help Them, Second Edition. Gavin Reid.
© 2011 John Wiley & Sons, Ltd. Published 2011 by John Wiley & Sons, Ltd.

The difference perhaps lies in the criteria rather than the character-istics of ADHD. As indicated above, some of the characteristics can be seen in children with dyslexia but these characteristics may not meet the criteria for an ADHD diagnosis. The factors that meet the criteria need to have persisted for at least six months to a degree that is maladaptive and inconsistent with developmental level. These are described in more detail below.

Assessing for ADHD

The American Academy of Pediatrics (AAP) indicates that the profes-sional criteria for a diagnosis of ADD/ADHD require the following:

- **Early onset**: Symptoms must have been present before age 7.
- **Duration**: A combination of symptoms must have been present for at least 6 months.
- **Settings**: The symptoms must be present in two or more settings (e.g. home, school, other social settings).
- **Impact**: The symptoms must have a negative impact on the individ-ual's school, family and/or social life.
- **Developmental level:** The symptoms are not due to the child's normal developmental level.
- **Alternative explanation:** The symptoms are not caused by another physical, mental or emotional disorder.

They also recommend that an evaluation for childhood ADD/ADHD should include:

- a thorough medical and family history;
- a general physical and neurological examination;
- a comprehensive interview with the parents, the child and the child's teacher(s);
- standardized screening tools for ADD/ADHD;
- observation of the child;
- a variety of psychological tests to measure IQ and social and emo-tional adjustment.

To be diagnosed with ADD/ADHD, children must exhibit multiple symptoms of hyperactivity, impulsivity or inattention. In addition, the professional assessing the problem will look at:

- **The severity of the symptoms**: To be diagnosed with ADD/ADHD, the symptoms must have a negative impact on the child's education, career, relationships or social life.
- **When the symptoms started**: Since ADD/ADHD starts in childhood, the doctor or therapist will look at how early the symptoms appeared. To receive a diagnosis, the symptoms must have been present before age 7.
- **How long the symptoms have been present**: The symptoms must have been going on for at least 6 months before ADD/ADHD can be diagnosed.
- **When and where the symptoms appear**: The symptoms of ADD/ADHD must be present in multiple settings, such as at home and school. If the problem only appears in one environment, it is unlikely to be caused by ADD/ADHD.

This list is fairly comprehensive and parents will appreciate the need to obtain a full assessment if they suspect ADHD. Most of the guidance on the diagnosis of ADHD stems from the DSM-IV criteria which are used by professionals' worldwide (significant changes in the criteria are being considered in DSM-V, see appendix 3).

Perspectives of ADHD

Parents will find that different categories of professionals will have different views on ADHD and they may also suggest different types of interventions.

In terms of education the following factors can be noted in children with attention difficulties:

- **Factors associated with free flight**: This means that the child will have little control over the thinking process – essentially what may be described as having a right hemisphere processing style. This means that learners with this style require some structure to help direct their thinking processes.

- **Unpredictability, inconsistency and impulsivity**: This again indicates that there is little control over learning and that many actions are impulsive. Indeed, many children with attention difficulties also show behavior difficulties which have occurred through their impulsive actions. Doing or saying things without first thinking it through.
- **Pacing skills and on-task factors**: These indicate a lack of control over learning and indicate that students with attention difficulties have a problem with pacing the progress of work and therefore may tire easily or finish a task prematurely.

Some characteristics that may indicate attention difficulties can include the following:

- difficulty sustaining attention during play/learning;
- fidgety and restless when sitting;
- difficulty sitting for any length of time;
- inability to complete tasks;
- unable to play quietly;
- disruptive when playing with others;
- difficulty listening;
- answers questions before they need to;
- difficulty following instructions;
- easily distracted by external stimuli;
- difficulty awaiting turn in group activities;
- losing materials necessary for tasks;
- unable to consider consequences of actions.

ADHD can be seen at a number of levels. These include the brain (neurological) and the processing level (cognition).

Neurological level

At the neurological level, in relation to attention difficulties, the following factors may be relevant:

- **Hemispheric preferences**: Usually, a child with ADHD is a right hemisphere processor.

- **Auditory distractibility**: This implies that they are easily distracted by noise of some sort.
- **Tactile distractibility**: Similarly, touch can be distracting, and often the child with ADHD may want to touch in order to be distracted.
- **Motor inhibition**: Often, children with ADHD have difficulty in inhibiting a response and may react impulsively in some situations.

Processing factors (cognition)

There is evidence to suggest that processing factors are implicated with attention difficulties. These factors can include:

- **Depth of processing**: If the student is not attending to stimuli, then it is likely that the processing will be at a shallow as opposed to a deep level. If this is the case, then the child will not gain much from the learning experience. This means that the learning experience will not be automatically reinforced. It may also mean that the child will become bored with the subject matter very easily.
- **Transferring learning**: This is important for reinforcing learning, for developing concepts and for efficiency in learning. This can sometimes be challenging for children with attention difficulties and for those with dyslexia.

Supporting children with attention difficulties

- **Avoid confrontational situations**: This is important as confrontation can lead to entrenched views and defiance. It is best to try to avoid confrontation when working with the child and trying to adapt to his/her specific needs as far as possible or desirable.
- **Listen to the child's concerns**: Often children with attention difficulties can become unhappy as they may not have much control over their actions but still have to face the full consequences of them. This can make them frustrated. It is important to listen to their views and perhaps even help them to express what they are trying to say by asking appropriate and non-threatening questions.

- **Avoid distraction**: This can be quite tricky as children with ADHD can be distracted very easily and can actively seek out distraction. You need to spend some time thinking ahead about the working environment – try to make sure there is a study area that is semi-enclosed, not to cut out all stimulation but certainly to cut it down. In this situation you can make the work periods quite short and intersperse them with breaks.
- **Keep instructions to a minimum and give them one at a time**: This is important as like children with dyslexia, children with ADHD can have a short concentration span and will likely forget if more than one instruction is given at any one time.
- **Provide reassurance on tasks**: Feedback is important but often children will need support before embarking on the task. This can be due to a low self-concept so it is important that their confidence is built up before embarking on challenging tasks.
- **Split tasks up**: It can be more productive to set short tasks rather than a long one. This is particularly important for homework as this is often a source of some tension.
- **Enable them to complete tasks**: If the task is not finished, then it will be better to work with your child to complete it. Although this is not ideal it is better than a notebook full of unfinished work. You may want to use an assignment pad to record homework and a specific folder to put work in on completion.
- **Provide routine:** Children obtain security from routine – it helps to establish patterns for their work. A routine, particularly in relation to homework, should be established and maintained as much as possible.
- **Provide outlets for active behavior:** This is important otherwise their impulse control can explode. Try to note the warning signs – if the child is under too much stress, then a timely release of stress can prevent an undesirable outburst.
- **Provide a clear structure at home**: This can go along with the routine, but try to structure all tasks – the child may need a framework and perhaps some key words to help with the task. The extent of the structure will depend on the tasks and the child, but it is important to be aware that children with attention difficulties need a structure.
- **Set a daily routine and stick to it:** Bedtime and preparation for school are much easier if there is a structure in place.

Organizing children with attention difficulties

Children with ADHD usually have difficulty with organization so it may be necessary for parents to take an active role in helping their child organize their work programme. Such help could include ensuring that notebooks have dividers and that separate folders are used for different activities. It is important to ensure that these folders are clearly labeled in addition to helping the child keep a daily record of tasks to be completed and those that have been completed.

It should be noted that there are different degrees of organization and some children can only tolerate a small amount of imposed organization. Their level of tolerance can depend on their learning style. Knowledge of your child's learning style can help to guide you in relation to the type of support that will be successful. It is a good idea to discuss your child's learning style with him/her. Learning style is discussed in a later chapter but some aspects of the learning environment that are worth considering for children with ADHD are discussed below.

The learning environment

Environmental factors can greatly increase or decrease the effectiveness of learning. Many people are not aware of this and often just accept the environment as it is, without making any attempt to adapt it in any way. In some instances it can be difficult to make a choice or to change the environment. But this is not always the case. If learners are aware of their environmental preferences, then they are in a position to make informed choices when they have some flexibility over learning. In most cases, certainly for younger learners, the learning environment often means the classroom or home. The environment is very influential and should be seen as an important resource that can help to access effective learning for children with attention difficulties.

The key aspects in the learning for children with ADHD include the following:

- **Design**: Is there a lot of space or does it have a crowded feel? People can react differently to these situations.

- **Color**: This can be important as some colors can be soothing while others may not. Try to find the colours that have a good impact on your child. As a general rule pastel colors tend to be better than bright, sharp colors.
- **Light:** You need to pay some attention to the kind of light your child is using. As a rule soft, low table lamps are preferable for children with attention difficulties rather than bright lights.
- **Sound**: This can be tricky as children with attention difficulties often need some background noise but too much can be distracting. It is a good idea to try to experiment with this and perhaps use different types of music.

Choosing a school: further consideration on the classroom environment

The ideal classroom for a child with ADHD is one in which classroom rules and expectations are clearly defined, the environment is organized and routines are structured. It is important that the child with ADHD should not be isolated in the classroom sitting by him/herself. It is best if the child is located near the front and center close to the teacher. Activities should generally be stimulating, interesting and meaningful, and involve a quite a bit of hands-on projects as opposed to board work or teacher talk.

ADHD – working partnerships

Effective communication is important and it is crucial that parents, teachers and other agencies including health, social work and voluntary sector, where appropriate, are involved in all aspects – assessment, provision and accommodations. It is important that parents know how and where to access information and that the school has information available to ensure that parental involvement is possible. Parents should be involved in the decision-making process and in the development of the individualized educational plans. Parents should ensure the school has opportunities for staff training and development and that they have effective liaison procedures at all points of transition, particularly the transition to high school.

It is important that as a parent you feel supported by the school. There are many different ways of ensuring this, but it is important that the school considers the need for structure and routine for the child's daily schedule and tries to reinforce the importance of learning self-control and self-regulation. This can be done at home. It is also important that you feel the school is promoting activities that can facilitate positive behavior in your child. For example, excessive punishment is negative reinforcement – you need to look for positive reinforcement that can promote motivation and particularly intrinsic motivation. This is when the child is self-motivated and that is usually the result of careful planning and sensitive application of behavior modification and reward schedules.

Resources for ADHD

There are many – perhaps too many – resources that can be used for ADHD. It is a major industry and it is easy for parents and teachers to be confused about what might be the most effective resources to purchase. The National Resource Centre on ADHD, which is a programme of CHADD (Children and Adults with Attention Deficit Hyperactivity Disorder) (http://www.help4adhd.org), provides excellent advice on this. It is one of the most popular websites. One section on parenting a child with ADHD (http://www.chadd.org/ AM/Template.cfm?Section=Especially_For_Parents) states that the aim is to empower parents. It is important that when you are looking at resources you try to obtain those that will empower your child, resources that can give him/her some responsibility to develop their own strategies and approaches to learning. CHADD also produce a free information and resource guide for members. The website http://www.help4adhd.org/en/education/rights/504 also provides a detailed explanation of parents' rights under section 504 of the Rehabilitation Act 1973 which ensures that a qualified child with a disability has equal access to education and should receive appropriate accommodations and modifications tailored to the child's individual needs.

In Australia ADDERS have an extensive website (www.ADDers.org) with parents' forums, games for children, information on research, support groups and resources. Some of the resources include free portable education software programs such as adders and ladders, a fun game for counting, alphabet soup for learning the sequence of the alphabet, and connections, which helps to learn the right connections or relationships between things. There is also one on math looking at learning and practice additions, one called divide tables on learning about division and multiplication and one on fractions. This is a valuable resource for parents of children with ADHD (http://www.adders.org/free-sen-resources).

There is a similar website for the UK – The National Attention Deficit Disorder Information and Support Service (http://www.addiss.co.uk), which has a dedicated resource center and bookstore. They also have a list of support groups throughout the UK which run as independent groups. The ADDDIS website also contains factsheets for parents and answers to questions which parents may want to ask, for example, is ADHD inherited? The answer is that if a family has one ADHD child, there is a 30–40% chance that a sibling will also have the condition and a 45% (or greater) chance that at least one parent has the condition. If the child with ADHD has an identical twin, the likelihood that the twin will have the disorder is about 90%.

Although these websites are hosted in different countries the information they contained is generic and can help parents wherever they live.

Summary

This chapter has looked at the condition known as ADHD and provided an indication of the diagnostic criteria for this condition as well as strategies to develop these children's learning skills. The chapter has also provided suggestions for parents to utilize at home and some aspects they may consider when looking at and communicating with schools. It is important to consider the overlap between dyslexia and ADHD as this underlines the view that we need to look beyond the label and obtain a broader view of our children's challenges and not expect the label to provide the solution.

Chapter 9

Self-esteem and emotional development

This chapter focusses on the emotional needs of children with dyslexia and how parents can identify and support these needs. There will be reference to the role and importance of self-esteem and strategies to develop positive self-esteem will be provided. Emotional well-being is crucial for effective learning, particularly for children with dyslexia. They are too often and too easily confronted with challenging situations and potential failure. They often have to use their emotional resources to get them through these difficult situations. It is important that they are supported at an early age so they can develop the emotional strength and positive self-esteem which will equip them for the future.

Even looking at what might be a typical day in the life of a dyslexic child you can see the possibilities of failure and a potential blow to the child's self-esteem.

Dyslexia: A Complete Guide for Parents and Those Who Help Them, Second Edition. Gavin Reid.
© 2011 John Wiley & Sons, Ltd. Published 2011 by John Wiley & Sons, Ltd.

7 am – slept in forgot to switch on the alarm. **Failure**

8 am – late for school as had to go back upstairs to my room get my friend Fraser's geography book, which I took home to catch up with work which I missed when I was doing extra English. Realized I still have not completed the work and will need to borrow it for longer. **Failure**

8.45 am – arrive at school – realized it is a PE day and do not have my gear with me –it is in my other bag (which is at my grandmother's house). **Failure**

9 am History – we begin with a test – I forgot to revise for it as I was catching up with geography. When finished test we have to select a worksheet from teacher's desk – they are graded – hard, OK and easy – I take the easy one (but I still have difficulty with some words) and make a guess at the answers. **Failure**

9.50 am English – not a good morning – we are doing a play and we all have a part – I have a small part – I am the messenger in *Antony and Cleopatra* – but always miss my cue because I have difficulty in following it. **Failure**

Recess – realize because I was hurrying to get to school I forgot to pack my snack – had no money so watched my friend snack. **Failure**

11.15 am PE – no PE gear with me so had to watch – practicing for school sports – pity I had a chance in the 100 metres. **Failure**

12.30–1.15 Lunch – luckily my lunches are prepaid so that was OK. I join a different line from my friends – forgot where I was supposed to meet them –by the time I found them lunch break was almost over. **Failure**

1.15–2.10 Science – I am working in groups for this but none of my friends are in my group. I watch as the others do most of the work – we all write the answers to the experiment together – I copy Ron's work but not finished when the bell goes so take Ron's notebook home with me. **Failure**

2.10–3.50 – last class of the day – Mathematics – (my favourite!!) left my calculator at home – but borrowed one from the teacher. Still got them all wrong – added 1 instead of 7 and messed up my 7 and 9's – have to do them all again but no class time left so take them all home. **Failure**

On bus home try to write up my homework and the things I still have to do – someone throws a ball from the front of the bus and it lands on my book. So put my books away and play ball with my friends. Homework not written up! **Failure**

Home: mother tells me to do my homework right away – have difficulty with mathematics so phone Ron – start speaking about the game next week – mother shouts at me after about 15 minutes – I say good bye to Ron – forgot to ask him and the math question. **Failure**

Help to prepare dinner with family – Mum asks me to go to corner shop to get some parsnips and cream and on the way out she shouted on me to get a newspaper too as she had not had time to buy one that day.

Came back after 10 minutes with nothing – mother had shouted the money is on the hall shelf – I had been so busy remembering what to get that I forgot the money. **Failure**

You can see from the narrative above that the word 'failure' appears 13 times. If this type of situation is repeated the young person will soon see him/herself as a failure and it will be difficult to reverse this.

Yet on each of these situations the failure could have been averted. This is shown below in reference to the main situations in this narrative.

1. Alarm – parents need to check this. Let the young person do it themselves but you can check it also.
2. Borrowing other students' books – it is worthwhile checking if your child has any other student's book. This is not the best way to learn and it might be that a visit to the school to discuss this is worthwhile, particularly if it is happening a lot.
3. PE equipment forgotten – this is all too common. It might be a good idea to use Post-it notes as an aide-mémoire and stick them on the bedroom wall, but it will be better to pack the bag the night before so it can be checked before the morning 'rush'.
4. Reading aloud in class – this is something that should be avoided. It is worthwhile discussing this with the teacher. But in situations like

plays it may be a good idea to go through this with your child and pay attention to the lines before he/she is to speak. Try to find out who in the class will be reading these lines so your child will know who speaks before him/her.

5. Working in groups – this is good for children with dyslexia but they need to feel part of the group. If you think this is not happening, then you need to speak to the teacher as group work can provide a really good opportunity to develop positive self-esteem, but too often the opposite happens.

6. Mathematics – children with dyslexia can easily mistake numbers that look alike and it is important that they have time to check and recheck their working. You may also have to speak to the teacher about this, but you can ensure your child is able to space out his work on the page and emphasize the importance of making the numbers clear and checking the numbers at least twice.

7. Bus – your child should not be trying to catch up with noting the homework to do on the bus – the bus journey should be an opportunity for socializing. It is important to speak to the school to ensure that your child has a clear account of his/her homework before they leave school.

8. Doing homework – while it is a good idea to get homework done as soon as your child arrives home, it is also a good idea to sit with him and go over the homework and help him to prioritize it. This will also ensure that he has all the information he needs to complete it.

9. Instructions – we need to remember that children with dyslexia will have difficulties remembering lists. They need to write down instructions and this is also an opportunity for praise when they do run an errand successfully.

You can see that it is possible to convert potential stressful and negative experiences into positive ones, ones that can lead to the development of a positive self-concept.

What is self-esteem?

Self-esteem is different from simply experiencing self-confidence. In fact, the two are different and some very confident people can have low self-esteem. Self-esteem can be equated more with emotional security. It is a perception of one's self and how that person thinks others see him/her. An individual's self-esteem can be greatly influenced by feedback they get from others. Positive feedback can result in positive self-esteem. It is important that children with dyslexia receive positive feedback otherwise they may develop low self-esteem and this undermines a child's confidence. One of the effects of low self-esteem is a reduction in motivation. Motivation at the best of times can be challenging for children with dyslexia, particularly if they experience early failure.

Often a reluctance to undertake a task can be mistaken for disobedience and difficult behavior when in fact it can be due to a lack of motivation resulting from low self-esteem.

Recognizing low self-esteem

You will find some factors below that can be characteristic of low self-esteem. Not all of them are a consequence of low self-esteem, but together a number of these can point towards it:

- Reluctance to apply him/herself to school work.
- Can act out in front of people to get attention.
- May avoid people and isolate themselves from others.
- Reluctance to show people their work.
- May take a long time to work out answers as they are finding the task challenging but may not want to ask for help.
- Can appear defensive, argumentative.
- May be anxious when working on school work.
- May be over-careful in checking work.
- May avoid eye contact.
- Can be isolated from peers or seek out younger children for companionship.

Often children's level of self-esteem is quite well established before they enter school. Initial experiences at school can have an effect on the child and children with dyslexia can be particularly vulnerable because often their early experiences are characterized by failure since all aspects of literacy are important in early education and they will find these challenging.

Strategies for developing positive self-esteem

Success

This is important as success can help children with dyslexia believe that they can do a task. This will also increase motivation. It is important to look for ways to make success a reality. It could be that for some children with dyslexia success needs to be measured in a different way from that for other children. The important point is that the child needs to recognize that he/she has been successful. So it may be that our expectations of what we mean by success have to change. For some children with dyslexia success can be simply attending school – for some going to school can be a frightening and fearful experience. It is important to note those experiences that can be stressful and to acknowledge success when they have been encountered. Success is not only about academic achievement.

Being part of a group

Children with dyslexia can feel isolated and different from others in their age group. It is a good idea to discuss with the teacher how he/she performs in group work. The teacher may have to monitor the child's interactions in the group to ensure that it is a positive and constructive experience. Group work can be excellent if it is a positive experience. Parents should ensure that in group work their child is not being left out or is not being given a full role in the group. Children with dyslexia can be very creative and can offer a great deal to a group.

Identify strengths

You will very likely be aware of your child's strengths and it is important that you can tell him/her what these strengths are. It is also important that you relay this information to the school. This will give them positive reinforcement and help to generate motivation as well as a positive self-esteem.

Give them responsibility

Some children with low self-esteem can respond well to a degree of responsibility. This is important and an effort should be made to look for situations where this can be possible and you can provide some responsibility as long as it is within his/her abilities.

Peer tutoring

If you are looking for additional tutoring for your child, you could first suggest peer tutoring to the school. This means working with one other child, usually an older child, and this can be beneficial.

Positive communication with the school

There is a great deal of research showing the positive impact of parent/school interaction.

The hidden effects of dyslexia

Dyslexia is one of the conditions that may not be obvious all the time. Some children with dyslexia can be quite accomplished at covering up and pretending to be able to do something when in fact they are not managing the task at all well. Often children with dyslexia are good in discussion. This can create an impression that they have an understanding of the topic, but they may not be able to display that in writing. Yet in terms of their oral presentation one can assume that they are entirely competent in the area. What one finds however is that children with dyslexia are often aware of their difficulties and shortcomings and it is this that can lead to low self-esteem. It is important for parents and teachers to ensure that the child has fully understood what is being learnt. It is quite important to go over the task with them orally first and then get them to repeat what they have to do.

Often one of the hidden effects of dyslexia is a reluctance to ask questions as the child with dyslexia may not want to appear that he/she has not understood the instructions or the question to be tackled. For that reason it is good practice to take time to go over the task orally and to ensure that your child's understanding is being monitored at regular intervals when the task is being undertaken.

Success through self-esteem and motivation

Small achievable steps

It is generally easier for children with dyslexia to learn new information in small steps. Many children with dyslexia are holistic learners and this means that first they need an overview of the topic, book or text. The key point is to ensure that each of the steps is achievable.

Progress

It is important that children with dyslexia are able to recognize and appreciate that they are making progress. Some may find this difficult and progression may have to be clearly displayed for them. A framework, or even a checklist, can help the learner note his/her progress.

Preparing for learning – emotional factors

For most of us it is too easy to overlook the importance of the role of emotional development in learning. We can be too preoccupied with results and performances to look at reasons underpinning these performances. The research shows that emotional development is important for the process of learning and has a big influence in the eventual success of a task. It is worthwhile spending time with your child to ensure that he/she is developing emotionally. This includes how they feel about doing a certain task and why they feel like that. The development of emotions can be seen at three levels – the cognitive (how people think), the physiological (the current state of bodily health and well-being) and the affective domain (their understanding and awareness of their own and other people's emotions). You can often tell if children are emotionally troubled. Warning signs can be reluctance to go to school or separation anxiety. They may also want to hide themselves away in their room and not want to talk about school work. There may also be changes in their eating habits and routine. They may also seem unusually unhappy and may go for longish spells feeling like that. Clearly, if this is the case there may well be a good cause for concern and the family doctor should be consulted and certainly the school, as the source of the difficulty may lie in some aspect of school life and work.

Emotional literacy and emotional intelligence

There has been quite a bit of emphasis recently on emotional literacy in schools. This is essentially being aware of one's emotions and the feelings of others. According to Killick (2005), emotional literacy provides 'a way of increasing the space that exists between feelings and actions' (p. 14). He argues this can be linked to emotional intelligence. Both relate to the capacity in individuals (and groups) to perceive, understand and manage emotions in oneself and in others. This is very important for social learning and for children with dyslexia who may need to use their social skills to compensate for the feelings they may harbor of not being as good as others academically.

Killick suggests that 'emotional literate children will have greater resilience to emotional problems' (p. 5) and it is often the case that emotional problems can underpin behavior problems. There are five pathways to emotional intelligence:

1. **Self-awareness**: That is self-knowledge so the child knows what they can do and what is challenging; they may also be able to develop their own coping strategies and can realistically anticipate the types of tasks that can be challenging.
2. **Self-regulation**: The ability to monitor their own progress so they will know if they have gone the wrong way when they are tackling a problem and will be able to self-correct. Many children with dyslexia have difficulty doing this.
3. **Motivation**: This is important for learning, but in some situations it is difficult for children with dyslexia to become motivated. Yet it is important as they will learn more effectively if they are motivated. One of the most important aspects of motivation is success and whether the learner perceives the tasks as achievable. It is crucial that tasks are selected to ensure the learner has some success and that it is broken down into small manageable steps.
4. **Empathy:** In order to be in touch with your own emotions you have to be able to show empathy and concern for others. It is for that reason that social skills programs in school are so important. These types of programs can help all children develop empathy and a caring approach towards others.

5. **Social competence**: It is important that children with dyslexia are given opportunities to develop social competence. Practice in social situations is important and parents can do a lot to help to arrange this type of situation. Success in these situations can lead to emotional stability and a sense of self-assuredness.

These factors are important for successful learning and for the development of emotional well-being.

Emotional stress and learning

There is evidence that children with dyslexia can display attention and behavior problems and the negative emotions that can be attributed to failure to acquire literacy skills can also lead to greater emotional problems (Hales, 2009; Miles, 2004). This can result in stress, particularly if the negative consequences of school failure are prolonged and not dealt with as early as possible. It is important for parents to be aware of the potential stressors that their child with dyslexia can experience. It has been found that higher stress levels can affect an individual's capacity to study and lead to poorer memory, which may decrease problem-solving abilities (Mueller, 1976). Children with dyslexia who are likely to be prone to stress when learning may have an increase in their processing difficulties due to the higher stress levels. Everatt and Brannan (1996) found that a difficult spelling task for students with dyslexia led to weaker performance in subsequent memory and problem-solving tasks. Studies which have compared dyslexic and non-dyslexic students have found that the dyslexic group is more prone to anxiety than their peers (Riddick, Farmer & Sterling, 1997).

Success through self-appraisal

One of the problems encountered by young people with dyslexia is that they may have difficulty realizing that they have been successful and can be poor appraisers of their own abilities. McLoughlin, Fitzgibbon and Young (1994) found that individuals with dyslexia had poor perceptions of their spelling abilities. Lawrence (1987) has argued that an individual's level of achievement can be influenced by how they feel about themselves, suggesting a potential downward spiral of poor achievement leading to poor self-esteem, which further affects performance. Equally, good self-awareness has been considered a factor in a successful adult life for the individual with a learning problem (Goldberg, Higgins, Raskind & Herman, 2003). These studies suggest that the role of self-esteem and self-perception of their own abilities is crucial for all dyslexic children and adults. It is important for parents to be aware of this.

Social factors

School is a social institution, but some children with dyslexia can find it difficult to fit into school. School is also heavily influenced by examinations, achievement and literacy. These can be challenging for children with dyslexia. The realization that they may not fit in can make them socially isolated and can be a chronic source of unhappiness.

Motivation

Many children with dyslexia find it difficult to become and stay motivated with some tasks. Parents are often looking for ways to motivate their child to read. There are different types of motivation and parents need to be aware of these different approaches.

Motivation by task

For many students with dyslexia the thought of certain types of tasks can be sufficient to demotivate them. If they have experienced repeated failure some will become totally demotivated and will not want to engage in learning new material at all. It is important, therefore, that children experience success before they become demotivated to this level.

It is for that reason that great care must be taken when developing tasks to ensure that they are motivating and importantly that the learner believes the task is achievable. It is important that the task is broken down into small steps and that every step represents an achievable and rewarding outcome for the learner. This should be done at school, but parents need to look at the type of tasks their child is taking home and assess whether or not they can be motivating and how they can be made more motivating for their child. A task will be motivating if it is achievable and captures the interest of the child.

Motivation by reward

Although rewards are useful they should be seen as a short-term strategy – one step towards self-motivation. Rewards are normally only successful in the short term and can help children who need a boost, particularly if they are finding the task challenging. Rewards must be also be accessible and the learner must value the reward that is offered. Ideally it is best if the reward is negotiated with the learner. This can be done by parents who have a good knowledge of their child and the types of rewards he/she finds motivating.

Social motivation – the influence of peer group

Social interaction can be beneficial for learners with dyslexia as it can help develop important social skills, such as turn-taking, sharing and listening to other people's opinions. The process of helping and working with others can in itself be motivating. Parents should try to ensure that the group and peer friendships are constructive and positive. This can be invaluable for the child with dyslexia.

Motivation by feedback

Every learner needs feedback to ensure he/she is on the right path. It is important that feedback is seen as different from merely 'correcting' work. Feedback should be positive or framed in a positive manner. Parents will realize that their child needs this almost continuous feed-back in order to reassure them and set them up for future tasks.

Motivation by achievement

The 'must be best' syndrome is quite widespread in today's competitive society and although this has some positive elements it can be seen as a very risky strategy and one that can place enormous pressure on the learner. It is not a desirable strategy for a child with dyslexia. Parents will also realize that achievement can be different for different learners. Obtaining an A grade can be considered an achievement, but it may not be an attainable goal for some students and therefore cannot be used as a measure of achievement. Just as in task motivation it is a good idea to break achievement down into small steps. This way the child with dyslexia will get started on the achievement ladder and can be motivating for subsequent tasks.

The key question therefore is, what do we mean by achievement? Achievement is not necessarily reaching the goal set by a teacher. Achievement depends on the learner and their readiness for the task. It is also important to consider the complete learning experience and appreciate the importance of the learning environment (Reid, 2007). Unrealistic expectations can often be the main cause of failure in school. It is important that expectations from both the children's and the parents' viewpoint are seen to be flexible.

Dealing with stress – individual approaches

- **Activity:** Most types of activity can help to alleviate stress. Children with dyslexia often feel more relaxed after exercise as long as the exercise is not of a competitive nature or too prolonged, otherwise it can result in additional stress and fatigue.
- **Sport:** This is a great stress reliever – it can also help to develop team building and peer friendships.
- **Music:** It is important that the right type of music is selected – the best idea is to get your child to try working and studying with different types of music to work out which, if any, is best.
- **Reflection:** Reflection means that children need to take time out from what they are doing to reflect on what they have done. Reflection can help them become aware of where they have been, where they are at and where they want to go. Often the pace of life in school is

fast and furious with packed syllabuses and high expectations. It is important therefore to allow time for self-reflection.

- **Talk:** Talking through a problem or a situation can help to clarify the situation in the child's mind. This should not be overlooked – it is important to give children the opportunity to do this. Some children may not be aware of the nature of the problem until they have started to articulate it.
- **Sleep/rest:** For many children with dyslexia school life can be hectic. The pace is fast and it can be exhausting. It is important to allow time for rest and of course sleep. The source of many periods of unhappiness and misery can be due to lack of rest and can be easily remedied.
- **Reading:** Many children with dyslexia find reading quite stressful. Yet if the book is interesting and at the right level reading can be a superb form of relaxation. It is important to try to engage children with dyslexia in reading but to do this it is crucial that the right level of reading materials is found. This applies to content as well as vocabulary. Many publishers now have a series of high-low books that have a high interest content but a low level of vocabulary for reluctant readers.
- **Hobbies:** There is certainly more emphasis in school on the development of interests and hobbies and parents should try to ensure that their child does have leisure outlets outwith school. Hobbies can promote the social competences that children need, and can also be a useful learning tool for developing specific skills. This can help in the transfer of learning from one situation to another – a factor that is crucial for effective learning and one that many learners with dyslexia have some difficulty with.

Motivation is a key factor in successful learning and it is crucial that attempts are made to ensure the child with dyslexia is motivated in all tasks, including the challenging ones. This can be done by ensuring that goals are set as well as short-term targets and rewards. Ideally, motivation should be intrinsic – that is, the learner is self-motivating. To achieve this the learner needs to have a desired goal and some determination to succeed. Children who experience barriers to learning, including children with dyslexia, can find motivation challenging as repeated failure will result in serious demotivation, a state often referred to as learned helplessness. It is crucial that the learner does not reach this state and for that reason early success is important when tackling new tasks. It is also important that both extrinsic (rewards) and intrinsic (self-motivation) factors are taken into account in learning.

Summary

This chapter has:

- Indicated the potential areas of failure in the school day for a child with dyslexia.
- Indicated how these potential 'failure' areas can be prevented.
- Noted the importance of self-esteem in learning.
- Observed that children with dyslexia can have low self-esteem which can affect their subsequent learning and have a crossover effect to other areas of learning and to school life.
- Noted the importance of positive feedback for self-esteem and for motivation.
- Indicated the role of emotional development and emotional literacy in successful learning.
- Indicated that it is important to encourage student responsibility when engaged in a task. This can give the student a sense of ownership over the task and this in itself is a great motivator.
- Provided some indication of the potential areas of stress for children and adults with dyslexia and how these might be dealt with.
- Considered the challenges of positive self-esteem and emotional development and the hidden effects of dyslexia, noting they may not be obvious but they can be very real!

Chapter 10

Empowering parents

It has been indicated many times in this book that communication between parents and schools is important as it can help to clear up any misunderstanding and help both parents and schools to work collaboratively and positively. In some situations this does not seem to be sufficient and it has been necessary for parents to pursue their legal rights and to take legal action against schools and education departments. It is important therefore that parents are aware of their legal rights. There is now legislation in a number of countries to provide parents with full rights to ensure that the educational needs of their child are met. This chapter will look at the legislation and the practical implications of this for parents. It will begin with a discussion and some guidance on choosing a school, the criteria that may show that a school is dyslexia-friendly and the issues relating to home schooling and inclusion.

Dyslexia: A Complete Guide for Parents and Those Who Help Them, Second Edition. Gavin Reid.
© 2011 John Wiley & Sons, Ltd. Published 2011 by John Wiley & Sons, Ltd.

Choosing a school

Choosing the most appropriate school for your child is very important. I have had many heart-searching and agonizing discussions with parents who were trying to decide on the best school for their child. It is no easy matter as there are many factors to consider. If at all possible I try to suggest continuity and familiarity. These bring security and emotional stability and this is important for effective learning. But in some cases the present school may not be the best choice. You may want to consider moving your child if you are not happy with the level of communication with the school. You have to feel comfortable in your discussions with the school as this can have a major impact on future working relations. In my opinion, this is the most important aspect – can you communicate effectively and freely with the school, and do they in turn respond constructively and positively? If you feel your child is not making sufficient progress, you may want to discuss this first with the school, before considering moving school.

There are a number of points parents may want to find out about when considering choosing a mainstream school. These include:

- Does the school have teachers who hold a recognized qualification for teaching children with dyslexia?
- Are those teachers who are not specialized in dyslexia encouraged to go on courses? Ask for evidence of this. You could obtain information on the school's professional development programs over the last few years and if they have included any whole-school awareness on dyslexia. This would mean they are committed to all teachers in the school having at least an awareness of dyslexia.
- Does the school have any special provision – units, facilities for one-to-one, school–parent programs for dyslexia?
- What specialized programs are being used for dyslexic students – is the main program a structured, multisensory language program such as one of those in the IDA Matrix of programs or the BDA dyslexia-friendly pack?
- How flexible is the school on subject and course choice? For example, do they insist on second language learning?
- Does the school have a policy on developing the emotional side of the child (sometimes called emotional literacy)?

- Is inclusion a high priority in the school? To what extent do they take learning differences into account when planning work and in teaching?
- To what extent does the school encourage creativity and do they have extension work/programs for gifted students?
- How does the school measure whether or not it is effective in dealing with dyslexic students – test results, research studies and performance indicators?
- School size and class size – this can make a difference. Children with dyslexia may become 'lost' in large classes and their needs may be inadvertently ignored because they appear to be coping. In a small class they cannot 'hide' to the same extent.
- Does the school have clear dyslexia-friendly policies and practices? The term dyslexia friendly is a useful one to consider. Some of the features of what might be considered dyslexia-friendly schools are shown below.

Dyslexia-friendly schools – what are they?

There is a growing number of schools in many countries, both in the state and independent sectors, that fulfill or strive to fulfill the practice of dyslexia-friendliness. The British Dyslexia Association has promoted the criteria that schools should meet for being dyslexia-friendly quite vigorously. In the US the International Dyslexia Association has guidance on what might make a school dyslexia-friendly. They have an excellent factsheet on multisensory structured language teaching and this is what is required for children with dyslexia.

In the UK the Council for the Registration of Schools Teaching Dyslexic Pupils (CReSTeD) has a number of categories for provision for students with dyslexia.

Dyslexia Specialist Provision Schools

The school is established primarily to teach students with dyslexia. The curriculum and timetable are designed to meet specific needs in a holistic, coordinated manner with a significant number of staff qualified in teaching dyslexic students.

Specialist Provision Schools

The school is established to teach students with Specific Learning Difficulties plus high functioning Autistic Spectrum Disorder. The curriculum and timetable are designed to meet specific needs in a holistic, coordinated manner with a significant number of staff qualified in teaching students with Specific Learning Difficulties.

Dyslexia Unit

The school has a designated Unit or Center that provides specialist tuition on a small group or individual basis, according to need. The Unit or Center is an adequately resourced teaching area under the management of a senior specialist teacher, who coordinates the work of other specialist teachers and ensures ongoing liaison with all mainstream teachers. This senior specialist teacher will probably have Head of Department status, and will certainly have significant input into the curriculum design and delivery.

Specialist Classes

Schools where dyslexic students are taught in separate classes within the school for some lessons, most probably, English and mathematics. These are taught by teachers with qualifications in teaching dyslexic students. These teachers are deemed responsible for communicating with the pupils' other subject teachers.

Withdrawal System

Schools where dyslexic students are withdrawn from appropriately selected lessons for specialist tuition from a teacher qualified in teaching dyslexic students. There is ongoing communication between mainstream and specialist teachers.

Maintained Sector

Maintained schools where the school's inclusion strategies support dyslexic students to access the curriculum; where there is an effective system of identifying dyslexic students; where there is a withdrawal system for individualized literacy support. There is positive, ongoing communication between mainstream and SEN staff, and the Senior Management Team.

Adapted from http://www.crested.org.uk/pages/gen_maintained. html.

Home schooling

Some parents may consider home schooling for a range of reasons. It is important to be aware of the challenges of home schooling. The IDA has an information fact sheet on this (http://www.interdys.org/ ewebeditpro5/upload/Why_Homeschool_a_Dyslexic_Child.pdf). But it does indicate that there is no 'magic bullet' for dyslexia and that intervention is best achieved through structured direct language instruction. There are courses that parents can undertake to help to equip them for this (see http://www.icepe.ie/) and in Canada parents can also access a training course on the Orton-Gillingham approach (OG) (www.ogtutors.com).

For effective home schooling you will need to take advice to ensure that your child is receiving a balanced curriculum and that you are able to develop a portfolio that can be used to apply for credits for a school or college. The AVKO Educational Research Foundation offers a number of good ideas and clear guidance in this respect (http://homeschooling.about.com/) and advocate a multisensory approach such as OG.

There are many examples of satisfied parents who have opted to home school but it does take a considerable commitment, preparation and training. Many of the parents who have succeeded with home schooling have undergone a full training course in an appropriate method such as OG. The comment below from one parent is typical of those parents who have succeeded with this option.

I realize that I should not put my own expectations on my son. When he cannot grasp a concept that I think should be easy, I no longer get frustrated. Instead, I take a deep breath and stay calm. If I were to get irritated at his difficulties, it would only set us back all the more. With a smile and a hug, I can see my son's face light up, and we get on with our lesson. There are still days of frustration, but on those 'dyslexic' days, we relax and take a break. It is slow going at times, but I know that the end results are well worth it. (http://lizditz.typepad.com/i_speak_of_dreams/ 2004/07/dyslexia_and_ho.html)

One parent who home schooled their dyslexic child indicated:

My dyslexic son looks at things differently from the rest of us, *on* and *off* the pages of a book. I never did give up on him. Our school year this year began the end of August. It is now the end of November and he has already read (for pleasure) eleven 500-page (on average) books.

For those of you who are teaching a child with dyslexia: Don't give up!

Ideas for Writing Practice

Narrate His Own Book
Many people with dyslexia are very creative people, which is the case with our son. He loves being read to and really enjoys a creative, exciting story. What we do is have him narrate his book and I type it for him.

Make His Own Comic Book
I also encourage him to draw and narrate his own comic books. I have him sound the words out as best he can on a separate piece of paper. I then show him the correct spelling and he copies that into the comic book he has put together.

Copy work
I don't think a small amount of copy work each day in a journal can possibly hurt. If your child likes poetry, for example, let him copy a small poem each day. (Adapted from http://www.thehealthyhomeschool.com/ dyslexia)

This parent also considered the following when deciding on the curriculum:

- Was it cost-effective?
- Can it be taught by a person with no previous training in special education?
- Are the resources to provide help with reading and maths accessible and affordable?
- Can the program you have selected be adapted for your child's age range?
- Is there a user-friendly teacher's manual?

The website http://www.learningabledkids.com/reading/inexpensive_ reading_programmes.htm has a number of inexpensive suggestions for reading programs for dyslexia that can be used at home. Many parents select home schooling because they feel that their child's needs will not be met in a mainstream school that is committed to inclusion because of the size and the diversity of needs. This need not be the case and it is important to look at schools individually – even schools in the same school district can show many differences in their approach.

Inclusion – is it right for your child?

Inclusion is a term that can cause parents anxiety. Many feel that in a school committed to the inclusive ideal their own child's specific needs may not be met. But in a fully effective inclusive school every child's needs should be catered for. This however is the ideal and often this ideal is not realized. Legally, parents have some weight to ensure their child's needs are met in an inclusive school. Accommodations need to be made to ensure that any learning differences are accommodated. This has presented challenges to the education system, although current legislation in most countries attempts to provide equality through access to a full and balanced curriculum. In England there is a national inclusion statement which includes a section on responding to pupils' diverse needs. This states that teachers should take action to respond to pupils' needs by:

- creating effective learning environments;
- securing children's motivation and concentration;
- providing equality of opportunity through teaching approaches;
- setting targets for learning.

An effective education for your child with dyslexia is a balance between social inclusion that ensures he/she is part of a positive friendship group and educational outcomes that can ensure that your child reaches his/her full potential. This means that resources and provision to achieve this can be different for different children. Inclusion should certainly be seen as a desirable product, but there are a number of routes to achieve this and parents should really view each school individually and assess whether it has the resources to meet their child's needs.

Parents should feel familiar with the school and be able to find their way around it.

Points parents may wish to consider are:

- Clear instructions on how the class teacher can be contacted and when.
- Clear signposts so that parents can navigate around the school comfortably.
- A set time when parents are welcome to drop into the school.
- Provision for working parents on how they may contact the school.
- Open evenings that are at a time and day suitable for most parents.
- Home−school notebooks can be very helpful for working parents.
- It is also worth considering that parents of dyslexic children may also be dyslexic themselves and this may have an impact on how parents can be used supportively.

Self-advocacy

There is a growing trend towards self-advocacy in education and in society. This means that children, young adults and parents need to be aware of their rights and to be able to speak up for these rights. But it also means that schools should help to equip children with the ability to articulate their needs. This is a skill that will benefit them in later life and particularly in the workplace. Parents also have a role to play in assisting their child in self-advocacy skills. Perhaps one of the best pieces of advice parents can give their child is to communicate with the school. It is too easy for children who are experiencing any type of difficulty in school to keep it to themselves or bottle it up to such an extent that it explodes in the form of unacceptable, inappropriate and sometimes explosive behaviour.

The difficulty for parents is that often the child finds it difficult to identify exactly what is going wrong and why. Even at the best of times, parenting can be a challenge. Parents have to be both disciplinarians and counselors. It is a question of balance, but there is no doubt that very often children with dyslexia will respond more to the counseling approach. Some suggestions for parents on counseling children with dyslexia include the following:

- **Self-esteem**: It is more likely that the child with positive self-esteem will open up and be more likely to discuss problems than a child with negative self-esteem. It is important therefore to make the child feel good as that can clear the way for the discussion of any difficulties.
- **Make a space for family or parent–child discussion**: If this takes place regularly, including when the child is not experiencing any obvious problems, it will set a pattern of discussion so that when a problem does occur it can be discussed in the normal pattern of family discussions.
- **Defuse the situation**. Try not to show the child any anxieties you may have because these will soon be felt by the child and make it less likely that he/she will want to discuss them.
- **Listen**: It is important to acknowledge and accept your child's challenges and views from his/her perspective. You may not always agree with them but you do need to listen. It is also important to have faith and confidence in your child's views and what he/she wants to do.
- **Use prompts**: Certainly ask questions about what they say to you, but let them take the lead. Try to avoid what you want to say to them until they have had an opportunity to express their views. At the end of the discussion, try to agree on some course of action even if it is

just to discuss the same issue the following week. But do not allow issues and concerns to drift.

- **Take what your child says seriously**: This may seem obvious but even if children raise what seems to be a trivial matter it will be a major issue to them and they need it to be taken seriously.
- **Involve the family if appropriate**: This can help to normalize the issue as everyone in the family, dyslexic or not, will experience some problems and difficulties, so the dyslexic difficulties will just be a variation of the normal course of family discussion.
- **Communicate with the school**: Inform the school if your child raises any issue that may be relevant to the school. That is not the same as complaining, but rather communicating with the school so that all involved with the child have the same knowledge. You need to suggest to your child that the school should know, of course.
- **Avoid confrontation**: This will put up barriers that will prevent free and relaxed discussion and make any counseling/supportive discussion impossible.
- **Praise and thank your child for discussing this with you**: This will make it easier for him/her to discuss any issues with you in the future.

Know your rights

Since the Salamanca Statement (UNESCO, 1994) there has been a considerable thrust towards equality in education in Europe. This trend has been noted throughout the world and there are similarities in educational philosophies – principally relating to inclusion, parental involvement, equity and student advocacy – in the US, Canada, Australia, New Zealand and throughout Europe.

The Salamanca Statement forged a powerful path on the road to educational equality and inclusive policies. The statement indicated that

> schools should accommodate to all children regardless of their physical, intellectual, social, emotional, linguistic or other conditions. ... Many children experience learning difficulties and thus have special educational needs at some time during their schooling .... Schools have to

find ways of successfully educating all children, including those who have serious disadvantages and disabilities ... emerging consensus that children with special educational needs should be included in the educational arrangements made for the majority of children. This has led to the concept of the inclusive school.

Statements like this have motivated governments to reform their education systems, but implementing this is quite another matter. In the US the Federal Special Education Law, called the Individuals with Disabilities Education Act (IDEA), includes a clear definition of learning disabilities. It states that 'Children with specific learning disabilities exhibit a disorder in one or more of the basic psychological processes involved in understanding or using spoken or written language. These may be manifested in writing, spelling, or arithmetic.' This includes conditions such as dyslexia. The law demands that every school in every city in every state must provide 'free and appropriate' special education programs for all children with special needs.

The publication Mapping America's Educational Progress (2008, http://www2.ed.gov/nclb/accountability/results/progress/nation.html) indicates that the aim is to have all children on grade level by 2014. You can see how your state is progressing towards that goal at http://www2.ed.gov/nclb/accountability/results/progress/index.html.

In New Jersey the mapping document indicates that 74% of the schools have made adequate yearly progress since the No Child Left Behind Act was passed and this is above the national average. New Jersey has passed a law that they will set up a Dyslexia Task Force, which will help determine the best methods for diagnosing, treating and educating special needs students. The 13-member panel will include the state commissioners of education and human resources, four legislators and seven members of the public (*New Jersey Real Time News*, 17 January 2010; http://www.nj.com/news/index.ssf/2010/01/nj_measure_will_benefit_readin.html#comments).

In Canada court action has been used to support children and parents ensure that dyslexia is identified and that the child is appropriately supported. The Canadian Charter of Rights and Freedoms has been quoted as support for parental rights. The Charter guarantees the right of all individuals to be treated equally before and under the law and to be afforded equal protection and equal benefit

of the law without discrimination (http://www.poynerbaxter.com/
Dyslexia/Canada%20News%20wire.htm).

In England and Wales the Special Educational Needs and Disability Act (SENDA) 2001 includes a Code of Practice. The Act
amends the Disability Discrimination Act 1995, to cover education.
The Act provides greater powers to the Special Educational Needs
Tribunal and places a duty on Local Education Authorities to provide and advertise both a parent partnership scheme and conciliation
arrangements.

The words 'disability' and 'discrimination' are key in the Act. The
Act states that schools cannot discriminate against disabled pupils (the
definition of disability is very broad and dyslexia can be seen in terms
of the Act as a disability) in all aspects of school life, including ex-
tracurricular activities and school excursions.

Parents can claim unlawful discrimination by putting a case to a
Tribunal. Under the Act it is unlawful for schools to discriminate in
admissions and exclusions, and a school cannot deliberately refuse
an application from a disabled person for admission to the school.
Discrimination is evident when a pupil is treated less favorably and
may be at a disadvantage because the school has not made 'reasonable
adjustments'. What is meant by 'reasonable' is not defined in the Act
as this depends on individual cases and can be a matter for the Tribunal
or an appeal panel to decide.

Essentially, the Act aims to incorporate parents as partners in the
education of their child. This is very important in relation to children
with special educational needs and parents need to be informed when
special education needs provision is made for their child.

The Code of Practice indicates that if a dyslexic child has needs that
cannot adequately be met, there may be a requirement for a statement
of educational need to be formulated in order to protect the child's
interests. The Code recognizes that all parents of children with special
educational needs should be treated as partners and should be empow-
ered to play a full and active role in their child's education. This also
means that the LEA will provide parents with 'information, advice and
support during assessment and any related decision-making process
about special educational provision' (Code of Practice, para. 2.2). One
of the means of empowering parents in England and Wales throughout
this process is the Parent Partnership Scheme (PPS).

According to the legislation children who face barriers to their learning will often require different levels of educational intervention to support their learning. This may consist in what is commonly referred to as Wave 2 or Wave 3 intervention. Wave 2 intervention consists of time-limited support for a child with special educational needs, focussing on a particular area of difficulty. This support is provided within the classroom, with the view to accelerate progress and address misconceptions that may have developed. Wave 3 intervention consists of more individualized support designed specifically for an individual child, again, with the view to accelerate progress. Some children with special educational needs will have a 'statement' outlining their individual needs and the specific provision needed. Getting a statement involves going through a statutory assessment of a child's individual needs and ascertaining the number of hours of support that child is entitled to. These hours of support must then be provided by the school but will often be funded by the local authority. The number of children eligible for a statement is dependent on the location and there is quite a bit of variation. In most cases such children will be educated within the same school as their non-SEN peers, but supported by an SEN Department within the school staffed by teaching assistants and organized by a Special Educational Needs Coordinator. The LEA has to take account of the SEN Code of Practice. Each school has its own policy, which details how the school implements the Code. Figures published in 2009 showed that 17.8% of pupils in English schools have special educational needs, a proportion that has steadily grown from 14.9% in 2005.

In England and Wales the failure of schools to diagnose and provide remedial help for dyslexia following the House of Lords decision in the case of Pamela Phelps helped to create an entitlement for students with dyslexia in higher education to receive support funded via the Disabled Students Allowance.

In Scotland by passing of the Education (Additional Support for Learning) (Scotland) Act 2004, the Scottish Parliament redefined the law in Scotland relating to the provision of special education to children with additional needs by establishing a framework for the policies of inclusion and generally practicing the 'presumption of mainstreaming' in Scottish education. The Act is an attempt to broaden the narrow definition of special educational needs which has typically been used to define children with special needs to incorporate additional support needs.

The Act sets out the responsibilities of education authorities and other agencies for helping young people with additional support needs. Amendments to the Act were agreed in 2009. These changes came into force in 2010, giving the authorities new duties and parents new rights:

- **Assessment:** Local authorities must respond to any reasonable requests for an assessment.
- **Provision:** Local authorities must make information available to all parents about the provision in their area for children with additional support needs.
- **Scottish Ministers** will also have to gather and publish information each year about the number of children with additional support needs in each local authority area; the main reasons for them needing support; the types of support provided; and how much is being spent (http://www.dyslexiascotland.org.uk).

Equality and rights

We have noted how in Canada the Canadian Charter of Rights and Freedoms has been quoted as support for parental rights. Similarly in the UK the government has passed the Equality and Human Rights Commission which includes a series of written guides to explain people's rights and responsibilities under the Equality Act 2010 which came into effect in October 2010. The Act brings together different pieces of legislation to make equality law simpler and easier to understand. Two versions of each set of guidances have been produced, one aimed at people who want advice on their rights and the other at those who have responsibilities under the law.

The guidances were published in July 2010 and cover two key areas of the new Act: Employment and Services, and Public Functions and Associations. The guidances can be accessed at: http://www.equalityhumanrights.com/legislative-framework/equality-bill/equality-act-2010-guidance.

Summary

Although this chapter has focussed on trends in some countries these trends have repercussions in virtually all countries. Additionally, 'the word' in relation to dyslexia has been spread by many 'ambassadors' and role models such as Sir Jackie Stewart, Sir Richard Branson and film producer Guy Ritchie who have all dealt with the challenges of dyslexia.

There are many examples of parents' support groups forming partnerships with others and engaging in many forms of lobbying, consultancy and support activities. Organizations such as the Dyslexia Association of Singapore and the Hong Kong Dyslexia Association have developed efficient organizations that can deal with all aspects of dyslexia from assessment to teacher training.

In New Zealand the Dyslexia Foundation of New Zealand (DFNZ) (http://www.dyslexiafoundation.org.nz/about.html) was formed in November 2006. Just six months after its launch, DFNZ was successful in having the New Zealand government recognize dyslexia in April 2007, after much hard work by the Foundation. In an accompanying statement, the Ministry of Education said it would be putting greater emphasis on assisting students with dyslexia, and would be implementing a range of initiatives to increase the level and quality of assistance given to these students. A ministry spokesperson said, 'We've completed a review of international research and are using this to refocus our current policies and programmes to better address dyslexia' (www.minedu.govt.nz).

The three steps of the Dyslexia Foundation – recognition, understanding and action – are critical to effectively addressing dyslexia, and are based on the following principles:

- **Recognition:** Identifying and naming the issue.
- **Understanding:** Noticing what this means for everyday life – at school, home and work.
- **Action:** Adjusting the approach to improve outcomes – at school, home and work.

Two other factors that have general application world-wide are the policy of inclusion and the notion of litigation. They may be connected.

Inclusion is a demanding concept for schools to implement successfully. It requires meeting the needs of diverse groups of children within the same educational setting. For this to be fully and successfully implemented requires time, training and resources. Although there are many good examples of governments attempting to provide training and resources, in many countries, and in many areas within countries, provision for dyslexia has been described as patchy by local dyslexia associations. There is optimism certainly and considerable amount of support and advice for parents and this does bring the much needed hope and advice that many parents need.

Chapter 11

Parents' and children's voices

The aim of this chapter is to highlight some of the experiences and views of parents of children with dyslexia.

The research for this chapter comes from the responses of participants of an online course for parents (www.icepe.ie), questionnaires and interviews with parents (and children) in different countries. It was interesting to note how the experiences of parents differed – even among parents living in the same areas – and it is also interesting to note the different types of pressures parents feel.

One of the points to emerge is that, however careful and sensitive the education authority/system or school district might be in developing procedures to identify and deal with dyslexia, there will still be some parents – sometimes a substantial number – whose needs are not met. It is also important to appreciate that every child is unique and that includes children with dyslexia. It is for that reason that an individual educational plan is often essential.

Dyslexia: A Complete Guide for Parents and Those Who Help Them, Second Edition. Gavin Reid.
© 2011 John Wiley & Sons, Ltd. Published 2011 by John Wiley & Sons, Ltd.

Communication between the school and parents is vital, but it is often not fully appreciated. Parents and schools can have different priorities and experience different types of pressures.

Some difficulties experienced by parents

The comments that follow are adapted from those made by parents participating in an online course on dyslexia (ICEPE, 2010). You will see that they express an enormous amount of anxiety:

- The possibility of their child repeating a year, sometimes with some pressure from the school. This needs to be carefully considered.
- Transition to secondary/high school. This is always an anxious time and parents need to find out well in advance if the school has a policy and procedures to help.
- Difficulty following a series of instructions, staying focussed and on task. This can be frustrating for the child and also for the parents – that is the time when the parents need to talk to other parents so that they realize they are not alone.
- Realizing the need to recognize the differences, that not every child with dyslexia is the same. One parent said, 'I always assumed that for best concentration and ability to absorb information a quiet, calm environment was best. No noise, no TV, no music or disruption. I assumed they would concentrate and absorb more this way. Now I realize that everyone is different – and whatever works, works!' (personal correspondence, 2010).

Dealing with anxiety

School can, and should, be an exciting period in a child's life. But for those who are not succeeding academically it can be traumatic and stressful. It need not be as many schools are tuned in to supporting students who have difficulties and this can minimize any potential stress. But there are key times which can provoke stress: the process of identification is one. Parents may have to attend formal meetings and put forward, sometimes forcefully, their views and opinions. One such parent comments about the feelings experienced on preparing for and attending a meeting such as this as well as the pressures:

> We would like to present our case from the perspective of spending thousands of hours researching our child's learning disability and consulting experts worldwide in regards to the most appropriate remediation and course of education. I have many peer-reviewed research articles proving that foreign language learning for a dyslexic child undermines their remediation (which is over learning the English sound/symbol relationships), is often unsuccessful educationally unless the teacher is well trained in OG methodology and negatively affects their self esteem as it is just another subject in their deficit zone [phonological processing/weak phonological memory]. (personal communication, 2010)

It is important that professionals recognize the potential anxiety as well as the intense preparation some parents make and appreciate that it is their responsibility to ensure that parental anxieties are kept to a minimum.

Parents will find discussing their concerns with other parents very helpful. This can noted in the advice provided by the course tutor (herself a parent).

> I can suggest some strategies to help with understanding and advocating for your child:
>
> • create a binder to keep all of the paper work together – organize it with dividers
> • be sure to take notes at meetings
> • bring a third party to the meeting with you, particularly if you are emotional about it. Perhaps a grandparent, friend, relative
> • educate yourself and find out about dyslexia or do a course on it
> • keep a phone log – include date and time of all phone calls and messages
> • give positive feedback to the teachers. A lot of teachers put in their own time to differentiate materials, have meetings, send emails, answer phone calls. Yes it is their job but a thank you note goes a long way!
> • request meetings early in the year and regularly and be persistent
> • go through the assessment and write down specific questions to bring with you to the meeting. It is easy to get off track and forget the questions that come to you at home

- create a list of strengths and interests — teachers need to know what your child does well and enjoys. (Reproduced with permission from Shannon Green, course tutor ICEPE, personal correspondence, 2010)

Parent-to-parent discussions

As part of the research for the first edition of this book I undertook a number of interviews with parents and also placed a parent questionnaire on my web home page. Parents were invited to complete the questionnaire on-line and all respondents provided address details in order that follow-up information could be obtained. The questions and the responses are shown below:

What are the factors that made it difficult for you as a parent of a child with dyslexia?

- helping to maintain the child's self-esteem;
- helping the child start new work when he/she had not consolidated previous work;
- protecting the dignity of the child when dealing with professionals/ therapists;
- personal organization of the child;
- peer insensitivity;
- misconceptions of dyslexia.

For this second edition I undertook interviews with parents and gathered information from courses I have been running for parents in person and online. Some of other factors to emerge from these sources include the following.

Curriculum choice

There is a lot of pressure on students — an overcrowded timetable is one such pressure. This can include the need to take at least one language other than their main one – often two new languages. While this can be good in terms of career and university choice it can add to stress.

Learning a new language can be demanding for children with dyslexia. There are a number of reasons, among them the need to learn a new vocabulary, a new grammatical structure and the tendency for the teaching of foreign languages to be verbal and auditory and usually at a pace which is too fast for the student with dyslexia.

Crombie and McColl (2001) make some suggestions which can help make modern languages more dyslexia-friendly:

- Use charts and diagrams to highlight the bigger picture and label them.
- Add mime and gesture to words.
- Add pictures to text.
- Use color to highlight gender, accents.
- Use games to consolidate vocabulary.
- Make packs of pocket-size cards.
- Use different colors for different purposes.
- Combine listening and reading by providing text and tape.
- Use mind maps, spidergrams.
- Allow student to produce his/her own tape.
- Present information in small amounts, using a variety of means, with frequent opportunities for repetition and revision.
- Provide an interest in the country, show films, etc.
- Rules and other information about the language should be provided in written form for further study and future reference.

Modern foreign languages should be accessible for all students with dyslexia. It is important for parents to be aware of this and consider how the materials are being presented to their child and reflect on whether this suits his/her learning style.

Helping with curriculum access

This is another issue that parents commented on a great deal. Yet all curricular subjects can be accessed by children with dyslexia. Although essentially this is the responsibility of the teacher it is also important for parents to be aware of how this can be managed. Some examples are shown below.

Social subjects

History, geography and social studies usually involve a considerable amount of reading and writing. This can be difficult for students with dyslexia and it can be challenging to present the subject in an accessible manner for them. There are a number of strategies that can be used:

- **Discussion**: this is a good reinforcing tool and should always be used as a follow-up to reading, such as history texts. The discussion should involve problem-solving activities (e.g. on the Wars of Independence or major political reforms). Learners with dyslexia will understand the text more fully if the information is relevant and meaningful to them; discussion can help to clarify this. The discussion should not be in the form of asking questions but rather jointly engaging in problem-solving activities.
- **Reading**: It is not essential for students to read every word in the text. They need to be taught how to read strategically, utilizing contextual cues. This means that they need to know the key words of the text and be able to understand the ideas and concepts in the text. This can also be achieved through pre-reading discussion. During this activity you can point out what the key words are and discuss why they are key words. Pre-reading discussion can also be provided by follow-up to watching a movie or documentary about the period or topic being studied.

Geography

Diagrams need to be labeled, using color as much as possible. Again, it is a good idea to provide key words and discuss the specialized vocabulary which can be found in geography texts.

Social Studies

It is important that difficulty in reading does not prevent students with dyslexia accessing higher-order thinking and problem-solving skills. It may be advisable to read some of the challenging texts to your child or put them on tape as it is important for young people with dyslexia to develop critical thinking in social studies.

Science

Students need to make full use of a laptop in the science classroom. This can be helpful for developing diagrams and for organizing and remembering information. A detailed and labeled plan of the science laboratory can useful as it can help the dyslexic student locate equipment and other materials they will need. Mind Maps™ can also be helpful as they provide a visual plan which is meaningful for the student. Mind Maps can also help with organization of information and recall of details.

It is also important to encourage independent learning and this can be reached through short, achievable targets. The student needs to be aware of exactly what is expected and know what they have to do to achieve the learning outcomes.

In subjects such as biology there is a considerable amount of factual detail to be remembered as well as technical words which are rarely used in everyday speech. Mind maps can be helpful here too. There are also technical words (e.g. homeostasis, ecosystem, respiration) and concepts to be mastered and these can be extremely abstract so it is important that your child has an understanding of them.

A great deal of the work in science subjects involves practical experiments and assignments based on practical work. There are certain skills associated with practical work such as understanding the instructions, which in fact may be quite complex, organizing the experiment, ensuring all the information and components are at hand and reporting on the experiment in a clear manner. These can be challenging for students with dyslexia.

Diagrams

Your child may need some help in developing diagrams for some topics. Factors you may want to consider are:

- making a plan, which will serve as a rough draft;
- deciding how much of the page is to be used;

- using color consistently, systematically and purposefully;
- labeling diagrams clearly and accurately;
- introducing fun into the activities which will make the work more meaningful.

English

The grammar aspects of English can be challenging for dyslexic students, but the critical thinking associated with English literature can be stimulating. The student with dyslexia may have gaps in their background knowledge as they may not have read as widely as other students. It is important to help them fill these gaps and this means that discussion and explanation of the concepts are important. Many literature classics are now available in DVD and audio and this can help the student develop a picture of the scene and the situational context of the novel or play. It may be better to commence any theme or topic with background discussion to develop ideas and concepts and then present the theme for the novel in visual or drama form before the student starts reading the book.

Strategies for parents

Every parent will have a different way of coping with their challenges but there are some common challenges and responses.

Emotional challenges

If a child is failing in literacy and finds school work challenging, then it is likely that he/she will suffer emotionally. It is important that this is addressed and preferably prevented. Children can be very sensitive, particularly if they feel they are in any way different from others. Some parents I have spoken to have been reluctant to accept a place in a reading unit for their child because they fear this may damage his self-esteem. Yet the reading unit will have the resources to develop his literacy skills and that in the long run it will do a lot to build his self-esteem. So it is crucial that any changes or moves such as this are treated sensitively, but they should not be passed over because of the fear of being singled out. These situations can and should be handled as a matter of priority.

Follow-up after assessment

This is a very important process and one that should not be rushed. You should prepare yourself with questions when you go to a meeting to discuss the results of an assessment. It is important to receive the answers you want to any issues about intervention. You may want to ask:

- Will all the recommendations in the assessment report be implemented?
- Will there be opportunities for withdrawal to small groups or one-on-one teaching?
- If so, what type of programs will be used?
- What is the school's policy on self-esteem and emotional development?
- Will my youngster's learning style be considered?
- What kind of experiences and training do the staff have on dyslexia?
- Does the school run any events to promote parent—parent communication?
- Will my youngster qualify for an Individual Educational Program?
- If so, what will my role be in developing this?

There may be other questions you want to ask and you need to be prepared to ensure you get the opportunity to ask them. If you do not get this, then be sure to put them in an email to the head teacher.

Self-esteem

There are a number of ways to help to maintain and boost children's self-esteem. One of the most obvious and most effective ways is to ensure that they achieve some success and receive genuine praise. In order for praise to be effective the child has to be convinced that their achievements are worthy of the praise. When children feel like a failure it is difficult to reverse these feelings and often they need to change their perceptions of themselves. This can be a lengthy process and ongoing support, praise and sensitive handling are necessary. Some suggestions include:

- Ensuring you discuss feelings with your child and not just results.
- Paired reading – this can be useful as it promotes working together.
- Mind mapping – this can help to give children a sense of ownership, that it is their own strategy and it is more meaningful to them.
- Memory games – this can be fun and rewarding, even simple games like covering up colored counters on a board and asking the child where the different colors are positioned.
- Learning styles – if the school does not know your child's leaning style, it is important for you to find this out. You can do this through observation – looking at whether he/she likes to:
  - learn new work visually, by listening or through practical experiential learning,
  - prefers to sit on a bean bag or the floor rather than at a desk,
  - prefers dim lights to bright lights,
  - prefers a quiet or noisy background when working
  - prefers to tackle a task one step at as time or in a more holistic multitasking way.

  From these observations you can work out at least some of your child's learning preferences.
- Opportunity for the child to benefit from discussion – this can also be important for self-esteem. Children like to express an opinion and it can be rewarding for them to be able to do this as it can have a positive impact on their self-esteem.
- Focus on areas of success – this is also important as it can promote positive self-esteem. It is important to reiterate this message in discussions with the school.

One parent suggested:

Self-esteem is a huge issue and one that is not helped by dyslexia being seen as a deficit! The continued emphasis on academic achievement and the issues of labeling are problematic for me. A major difficulty with the teaching profession is attitudinal — a lack of knowledge on dyslexia is apparent, although I have found there are also some exceptional teachers, but it is always difficult for a parent to know what advice to take. By the time they are in a position to decide it can be too late, or less effective than it could have been.

But discussions with schools can be very positive and some parents have good experiences:

I am very aware that I have been very fortunate that the education services in our education authority have provided teachers with up to date training in dyslexia and this has greatly benefited me and my dyslexic children. Having a teacher who is very aware of dyslexia and understanding is incredibly supportive.

One parent from Ohio who decided to home school her dyslexic son listed the struggles that had to be endured. These include being 'accused of not understanding him, accused of showing favouritism between him and his other siblings, teaching him to read, keeping his attention and making him want to learn, finding the right resource and finding people who are supportive to me'. These comments may well be familiar to many readers. In fact, I asked a former colleague who is a parent of an adult dyslexic daughter, who is now a very success-ful professional, of her lasting recollections as a parent of a daughter with dyslexia. Although her daughter had left school well over 10 years earlier my colleague without too much hesitation suggested two key fac-tors. First was not having her daughter's 'able and gifted' attributes rec-ognized by the school. She was essentially treated a slow learner. Sec-ondly, the emotional damage — indeed the lasting emotional damage — that can result even when the outcome is favorable, in terms of the person emerging as a skilled, mature adult succeeding in a demanding profession. It is reasonable to suggest that most parents are aware of the emotional factors that can accompany dyslexia. But they may not be aware of the potential longevity of these factors even when life events become favorable for that person.

Key issues

Some of the key issues to emerge from my discussions with parents include the following:

Frustration

One of the key issues to emerge is the frustration that parents can experience with the education system. This may not necessarily be a problem with the system, but a problem stemming from a breakdown in communication and different priorities and agendas.

Without question all schools and all teachers want to do their best for all children. Schools however have to meet the needs of individuals as well as the common needs of all learners. Teachers have also to meet the demands placed on them by the management and the education system. These demands are usually set by politicians and are often based on principles relating to accountability and results. These principles can present a difficulty in relation to dyslexia because progress made by children with dyslexia may not always be easily measured, and certainly not by conventional means. For example, for some children with dyslexia merely attending school can be a measure of success, but schools may not record this as progress and would rather focus on progress on attainments such as reading, spelling and writing. This is understandable but children with dyslexia may not make significant progress in this area at least in the short term. This can lead to some frustration on the part of parents and highlight very clearly the different agendas that exist between home and school. This underlines the importance of effective and shared communication.

Trust

Different perspectives can lead to a degree of mistrust. This is obviously a negative emotion and one that seriously damages the relationship between home and school. It can sometimes be difficult for parents to place their trust in a system that may not even seem to recognize dyslexia, but this is exactly what they have to do! Some parents who responded to the questionnaire suggested that they are a source of information on dyslexia for the school. It is a question of balance – of placing some trust in the education system, but also ensuring that you are aware of exactly what is going on in school regarding your child's education. There may be differences of opinions between home and school, but these should not break down any trust between the two. Parents are permitted to question and to seek explanations from the school on how their child is being educated but it is best to approach this in a constructive manner.

Balance

Parents often ask how they can balance the stress their child can experience in school work with life at home. This can be difficult as often the stress that is experienced at school can spill over into home life, especially since potential stresses, such as homework, can take up an undue amount of time at home. One parent indicated very strongly in the questionnaire that work at home should be fun. This may be difficult to achieve without making light of the work that the child has to do, but what this parent meant was that the family should try to provide a fun environment and one that is free from stress. She suggested the family should try to provide fun-type activities or games that can provide learning strategies for the child. This can be the use of mnemonics or even board games, both of which can be useful for developing memory skills. One parent from south-west Scotland suggested that for her games were extremely important in ensuring that her son did not take the stress at school into the home. She suggested the following:

> 'Kitchen cupboards' is a favourite, you have to identify all the products in the kitchen, play around with the products using part of the name, adding it on to part of another product's name. For example, we may take flour, marmalade, milk, washing powder and work our way through the different combinations of sounds from each of the products. From this we make up silly products like 'marwashder'. My son remembers the sounds and combinations much more easily when I relate it to some fun activity.

Understanding

Another of the issues relates to understanding. Many parents indicated that schools, or some teachers in schools, did not have much knowledge of dyslexia. This clearly varies from country to country and indeed within a single country from area to area. Also the level of knowledge of dyslexia within a school will be different. Parents need to realize this and may have taken it upon themselves to inform the school of some of the current interventions and thinking in dyslexia. At the same time, however, there does appear to be a considerable thrust in schools, and within education authorities, to increase teacher training and whole-school awareness of dyslexia (Reid, 2001, 2009).

Having spoken on dyslexia to parents' associations in many countries this is becoming very apparent and almost without exception a scheduled and advertised talk to a parents' association will include many teachers in the audience. It is important that parents understand what dyslexia is and this should be explained to them as soon as their child is assessed. It is just as important that teachers also know the different aspects relating to dyslexia.

Emotions

As indicated above, emotional factors are an important consideration for parents and can be a real concern to children and adults with dyslexia. Indeed many parents can themselves become emotionally affected due to the anxieties they experience and the frustrations they encounter. As a parent of a young man with autism I know only too well the emotional and the long-lasting impact of supporting and living through crises and trauma. Parents do become affected if they do not seek out the best form of support (usually other parents), and if they continually see their child's education in terms of a 'struggle'. One parent remarked at the end of the questionnaire, 'I am very cynical'. This is unfortunate as this emotion can be destructive but it can also be appreciated why in some situations parents feel like this.

An interesting university study ('I feel very, very small': Reflections on Living with Dyslexia) was conducted by Terras, Minnis, Mackenzie and Thomson (2004) jointly with the Dyslexia Institute Scotland. The study was conducted on six adults with dyslexia and concluded that dyslexia was experienced by the group as having a negative impact on their:

- self-esteem;
- social/emotional well-being;
- relationships;
- daily life, education and choice of career.

Low self-esteem is often accompanied by negative emotions. In the above study one respondent said: 'If you are comfortable in the environment you are in you get on well, but if you feel threatened in any way you will draw into yourself'. This highlights a crucial point about the environment. Children, and adults, learn more effectively if they feel comfortable in the school. They must feel they belong there and that they are being treated fairly. One adult reflected: 'If you are dyslexic you are bullied all the time'; another said: 'I just disappeared into a corner somewhere and just hoped the teacher wouldn't get me'.

Yet it should not be all doom and gloom. Many people with dyslexia have succeeded to a high level and have become confident and well-adjusted adults. This is the hope of every parent of a child with dyslexia – and to be fair the goal of every teacher. There are however many influences along the way that can prevent this. Yet there is more support available in dyslexia than ever before and more scientific advances that allow parents and teachers to understand the causes and characteristics of dyslexia.

Summary

This chapter has outlined some of the concerns and anxieties of parents using the voices of parents themselves. One of the striking points is that parents often have to take the initiative and many have done this very successfully. It is also apparent that some parents have benefited from good communication with the school and dialogue with teachers who are knowledgeable about dyslexia. Parents nevertheless can have a number of anxieties relating to the extent to which their children can reach their potential. This is understandable but parents and children should be optimistic. It is now well known that there is a positive side to dyslexia and it is important that this is recognized and harnessed.

Although many of the points discussed in this chapter come from parents who responded to a questionnaire they are applicable to all parents and can be generalized to parents in different countries. The message is the same for all – be positive and optimistic.

Chapter 12

Beyond school

It is important that parents are aware of the opportunities for dyslexic people at college and in the workplace. They also need to be aware of the challenges and how to prepare for and deal with them. This chapter shows that there is a great deal that has been achieved in this area in most countries and that the legislation particularly in the US, Canada and the UK has benefited young people with dyslexia at college and at work.

Initiatives such as the Employer's Guide to Dyslexia in the UK (BDA, 2005) have helped to establish a firm basis for developing awareness and effective workplace support for adults with dyslexia. Similar supports are available at college and universities. In the US, the Americans with Disabilities Act 1990 is the relevant Federal law; section 504 of the Rehabilitation Act 1973 uses the term 'academic adjustments' when referring to ways of supporting students with dyslexia. The term 'reasonable accommodation and support services' is also used because that emphasizes the institutional responsibility for addressing the person's academic needs as a result of dyslexia.

Dyslexia: A Complete Guide for Parents and Those Who Help Them, Second Edition. Gavin Reid.
© 2011 John Wiley & Sons, Ltd. Published 2011 by John Wiley & Sons, Ltd.

In the UK universities are required by law to effectively support disabled students. The Special Educational Needs and Disability Act 2001 (and its 2004 revisions), commonly referred to as SENDA, places three obligations on universities:

1. Not to unreasonably discriminate against disabled students.
2. To make reasonable adjustments to facilitate their learning (though not at the expense of academic standards).
3. To be anticipatory, requiring departments to plan ahead for the needs of future students.

The term reasonable adjustment which is used in the SENDA legislation is open to interpretation but is usually considered as: 'a necessary accommodation or alteration to existing academic programmes, offering individuals the opportunity to demonstrate their ability' (Association of Dyslexia Specialists in Higher Education, 2010). It is important that parents are familiar with this type of information as they are in a good position to guide and advise their son/daughter.

Monitoring performance

It is reassuring for parents and for adults with dyslexia to be aware of the accommodations that can be made by colleges and universities in relation to assessment of performance on the course. Most universities have published policies on this and these can be viewed by parents as well as the people with dyslexia. You should in fact ask to see the university's policy on dyslexia. An example from the University of Swansea is shown below.

Assessment and Examination Provision

- The university has a policy of anonymous marking, but in order to comply with SENDA students with SpLDs may choose to have their examination booklets and coursework work identified by means of a stamp, sticker.

- Extensions to deadlines should be considered but successive extensions may not help the student.
- 25% extra time in examinations and class tests (including practical sessions) is commonly recommended by Needs Assessors and Educational Psychologists for students who have been assessed with SpLDs. However, the Needs Assessor or Educational Psychologist may recommend other accommodations, for example, the use of a reader. These recommendations should be adopted at the request of the student and after discussion with the Disability Office.

Alternative Forms of Assessment

- Alternative forms of assessment may be necessary but in the case of professional examinations or where accuracy in written language is essential this may not be an option.
- Whilst ensuring that a reasonable adjustment is made, academic standards must not be compromised. It is important that the student is involved in discussions concerned with an alternative assessment format. If it is not possible to make any adjustment, it must be clear on what grounds the decision has been made.
- If a student is assessed as having a SpLD during the course of an academic year and is borderline for a module, re-marking completed course work within that year should be considered, where practicably possible. Students who were found to have dyslexia in subsequent sessions would not have papers re-marked from earlier academic years.

Adapted from: http://www.swan.ac.uk/study/current/StudentSupport Services/DisabilityOffice/DyslexiaPolicies

It is also important for parents to know that in the UK there is a national association of dyslexia specialists who cater for the needs of students with dyslexia. The Association of Dyslexia Specialists in Higher Education (ADSHE) was formed in order to share knowledge and inform good practice between all the universities. The aim of the association is to work towards establishing parity of provision so that any dyslexic student will be assured of appropriate support throughout the higher education sector anywhere in the UK (http://adshe.org.uk).

The association indicates that students should be aware of the reasons for referral for an assessment, the content of the assessment itself and the follow-up process, including the importance of consent to disclose. They also indicate that a minimum time-scale for the return of diagnostic reports to students should be established. A survey of the ADSHE membership found that two weeks is widely regarded as best practice, although five weeks is not uncommon. Longer than two weeks could be detrimental to the student and prolongs an already protracted procedure.

One of the important procedures that ADSHE recommends relates to post-assessment feedback to the student. They indicate that this is essential in order to ensure that the student understands the report's findings and implications. Feedback should be handled sensitively by someone with a clear understanding of the issues involved. At the same time it is important to obtain an explanation of the Disabled Students' Allowances system so that parents and the student are aware of what they may be able to claim.

Supports

It is important that parents are aware of the supports for students with dyslexia. Supports that may be available include:

Extra time

To complete course work, continuous assessment and examinations can be provided. The reading fluency of a student with dyslexia may be slow and they may also have processing speed difficulties, particularly with print. For these reasons they may qualify for 'time and a half' to ensure they are able to plan, proofread and re-read their answers.

Re-read text

Many students with dyslexia will find it necessary to re-read text to grasp its meaning. This is characteristic of dyslexia and additional time can be allowed for this.

Reader

Some can benefit from a reader to read examination questions to ensure that the student has not misread or misunderstood the question. This will also apply to multiple-choice questions as these types of questions require quite a bit of additional reading.

Word processing

The use of a word processor in exams can also be permitted, particularly if the student's handwriting deteriorates when writing at speed and often they may have difficulties with the organization of written work.

Proof reading written work

Some students will require drafts of written assignments to be proof read before formal submission.

Planning

Assistance in planning, particularly when students have to meet deadlines, can be helpful. This can involve guided reading and assistance with interpreting the question. Pre-task discussion may help.

Reading comprehension

It is important for the student to prepare for reading a course text, particularly if specific information or ideas are needed. A variety of approaches should be tried until suitable strategies are identified. For example students should:

- ask themselves what they want to obtain from the text in advance;
- note key words and issues;
- list any people or places needed;
- make a rough outline of the text so that they know the geography of the book,
- look at different sections before reading the main body of the book;
- look at the list of contents and the index as they give a good overview of the content of the book;

- read the introductions and summaries of the chapters;
- read the chapter headings as they will help to build up a picture of the content.

Resources

Posters, charts and diagrams, time-lines and visuals can help the student plot the detail of theory or a sequence such as 'child development stages' in psychology or the plot in a play in English literature. This can ease the burden on memory.

Study skills

These include essay planning and organization of written work as well as memory. One of the keys to success for the adult with dyslexia is organization. This can be dealt with by making a study plan, which may include the following steps:

- Select the topic you are going to study. Try to be exact – if there are several topics for one area, select just one and write down some questions that relate to that area.
- Compile notes for the topic and refer frequently to the questions you have written down.
- Read through your notes and make sure they still make sense. You may need to re-read any point you have not understood.
- Make a note of the key points in your notes.
- It might be an idea to dictate the key points using a voice-activated tape-recorder, then listen to the tape.
- Prepare a mind map or diagram from your notes.
- You may want to write linear notes from the diagram.
- Discuss the diagram with a parent/friend to ensure that you have fully understood it.
- At this stage look at some exam questions or questions relating to the topic.

Study skills are essentially about how students organize their work. This is the key and this also involves practice.

Learning style

It is important that people with dyslexia are aware of their learning style. This can determine the best way for them to learn. For example, kinesthetic learners benefit from experiential learning while visual learners need to see diagrams and pictures. Time of day and the study environment are also important and learners need to know their environmental learning preference.

Technology

The use of a dictaphone (MP3 player) to tape lectures can be useful and other technology can be accessed. Most universities have a department that can advise on the best type of technology for students with dyslexia. The CALL Center at the university is a good source of information on technology that can be available to the public (http://www.disability-office.ed.ac.uk/technology/resources/callcentre.cfm).

Notes

Printed notes prior to lectures presented with a summary of the lecture with the key points highlighted can be very useful and should be requested.

Key words

It is important to note key words when taking notes or reading over a textbook. This will also be less of a burden on memory.

Memory strategies

These include:

- Repetition – opportunities for repetition will reinforce and help the student over-learn information which is essential for learners with dyslexia.
- Prioritizing – this involves helping the student decide what to do first and what is less important. This can help to reduce the burden

of trying to read too much of the same type of information for an assignment.

- Organizing information (important for memory) — the key here is to rearrange the information so it can be more easily understood and retained. The student may benefit from using headings to help to organize information. Visuals can also reinforce this. This helps to personalize the information which is crucial for retention and recall.
- Mind mapping — many students with dyslexia find this useful. Mind maps are a good way to use visuals and this strategy can also help with organization as Mind Maps™ can also show the relationship between different facts and concepts and therefore help to give the student a deeper understanding of the subject and the connections between different aspects of it.
- Chunking is an excellent strategy for organizing information and can also help with retention.

Over-learning

Students with dyslexia need to over-learn material. 'Little and often' is a useful phrase to remember. Most students with dyslexia will manage their own learning when it is broken into small manageable chunks and when they take short, frequent breaks. The aim is to work towards independent learning where one should be striving to achieve autonomy in learning. Responsibility should shift from the tutor to the student as soon as the support program is established.

According to Professor Bob Burden, who led the Networking Day in 2009 (arranged by ADSHE), learning includes three dimensions: the cognitive dimension of knowledge and skills, the psychodynamic dimension of motivation and emotions, and the social dimension of communication and cooperation (www.adshe.org.uk). It is important to appreciate the social, emotional and the motivational aspects of learning.

Questions and concerns of young people

The future of young people with dyslexia after they leave school can be of some concern to parents, and of course to the young person him/herself. Some of the questions and concerns that young people often harbor include:

- What type of work will I be able to do?
- Are there any professions/occupations I should avoid?
- Will I be supported in a college or university course?
- What are the legal issues?
- Will my employer consider and take my dyslexia into account?
- Should I declare my dyslexia in my application forms?
- How can I develop strategies to deal with dyslexia?

Some suggestions for dealing with these are shown below.

What type of work will I be able to do?

The short answer to that is a simple – anything! If the young person has an interest in journalism, medicine, law or accountancy, then with support he/she can achieve that ambition. Certain occupations can be more challenging because of, and indeed depending on, the nature of the dyslexic difficulties, but no occupation should necessarily be ruled out.

Below there is a list of popular professions and the type of challenges that can be faced by young people with dyslexia who may want to enter one of these professions. Although this book is for parents it is still important that parents are aware of the challenges the young person can face as often parents are the most readily available support for the young person, particularly when in the transitional stage from school to college or to work. The young person may no longer have access to the sources of support they had at school and not yet have made any contacts with the information sources and support at college or in the workplace.

Every profession, no matter how dyslexia-friendly, will contain some elements or tasks that can prove difficult for a dyslexic person. But the important points are that the dyslexic person is not excluded from any occupation because of his/her dyslexia. Secondly, it is possible to work out accommodations, preferably with the backing of the employer, to support the dyslexic person in the workplace (Table 12.1).

Table 12.1 An A–Z of professions, challenges and accommodations for dyslexic people (© Gavin Reid)

Profession	Challenges	Accommodations
Armed Forces	Entry qualifications, organization, report writing, reading fluently, remembering instructions.	Lot of support available in the US and UK. Recognizes the importance of supporting dyslexic people as they can have excellent attributes for this profession.
Accountancy	Close and accurate number work, tables and statistics, memory work, examinations, detailed and accurate knowledge of tax legislation.	Use of technology, working in teams, using dictaphone for reports, working as part of a team, secretarial support.
Art careers	Usually very well suited for dyslexic people but they can experience difficulty in examinations, ordering and sequence of practical work, also sometimes quite a bit of theory attached to some courses and also art history.	Use visual strategies, mind mapping to remember information, time management support, additional time for exams and for assignments.
Building trades	Examinations, remembering quantities, ordering materials, figures, time management, keeping up to date with new methods and materials.	Work in pairs, use calculator, regular courses to keep up to date. Working as part of a team.
Computer work	Usually very popular choice for dyslexic people. Examinations may include some mathematics, writing reports and letters, filing software and general administration work.	Spend time to organize data and get some assistance with this if possible. Need to focus so can get support with tasks and identifying the key points in a task. Working in groups.
Dentistry	Examinations, organization, memory, record keeping, remembering procedures.	Study skills support, memory strategies, mind maps for procedures. Working collaboratively.

Engineering	Usually a popular profession for dyslexic people, mathematics, accuracy in figures and measurements, report writing. Knowledge of building techniques.	Have formula pre-prepared, work in teams, use mind maps for techniques and materials. Use a template for writing reports.
Fire services	Memory, report writing, concise instructions.	Usually team work is important.
Garage work	Report writing, work records, visual memory, visual skills, maybe mathematics and formulae.	Customer relations important, working as part of a team, experiential and practical techniques.
Hairdressing	Ordering stock, remembering different lotions for different purposes, examinations.	Develop customer relations and social skills, chart as a memory aid for different creams and lotions.
Insurance work	Mathematics, statistics may be necessary, accuracy with figures, report writing, calculations.	Use technology, calculators, software programs, dictaphone for letters, secretarial support.
Journalism	Reading and writing at speed, summarizing information, grammar and accuracy. Accuracy of details.	Use dictaphone for interviews, use good word processing package with advanced spell check such as Texthelp© voice-activated technology, creativity.
Law	Entry qualifications may be high, a lot of reading, need to remember facts and details, need to be able to summarize information and sequence events.	Use secretarial support, use dictaphone, some good word processing packages available for helping with summaries and with memory and organization.

(Continued)

Table 12.1 (*Continued*)

Profession	Challenges	Accommodations
Librarian	Accuracy in cataloguing, reading, ordering books sequencing, organization of catalogues and information.	Take time to check and re-check. Ensure that you are familiar with the recording, shelving and filing system at the outset. Develop new systems that can be more beneficial.
Musician	Remembering the music scores, timing, reading the music sheet at speed.	Mind mapping, individual strategies, color coding, practice.
Nurse	Exams, medical terminology, time keeping, reading medicines, prescriptions, keeping up to date with new information.	Working in teams, more time to check medicines, extra time for exams. Regular professional development to keep up to date, working in teams.
Optician/ optometrist	Examinations, accuracy with figures, practical work, record keeping.	Take extra time to check figures, develop own system for keeping records.
Police force	Entry qualifications, accuracy in reading, responding quickly, writing notes at speed, summarizing information for incident report, presenting information form notes/court work.	Use dictaphone to record notes, work in teams, develop a pro-forma for report writing, use short heading for recalling information for court work and interviews.
Restaurant work	Counting accurately, remembering orders, ordering materials, remembering composition of dishes, change of menu, remembering specials.	Write down everything including table number, try not to get flustered and develop good polite customer relations, use mnemonics for remembering dishes.
Salesperson	Remembering orders and product information, new products and names of suppliers.	Use lightweight laptop computer to record information, use mind maps to remember product information and suppliers.

Teaching	Popular choice but you need to be aware of your weaknesses, e.g. spelling and try to compensate for these when you are teaching, planning lessons, diary keeping, organization of classes, lesson plans, assessment information.	Use strategies to ensure that you use your strengths. Plan well ahead so that you are not unawares by any situation. Work in teams if possible. Discuss issues with your line manager. Professional development courses.
Vet	Long course, examinations, practical work, accuracy, memory, keeping up to date with new medicines.	Use visual diagrams, work in teams, use the support assistance that is available, go on frequent professional development courses.
Youth worker	This is also a popular choice for adults with dyslexia, examinations, memory work and punctuality will be important.	Work in teams, make sure that any legal and statutory implications of your work are explained to you rather than you having to read regulations.
Zoo worker	Remembering routine, ordering materials, different types of diseases and knowledge of all the species and feeding materials.	Make a mind map of any duties such as time of feeding animals and type of food, ensure that the safety requirements are explained to you.

Table 12.1 shows that all professions, even those that are popular with dyslexic adults, such as art and engineering, present challenges. Nursing and teaching are also popular career choices. Parents therefore will realize that dyslexia does not end with school. School can prepare the young person for adult life and parents need to ensure that their son/daughter obtains appropriate career advice at an early age – before they decide on subject choices at secondary school. This is one of the most crucial aspects for a successful employment outcome for a young person with dyslexia.

Questions and issues

Are there any professions/occupations that should be avoided?

Some occupations can be more challenging than others and may have more demanding entry qualifications for training courses (e.g., medicine and law). This should not prevent the young person from applying for these courses as they will be supported if they receive a place. There is now more support at school, more young people with dyslexia are achieving higher grades in school and are gaining entry qualifications for demanding courses such as law and medicine. This has a positive knock-on effect as tutors on these courses are increasingly gaining experience in dealing with dyslexic students, becoming more aware of what dyslexia is and more knowledgeable on the type of support required in both practical and theoretical work. There is still a long way to go before all the staff in every university are comfortable and familiar with dyslexia, but that day will come and aided by legislation the needs of all students with dyslexia can be met.

Will I be supported in a college or university course?

The simple answer is yes! Most countries have legislation to support all students with a recognized disability and dyslexia is recognized in terms of the legislation as a disability. Most universities have guidance for students with dyslexia or even those who suspect they might have dyslexia, but have not yet been diagnosed. This guidance can normally be accessed from the university web page.

It is important to remember that the degree of severity of dyslexia can vary considerably. But all universities will have a disability coordinator and student support departments in the United States and in most other countries. The coordinator is a good point of contact for the student and can help with preparation and planning in advance of starting the course.

The legislation discussed in an earlier chapter of this book indicates that is unlawful:

- To treat a disabled person less favorably for a reason relating to a person's disability.
- To fail to make reasonable adjustments to avoid substantial disadvantage to the disabled person.

This also applies to the arrangements for admitting or enrolling students with a disability and in the provision of student services to those with a disability. These services might include:

- teaching, including classes, lectures, seminars, practical sessions, field trips;
- learning facilities such as classrooms, lecture theaters, laboratories;
- learning equipment and materials, such as laboratory equipment, computer facilities, class handouts and lecture notes.

One of the key points in legislation is the notion of 'reasonable adjustment'. This means that colleges and universities must take reasonable steps to ensure that a student with dyslexia is not placed at a substantial disadvantage in comparison with other students.

The issue that remains however is the terminology – the use of the term disability.

David McLaughlin from the Adult Dyslexia and Skills Development Centre in London suggests that if dyslexic people are to be fully included in society, the emphasis should be on *empowerment* or enablement rather than a model of disability that perceives the 'dyslexic as a victim'. He suggests that empowerment comes from:

- **Self-understanding**: Dyslexia is often referred to as a 'hidden disability'. Dyslexic people therefore have to advocate for themselves, and can only do so if they have a good understanding of the nature of their difficulty, how it affects them and what they need to do about to improve their performance.

- **Understanding by others, particularly employers**: If dyslexic people have to deal with managers and colleagues whose understanding of the nature of dyslexia is limited, it is likely the dyslexic person will be excluded rather than included.
- **Contextualization**: It is important to recognize that dyslexia is contextual (Reid, 2009). This means that the work environment and context are important and the degree and the extent to which dyslexia will affect the individual will depend on the actual task demands and the work environment.

Will my employer consider and take my dyslexia into account?

In terms of equity legislation in most countries, employers must take dyslexia into account. There are many loopholes, but employers need to ensure that they have made appropriate accommodations to support the dyslexic employee. Much depends on the understanding of the employer and it can be difficult for the dyslexic young person if the employer is not sympathetic to dyslexia. It is always best to avoid confrontation and recourse to the law, but that is always an option.

It does not require much effort for the employer to take dyslexia into account. It may mean teaming people together so that the dyslexic person is with someone who can support him/her (and similarly the dyslexic person can support others who are not dyslexic!), providing some software that can help with spelling, organization and summarizing information. Providing more time for some kind of tasks (e.g., those that require a substantial amount of reading and writing) and perhaps ensuring that the dyslexic person is employed in an area that will highlight his/her strengths and not their difficulties.

Should I declare my dyslexia in my application forms?

This is usually the best course of action and I always strongly recommend that a dyslexic person does declare his/her dyslexia on their application form. This should not discriminate against them as the law is on their side and it also informs prospective employers at the outset. This means that if the dyslexic person is employed, employers will be made aware of the accommodations that they will need to make.

In some professions the applicant may think that dyslexia will not be an issue because of the nature of the work and so may be inclined not to declare it to an employer. This needs careful thought as job descriptions can change, with or without promotion to another post. It is better therefore to let the employer know at the outset so that if a promoted post or change of duties occurs, the employer will be aware of the need to make appropriate accommodations.

How can I help myself?

This is an important question as it really is up to the individual how they deal with their dyslexia. Self-help is usually the best type of help as the individual has control over this. Others can tell the dyslexic young person what might be best, or how to deal with a certain challenging situation at work, but each dyslexic person is different, each is an individual, and therefore the most effective way to deal with any challenging situation is on an individual basis. It can also be best if the young person with dyslexia takes the lead.

This though may be easier said than done for some young people. Parents can help by discussing with the young person how they tackle situations and how they may improve on their method. It could be that after discussing it with a parent or family member they realize that all they need to do is to improve on their filing system, diary keeping or prioritizing some areas of work or changing the sequence of tasks. A parent can provide a listening ear and pass on supportive and non-threatening advice. But the person him/herself must act on it.

Career advice

Some occupations are more dyslexia-friendly than others. Some can utilize the dyslexic person's strengths rather than expose their weaknesses. There are dyslexic people who are in the wrong job, that is,

they are in a situation where the demands of the task outweigh the resources and competencies they have at their disposal. Career guidance/
counseling specifically aimed at dyslexic people is a top priority but is
sadly neglected in some countries.

Without doubt ongoing career advice is important. It allows the
young person to have several choices and if one does not work out,
they will be able to discuss this with the careers advisor. Key points for
career advice would be before subject choice in secondary/high school;
before applying to college or university; when applying for a job and
after having been in employment for a period of time. It is important to
discuss how the dyslexic person may see him/herself advance in their
career. Some questions a parent/young person may want to know from
a careers advisor include:

- entry qualifications for course;
- availability of places in training courses;
- length of training;
- amount of written skills needed for the occupation or course of
  training;
- competition;
- career prospects;
- location of employment;
- time pressures associated with the work;
- whether the work demands accuracy with figures.

Transition to work

There are a number of factors that need to be considered when applying
for and commencing employment. These are the interview, preparation
for employment and settling in to new employment. Although at this
stage young people tend to be independent of their parents that is
not always the case and parents can provide advice and certainly be
on hand to give advice if the young person asks for it. Parents at
this stage need to maintain a balance between being on hand to give
advice if necessary, and allowing the young person to gradually develop

independence and take responsibility for their decisions. In many ways this is what parenting is all about, but young people with dyslexia can have additional sensitivity related to their dyslexia and can be slightly more vulnerable at what can be a challenging time for young people.

The interview and the job

Young people need advice and support before a job or college interview. Again, parents may be a good source of this advice. There is some general advice that parents can provide, or indeed the young person themselves can consider. This includes:

Preparation for the interview

- Try to ensure you know exactly where the interview is being held – if possible check out the area and the venue of the interview the day before so you will know exactly where the interview is being held. This will be one less thing for you to think about and it will make it easier to concentrate on the interview itself.
- Ensure that you arrive in good time – not too early, but certainly not at the last minute. It is important to be relaxed before an interview and rushing at the last minute will create panic not relaxation.
- Try to have some idea of how long the interview will last – this will help you pace your answers and you will have an idea of how long there is to the end. This can help you to work out when to ask any questions you wish to ask.
- Try to find out who will be interviewing you and how many people will be present – this may cut out the unexpected.
- Take advice on how to dress for the interview.
- Rehearse an answer in your mind to a possible question you may be asked about your dyslexia and how it has affected you. You may wish to describe how you have coped with it and your strengths that you have used to overcome any difficulties.

Preparation for employment

- It may be a good idea to have a pre-meeting with your employer to reassure you that your dyslexia will not be a problem in the type of work you will be doing.
- If your employer is not aware of what dyslexia is, this might be a good time to tell him/her.
- Try to work out the best route that you can take to work so that you will not be late on the first day.
- The best preparation for any job is to be relaxed before you start. Starting a new job can be quite exhausting and you will need to be in peak condition, so it is best to rest beforehand.

Settling in to new employment

Often it can take a young person a little time to settle in to a new occupation. The challenges of new employment are different for each person and also depend on the type of work that is to be carried out. Once you know exactly what your duties are you may want to try to anticipate the kind of duties that may cause you some worry. General workplace difficulties include:

- filing documents/retrieving files;
- following detailed instructions;
- remembering routines;
- writing letters and memos;
- writing reports;
- summarizing and presenting ideas in presentations;
- getting the times and places of meetings wrong;
- missing appointments.

These difficulties can be managed by:

- reading words slowly and carefully;
- breaking sentences down into short phrases;
- skimming text to get an overall picture before reading for detail;
- using color coding for different pieces of information;

- labeling box files and filing trays;
- making a checklist of tasks to be completed and possibly working one step at a time.

If I were to identify any one aspect that is crucial to the above it would be communication. Parents in their supportive role can ensure that the person with dyslexia has the confidence and the opportunity to communicate with employers and is able to ask the right questions.

Summary

This chapter will help parents understand the demands placed on the young person with dyslexia who is about, or has recently, left school. Although the young person is gaining in independence and is less reliant on his/her parents for direction, parents' views are still often sought by the young person. The objective of this chapter therefore is to help parents by providing some guidance that may help them advise their son/daughter. I have mentioned in this chapter that dyslexia can be described as contextual. This means it can have a varying impact depending on the situation, the nature of the work or the type of course of study that is to be completed.

This chapter answers some fundamental questions that can be of interest to parents, teachers or careers personnel and by teenagers with dyslexia. To recap, these questions are:

- What type of work will I be able to do?
- Are there any professions/occupations I should avoid?
- Will I be supported in a college or university course?
- What are the legal issues?
- Will my employer consider and take my dyslexia into account?
- Should I declare my dyslexia in my application forms?
- How can I help myself?

By answering these questions it is hoped that this chapter has provided some advice and guidance to parents. Parents can be in a difficult position as they want to help but at the same time need to allow the young person a degree of independence. In treading this delicate balance it is best if parents at least have some knowledge, understanding and even facts at their fingertips. This will enable parents to provide the type of advice, and more importantly, the support the young person may need.

Chapter 13

Issues for parents to consider

This chapter looks at the issues parents face and how they can deal with them. Some comment will be made on policies and associated practices in a number of countries. There is an attempt to draw these together and provide some tips for parents irrespective of the country they live in.

What role can parents play?

Parents have often asked me that very question. How can they be useful and complement the work of the school? The role parents can play is of great importance. They are a key element in the whole network of action and support. In some cases parents can actually inform schools of new ideas and resources as often parents seek out specialized and specific information that schools are unaware of. At the national and international level parents have played a key role. They have informed governments and participated in policy-making forums at local, national and

Dyslexia: A Complete Guide for Parents and Those Who Help Them, Second Edition. Gavin Reid.
© 2011 John Wiley & Sons, Ltd. Published 2011 by John Wiley & Sons, Ltd.

international levels, all of which have had a significant impact on policy and practice. Thriving organizations such as the International Dyslexia Association (IDA), British Dyslexia Association (BDA), the European Dyslexia Association (EDA), Dyslexia Foundation of New Zealand and Dyslexia International have had, and continue to have, an impact on policy and practice throughout the world. These organizations are a great source of support for parents by publishing regular newsletters and organizing events. There are however other avenues open to parents and by far the most accessible is through direct communication with the school. This, without doubt, needs to be the parents' first call, as communication at this level has the potential to deal with current and future anxieties. Yet in practice this may be difficult for some parents as they do not want to be labeled troublesome. Many schools now are promoting more open-door policies and welcoming parents more and more into the school.

TeacherNet suggests many ways that schools and parents can liaise, including more participation in school management, although they recognize that increased parental involvement in school management won't be achieved overnight. Initiatives such as this do represent a significant change in culture and behavior for both parents and schools and this type of initiative will benefit all, including parents, children and families as well as the school and the wider community.

Teachernet (http://www.teachernet.gov.uk/wholeschool/ familyandcommunity/workingwithparents) has publications that can be obtained on the following areas:

- **Parents as partners**: The case for greater parental involvement.
- **Parent councils**: Including information on how they can be established.
- **Parent champions**: How parents can support school improvement.
- **Parent satisfaction**: How monitoring parental satisfaction can help to raise standards.
- **Fair and equal access to schools.**

These initiatives are not new; in fact as far back as 1993 some educators were actively promoting initiatives like these. Peel and Foster (1993), from East Carolina University, when researching the decline in parental involvement, asked themselves: 'Do parents drop out or are they pushed?' They selected middle schools because at that stage children declare their independence by asserting themselves more, become increasingly less dependent on their parents and trying to look and behave like everyone else in their peer group. This can make it more challenging for parents to be involved in the school. Yet they assert that there is ample research to demonstrate that parental involvement correlates with children's success in school. They developed the strategy which they called the five P's – people, places, policies, program and processes. The five P's, they argue, provide a structure by which schools can assess their current status and develop specific plans to invite parents to become more involved.

'Places' refers to the school facility, the entrance, offices, classrooms, waiting areas and hallways, which can all reflect the school's attitude to visitors. 'Policies' refers to written and unwritten guidelines, the framework that outlines school rules and the organizational structure that allows the school to function efficiently. 'Programs' offered can say a lot about the school. Are programs available to parents' need? Do they encourage a wide spectrum of roles for parents? 'Processes', they argue, can either develop or destroy the school's rapport with parents. 'Processes' involve all the procedures and plans that help to establish ongoing and long-term development of parental participation. In creating inviting schools, the 'how' is as important as the 'what'. How the staff interact with parents is crucial in encouraging parents to accept the invitations offered by the school. The 'P' for people represents the level of understanding that people have of each other and the effort they make to establish relationships based on mutual trust and integrity. Staff members who understand and accept their responsibilities in developing relationships with parents will determine appropriate and effective means of dealing with each family. The authors also indicate four principles: optimism, trust, respect and intentionality. Although this was written some time ago it is as relevant today as it was then and very relevant for parents of children with dyslexia.

The authors also suggest some strategies. These include:

- **Homework:** Help-lines for both parents and students.
- **Directories:** With the numbers of all professional personnel who are responsible for student assistance.

- **Recognition:** Of all parent efforts.
- **Social:** Events that involve parents in opportunities to discuss their interests, communication bulletins and newsletters to inform and share news about students, the school, parents, teachers and the community.

The use of a label

This has been referred to at different points in this book but it is a central issue for parents. Parents can experience concern at the lack of diagnosis or of a label. There is usually a strong belief among parents that a label (identification of the special need) is necessary if their child is to get appropriate help. While this may well be true in some instances, particularly if the child is significantly lagging in attainments and additional resources or a review of provision is needed, in many cases the label is not the most important factor. The most important is for the school to be aware of the child's progress in all aspects of the curriculum, to communicate this to parents and together discuss how the school (and parents) plan to deal with any lack of progress.

The lack of a label can however be frustrating for parents, but they do need to seek an explanation for lack of progress and this can be done through a full assessment. A label, of course, is helpful and in some situations, such as examination support, can be essential. Heaton (1996) found that many parents felt considerable relief when the label 'dyslexia' was provided. She quotes one parent as saying, 'I was so relieved to know that it had a name' (p. 15) and another, 'my family had begun to hint she might be mentally retarded because she was illiterate. I could never explain why I knew she wasn't, so the diagnosis helped me a lot' (p. 16). It is important, therefore, to consider that a label can often be accompanied by acceptance, and this can pave the way for constructive collaboration between home and school. Fawcett (2001) suggests that anxieties can arise from the potential conflict between the views of individuals and interest groups who may have different agendas. This potential conflict can be found between parents and teachers in particular, and indeed may drive parents and educational administration into opposition. It is important that this is avoided as anxieties and stresses can usually be felt by the child. It is important that the aims of the school in relation to any particular child are made clear to the parents and that parents and teachers share a common agenda in relation to the child's progress and level of work.

Effective communication with the school can provide parents with considerable support. A diagnosis and, if appropriate, a label can provide some reassurance and relief on the part of the parents. Whether or not a label is used it is important that schools have a good knowledge of the child's individual learning profile and specific teaching approaches that should be implemented stemming from the profile. Consistency is also important, and periodic reviews should provide guidance on the effectiveness of the approaches being used and whether particular approaches should be continued. Parents need to ensure that they are informed well in advance of any review.

Reid (2004) interviewed a number of parents of children with dyslexia. Some of the responses included the need to:

- maintain the child's self-esteem;
- help the child start new work when he/she had not consolidated previous work;
- protect the dignity of the child when dealing with professionals/ therapists;
- help in the child's personal organization;
- offset peer insensitivity;
- overcome misconceptions of dyslexia.

These responses touch on some of the key areas, particularly the emotional aspect of dyslexia. They also touch on the misunderstandings and misconceptions that can exist on dyslexia. Some of the other key issues that parents have to deal with include the following.

Frustration

Frustration can be experienced when the agenda and the priorities of the school and the parents are different. Many parents have contacted me directly indicating that this is one of the most serious areas of frustration they experience. This underlines the importance of effective and shared communication. The type of support parents can obtain from support groups can be helpful in this respect too.

Trust

Not all staff in schools will be familiar with dyslexia. It can sometimes be difficult for parents to place their trust in a system that may not even seem to recognize dyslexia, but this is exactly what they have to do! Parents can have a role to play in providing information on dyslexia to schools; it does not need to be the other way round.

Understanding

Knowledge and awareness of dyslexia varies from country to country and indeed within countries and school districts. Having spoken on dyslexia to parents' associations in many countries this is very apparent and almost without exception a scheduled and advertised talk to a parents' association will include many teachers in the audience. It is important that parents understand what dyslexia is, and this should be explained to them as soon as their child is assessed. It is equally important that teachers are aware of the different dimensions of dyslexia.

Culture

We live in a multicultural society and cultural factors can have a big impact on the communication between home and school. It is important that schools respect the different cultures of the parents and ensure that this is a bonus for the school and not a challenge. It is important that as a parent you ensure the school is culture-friendly and culture-fair in how they support their students and parents.

In terms of diagnosis it can be argued that it is important for schools to consider the cultural information parents give as this will provide a more complete picture of the child in a range of settings, including those not involving language skills. Schools should be alerted if the child lacks interest in books, there is discrepancy between listening comprehension and reading skills, or difficulties with phonological awareness as this can indicate either that culture and language differences are not being taken into account or the child has a learning disability.

It is important to view children who are bilingual as individual learners and to take into account the particular learning styles of each individual. You need to ensure that schools are taking this into account. For example, is the learning environment conducive to the learner's cultural experiences and learning style? This can have implications for different cultures, as there may be a culture-dominant learning style.

It is important for parents to ensure that teachers have an awareness of the cultural background of the students. Berryman and Wearmouth (2008) suggest that when teachers give students' home cultures a central place within the pedagogy of the classroom, student learning is more effective. They suggest that one of the reasons for this is that the learning of new concepts is linked to prior knowledge stemming from outside the classroom. It can be argued that the greater the distance between the world of the teacher and that of the child, the greater importance culturally responsive pedagogies may have. Bishop and Glynn (1999) suggest that when there is a cultural mismatch between the teacher and the student it must be the teacher who makes the cognitive adjustment. This has implications for informing the school of the cultural preferences of the student and the school will need to select reading material based on this information.

Bilingualism is one of the key challenges facing educators in relation to the identification of dyslexia. This is a challenge because syndromes such as dyslexia do not occur for only one reason; usually, there are a number of factors that contribute to this type of literacy difficulty, and if a child is also bi/multilingual, then this will be another factor that needs to be taken into account throughout the assessment. It has been noted that cultural and language factors in many standardized tests (Everatt et al., 2004) can militate against the child whose first language is not English. Many standardized assessment strategies have been developed for use with a monolingual population, and this can account for the underestimation or, indeed, the misdiagnosis of dyslexia in children who are bilingual.

Practice

It is important that any Individual Educational Program (IEP) that is developed is a result of wide-ranging deliberation between professionals and parents.

Critical literacy

Many parents may not have heard this term before. According to Eames (2002) critical literacy can be placed at the highest stage of the literacy hierarchy. She suggests that critical literacy involves constructing meaning from text and that such meanings are achieved during interaction of reader and text, during discussion of text and when listening and responding to others. This has important implications for children with dyslexia and particularly young adults who may not have efficient decoding skills. Wray (2006) acknowledges that critical literacy is not a new concept and can be recognized as critical language awareness, critical social literacy and critically aware literacy. He argues however that there are some common threads running through the different approaches to critical literacy. One of the crucial factors rests on the assumption that being literate is not sufficient. He argues that teachers who engage in critical literacy 'will encourage students to investigate, question and challenge relationships between language and social practices that advantage some groups over others' (p. 21). He also argues that critical literacy often challenges the racial and class tensions that can characterize some societies. Wray therefore suggests that critical literacy is 'about transforming taken for granted social and language practices or assumptions for the good of as many people as possible' (p. 21). It is important that students with dyslexia can be encouraged to access these higher level concepts. Too often the priority is to develop reading accuracy while higher-order thinking skills are seen as less important. It is suggested therefore that one of the other key points about critical literacy, particularly in relation to children with dyslexia, is that it can help to engage the reader, especially if the reading activity is structured around the ideas relating to critical literacy.

Metacognition

This is another term that may be new to parents but it will often be found in psychologists' and school reports. It means being aware of how one learns and benefiting from this for future learning – in other words, being able to transfer learning form one context to another. There is a view that children with dyslexia may have poor metacognitive awareness, particularly in relation to print and literacy (Tunmer & Chapman, 1996). When children are learning to read words they develop 'recognition', then 'understanding' and then 'transferable' skills, which means that they need to develop concepts and an understanding of the text before they can use the new word or text in other contexts. This transfer of skills is crucial to the development of metacognitive awareness. To achieve metacognitive awareness, children usually develop schemata (children's specific understanding, from their perspective, of a situation or text). To achieve schemata of a situation, children need to be able to express their understanding of the situation verbally or in written form, and identify the specific concepts and how these relate to the overall picture. The teacher, through a process called scaffolding, helps to build up this understanding and the conceptual and schematic development of the child.

The awareness of schemata is important to the understanding of text for all children, but particularly for children with dyslexia and can also have important implications for children who have a bilingual background. Therefore, the child who for some reason activates inappropriate schemata will not fully understand the text and may even elicit the wrong meaning from a piece of text.

One of the most effective means of developing schemata and ensuring the child has an appropriate schema is through pre-reading discussion. This sets the scene, introduces the characters, describes the situation and provides some of the keywords and concepts. Pre-reading discussion can involve the parents and can be initially in the child's first language, particularly with children whose English is not well developed. Texts relating to the cultural experiences of bilingual learners will assist in the development of schemata and the subsequent development of metacognitive awareness. Parents can play a key role in pre-reading discussion and can discuss the text with the child prior to the reading activity.

Early identification

Parents often ask how early dyslexia can be identified and when it is the best time to have their child assessed. This touches on one of the key issues in the assessment process – early identification. How such identification should take place and when it can most effectively and most sensitively be conducted are matters of some debate. Knight, Day and Patton-Terry (2009) suggest that it may not be desirable to diagnose and label a young child who is not reading as dyslexic, but as early as three years of age, some children display behaviors that indicate that they are not developing oral language, phonological awareness or motor skills as one would expect. They argue that some of these children will be diagnosed with dyslexia, while others need intervention to allow them to have the necessary experiences to become readers. The point is that the children in both groups are at risk for developing reading difficulties. This is the essence of early identification – not to label but to identify those who are at risk of developing difficulties in acquiring literacy. There is no doubt that early identification is crucial and can make a significant difference to the achievement outcome of children who are at risk. Knight, Day and Patton-Terry (2009) provide evidence of early identification of reading difficulty along with targeted, research-based interventions improving children's chances of becoming more effective readers (Henry, et al., 2004; Lynch, 2007; Southern Education Foundation, 2007, 2008). For parents it is important that they are aware of the early indicators of dyslexia (see Chapter 3). It is also important that they are able to communicate their concerns to the school as early as possible. There is no real advantage to delaying this and an assessment can take place at any age. Parents need to be aware of this.

Overlap

It has already been noted that dyslexia can be seen within a continuum. This means that it can overlap with other specific difficulties. The term 'co-morbidity' is often used to describe the overlap between the different specific learning difficulties and this means that that there is likely to be some overlap between several of these as they tend to be factors associated with left hemisphere, language-associated functioning. Moreover, since neurological processing activities tend to be interactive rather than independent, it is likely that children with dyslexia will share some of the characteristics with children diagnosed as having a specific language impairment or similar syndrome.

Came and Reid (2007) suggested that teachers could focus on a core of common concerns. This implies that many children will share some of the same difficulties even though they have been identified with different syndromes. For example many will have:

- attention difficulties;
- memory problems;
- organizational difficulties;
- difficulties with processing speed.

They propose that tackling those four areas alone will help to meet the needs of most children identified with dyslexia, dyspraxia, ADHD or dyscalculia. So rather than focus on the label, they suggest that teachers should focus on a core of common concerns. This means that teachers will not feel deskilled as often when faced with children with labels. It is not unusual for dyslexia, dyspraxia and to a certain extent ADHD to share some common factors. Parents need to be aware of this overlap as it can be confusing for them. Many parents however feel that it is best if the school only caters for dyslexic students and this is based on perfectly sound reasoning as there are a large number of schools that do that in the US, Canada, the UK and elsewhere. It is also important to appreciate that even if the school is not dedicated to dyslexia, they can still implement and utilize specialist programs and strategies that can be beneficial for a range of the specific learning difficulties.

Alternative therapies

Parents are often confronted with choices and this includes whether they should use what are described as alternative interventions. Often these approaches are heavily advertised and promoted but may not be available in mainstream schools. They can be popular, innovative and often have media appeal and in some cases extravagant claims of success. That is not to say they are not helpful; some of the evidence, in fact, seems to support the benefits of some alternative forms of interventions.

Fawcett and Reid (2009) suggest that alternative approaches can be attractive to parents and to schools because of the state of 'unreadiness' of the current administrative and school systems to provide informed and consistently applied identification and classroom-based intervention focusing on individual needs. If, they argue, practice in schools was informed and consistent, then alternative approaches would not be able to penetrate the traditional educational area. Fawcett and Reid point out the main concern is that the alternative approaches have often not undergone stringent and robust clinical trials. They indicate that the gold standard in experimental design for evaluating interventions is the double-blind placebo-controlled study. It is taken from the medical field where it is widely used to evaluate the effectiveness of new drugs, and whether or not they have harmful side effects. A double-blind approach means that neither the experimenter, the child, the teacher nor the family know which approach the child is receiving, either the therapy which the study is testing, or whether they have been given an alternative (a placebo). It is important to make sure that studies are double-blind to overcome any tendency for performance to improve simply because the child or the experimenter expects this or wants it to happen. In some studies, a crossover technique is used. This means that half the children receive the placebo in the first set of trials. This is held to be ethically sound, because no one is deprived of an intervention thought to be beneficial. A stringent and well-controlled system would mean that the trial supervisor was not aware of who received placebo and who received treatment. This approach is relatively easy within a medical setting, but is less easy to adhere to in an experimental educational setting. There has been considerable debate on whether or not the approaches typically used in the education system, for both traditional and alternative interventions, have been sufficiently researched. Improvements in reading and spelling scores which can be attributed to a specific approach or program may reflect the commitment of the teacher and the parent rather than the effectiveness of the intervention.

There are many views on the efficacy of alternative treatment programs. These programs are usually not harmful, most however are expensive and some risk is attached to enlisting wholeheartedly in any one program. It is important that enthusiasm for any particular treatment or intervention does not minimize the effect of good classroom teaching and the importance of parent–teacher liaison. There is an abundance of well-researched teaching and learning programs (see IDA matrix of programs in chapter 5). Silver (2001) makes illuminative comments on 'controversial therapies' and suggests that the process from initial concept to acceptance of a particular treatment approach is slow and can take years. Research needs to support a particular approach and the results need to be published in peer-reviewed journals. There is a great deal of anecdotal evidence that often convinces parents of the value of certain approaches. These usually stem from people who have benefited from the treatment or whose children have. These views are not to be discounted, although it must be acknowledged that what works for one child may not be successful for another.

Self-esteem

This is an important issue for parents as they can be a good judge of the level of their child's self-esteem. They will know if they find any aspect of learning stressful. It is important that any feelings of failure that can result in low self-esteem are addressed and preferably prevented. This point has been made throughout this book.

There are a number of ways of helping to maintain and boost children's self-esteem, but one of the most obvious and most effective is to ensure that they achieve some success and genuine praise. In order for praise to be effective children have to be convinced that their achievements are worthy of the praise. When children feel a failure it is difficult to overcome that feeling and often they need to change their self-perceptions. This can be a lengthy process and ongoing support, praise and sensitive handling are necessary.

When discussing this with parents some have indicated that the following have been useful for developing self-esteem:

- **Using paired reading** as a strategy as it provides 'togetherness' between parents and child. It is also a well-researched and successful strategy for developing reading.
- **Mind mapping** is a popular strategy that can help to boost the dyslexic person's memory and organization skills. It can also help

them develop independence as they can adapt mind mapping in their own way and this gives them both success and independence.

- **Memory games** can be carried out at home and on family excursions. Word searches and puzzles can also be good for developing memory and vocabulary in a fun way.

- **Learning styles** – it is important to be aware of your child's preferred learning style. That means whether they are visual or auditory learners, whether they prefer experiential learning or watching, and the type of environment they prefer to work in – a quiet room or background noise. These factors can all make a difference to how the child can be motivated and whether he/she can persist with tasks.

- **Discussion** – this is important as the person with dyslexia can often be good at oral work but have difficulty with written work. So encouraging discussion plays to their strengths and can give them confidence and build self-esteem.

- **Self-advocacy** – it is important to help children with dyslexia develop confidence so that they can stand up for themselves and advocate for their needs to be met. This is particularly important in college and in the workplace. But this will not happen without preparation and parents need to prepare their child from an early age. Self-knowledge and knowledge about dyslexia can both help to do this.

- **Developing strengths and talents** – parents need to look for every opportunity to develop their child's strengths and to help them appreciate their strengths and particularly how they can use these to develop their self-esteem. These strengths can also be used to help overcome their weak areas. You can see an example of how the strengths can be noted in the extract below from a report of an assessment I recently conducted.

Strengths

- Josh* scored in the high average range in the visual /perceptual area.
- His vocabulary came out quite strong in the assessment.
- His score in the receptive vocabulary scale which was above average is particularly encouraging.

- His level of reading comprehension is very encouraging as it indicates that he has considerable potential in this area.
- He performed well in listening comprehension.
- He is a good communicator and conversed happily throughout the assessment.
- He can be very creative and enjoys art.
- He has excellent word processing skills.
- He scored comfortably in the average range in the cognitive assessment.
- He persisted well with all the tasks.
- He excels in sport and the reports from school indicate that he is an excellent team player.

*Not his real name.

Other issues

- **Developing consistent work habits:** It is worthwhile to spend some time developing a routine. This will give your child security, but it will also provide a framework so that they can take responsibility for organizing their own work. Providing a routine can be good for challenging aspects such as homework.
- **Homework:** This can be quite a challenge for parents as homework can be a real issue for children with dyslexia. They may not even have the homework tasks available and it is important to ensure that they do get the details of the homework copied down accurately. It is a good idea to set a time for homework and not to expect too much. Short tasks are better than lengthy periods of homework. Try to sit down and discuss the homework beforehand to make it more enjoyable. It might be a good idea to discuss a pleasant task that they can do after the homework is done. This can be motivating. It is worth reminding your child that many famous and successful dyslexic people past and present have also struggled with homework. Reflect on the words of Agatha Christie, the prolific author: 'I myself was always recognised as the "slow one" in the family. It was quite true, and I knew it and accepted it. Writing and spelling were always terribly difficult for me. My letters were without originality. I was an

extraordinarily bad speller and remained so . . .' (DITT Newsletter, no. 27, Spring 2007, p. 16).

Comment

While it is clear that there can be many issues that are challenging for parents it is also worth bearing in mind that parents can draw on considerable resources to support them – contact and constructive communication with the school, support groups and web-based resources can all be a lifeline for parents. The key point is that parents need to have the confidence and the opportunity to utilize these supports. Confidence can emerge from knowledge – knowledge of the field of dyslexia and knowledge of their child. Parents already have a head start in knowledge of their child and there is no reason why they cannot also become knowledgeable in the field of dyslexia – they have much to offer.

Appendix 1

Assessment

This appendix contains some brief information on some of the tests you are likely to come across in psychological reports. This is by no means an exhaustive list as the choice of tests can vary depending on the psychologist and the purposes of the assessment and the test.

Background information on the WISC-IV

Wechsler Intelligence Scale for Children, 4th ed. (WISC-IV) (2005)
The WISC-IV is an individual test that does not require reading or writing.

Purpose of the test: the WISC-IV was designed as a measure of a child's intellectual ability.
Test age range: 6'00 to 16'11 years.
Scores: Provides a full-scale IQ and factor scores – Verbal Comprehension, Perceptual Reasoning, Working Memory and Processing Speed.

Dyslexia: A Complete Guide for Parents and Those Who Help Them, Second Edition. Gavin Reid.
© 2011 John Wiley & Sons, Ltd. Published 2011 by John Wiley & Sons, Ltd.

Information: The WISC-IV is the fourth generation of the Wechsler Intelligence Scale for Children. Its predecessors, the WISC-R and the WISC-III, were the most popular and widely researched test of children's intelligence in history.

Scoring: The average IQ is 100; 110−120 is viewed as high average and over 120 is high. The average range is 90−110, below that is seen on the below average to well below average range. An IQ of around/below 70 is viewed as an indicator of severe learning difficulties.

Description of tests

Wechsler Intelligence Scale for Children (WISC-IV)

The subtests are grouped by scale membership, i.e., *Verbal Comprehension* (Similarities, Vocabulary, Comprehension, Information and Word Reasoning); *Perceptual Reasoning* (Block Design, Picture Concepts, Matrix Reasoning and Picture Completion); *Working Memory* (Digit Span, Letter-Number Sequencing and Arithmetic) and *Processing Speed* (Coding, Symbol Search and Cancellation).

The Verbal Comprehension Scale assesses the development of a child's language skills. It includes tests of expressive vocabulary, comprehension, reasoning and general knowledge.

The Perceptual Reasoning Scale assesses the development of a child's visual perceptual skills – there are tests of spatial analysis, visual perceptual reasoning and observation.

The Working Memory Scale assesses the student's working memory and attention and the Processing Speed Scale assesses motor (manual) skills and speed of information processing.

Comprehensive Test of Phonological Processing (CTOPP)

Richard Wagner, Joseph Torgesen and Carol Rashotte

The Comprehensive Test of Phonological Processing assesses phonological awareness, phonological memory and rapid naming. Persons with deficits in one or more of these kinds of phonological processing abilities may have more difficulty learning to read than those who do not.

The Dynamic Indicators of Basic Early Literacy Skills (DIBELS)

http://dibels.uoregon.edu

DIBELS is a set of standardized, individually administered measures of early literacy development. They are designed to be short (one-minute) fluency measures used to regularly monitor the development of pre-reading and early reading skills.

Dyslexia Screening Test (DST)

Fawcett and Nicolson (1996)
This screening instrument can be used for children between 6'6 and 16'5 years of age, although there is also an alternative version developed by the same authors for younger children, Dyslexia Early Screening Test, and an adult version (Nicolson and Fawcett, 1996). The test consists of the following attainment tests: one-minute reading, two-minute spelling, one-minute writing. Additionally, there are the following diagnostic tests: rapid naming, bead threading, postural stability, phonemic segmentation, backwards digit span, nonsense passage reading, verbal and semantic fluency.

The dyslexia screening tests can be accessed by all teachers.
Email cservice@harcourtbrace.com

Gray Oral Reading Tests, 4th ed. (GORT-4)

J. Lee Weiderholt and Brian R. Bryant
GORT-4 provides an efficient and objective measure of growth in oral reading and an aid in the diagnosis of oral reading difficulties. Five scores give information on a student's oral reading skills in terms of:

Rate – the amount of time taken by a student to read a story

Accuracy – the student's ability to pronounce each word in the story correctly

Fluency – the student's Rate and Accuracy Scores combined

Comprehension – the appropriateness of the student's responses to questions about the content of each story read

Overall Reading Ability – a combination of a student's Fluency (i.e., Rate and Accuracy) and Comprehension scores.

TOWRE – Test of Word Reading Efficiency

Joseph Torgesen, Richard Wagner and Carol Rashotte

TOWRE is a nationally normed measure of word reading accuracy and fluency.

The Woodcock Johnson III Tests of Cognitive Abilities Richard W. Woodcock, Kevin S. McGrew and Nancy Mather, 2001, 2007 Ages: 2.0 to 9.0+ years

The WJ III Tests of Cognitive Abilities standard and extended battery tests 20 different factors including verbal comprehension, visual –auditory and spatial relations as well as memory, rapid picture naming and planning. It covers intellectual abilities and provides a general intelligence score based on a comprehensive cognitive battery. www.woodcock-johnson.com

The Woodcock-Johnson III Tests of Achievement (WJ III ACH) (Woodcock, McGrew, & Mather, 2001, 2007) Riverside Publishing— A Houghton Mifflin Company, USA

Includes 22 tests for measuring skills in reading, mathematics, and writing, as well as important oral language abilities and academic knowledge. Two parallel forms (Form A and Form B) contain all 22 tests. The Woodcock-Johnson III Tests of Achievement, Form C/Brief Battery (Brief Battery) (Woodcock, Schrank, McGrew & Mather, 2007) includes a third form of nine of the most frequently used reading, mathematics, and writing tests. www.woodcock-johnson.com

Detailed Assessment of Speed of Handwriting (DASH) (2007)

Barnett, A., Henderson, S.E., Scheib, B. & Schulz, J. (Pearson Assessment) Age Range: 9:0 – 16:11 years

Comment:

The assessment includes five subtests, each testing a different aspect of handwriting speed. The subtests examine fine motor and precision skills, the speed of producing well-known symbolic material, the ability to alter speed of performance on two tasks with identical content and free writing competency. www.psychcorp.co.uk

Wechsler Individual Achievement Test (WIAT-II and III) (2005 and 2010)

Pearson Educational Age Range: 4:00 – 16:11 years Also US norms from 17 – 85 years.

Comment:

The WIAT-II and WIAT-III assesses reading, language and numerical attainment. Contains three measures of reading – word reading, reading comprehension and pseudoword decoding, two measures of numerical attainment – numerical operations and mathematical reasoning, two measures of written language attainment – spelling and written expression and two measures of oral language attainment – listening comprehension and oral expression. Subtests can be used separately.

The WIAT-III has five new subtests: Oral Reading Fluency; Math Fluency (Addition, Subtraction, Multiplication); and Early Reading Skills as well as Enhanced Listening Comprehension, Oral Expression, and Written Expression subtests.

www.pearsonassessments.com

Wide Range Achievement Test (WRAT 4) (2006) Wilkinson, G.S. & Robertson, G.J.

Pearson Educational Age Range: 5 – 9:5 years

Comment:

The WRAT 4 includes tests of word reading, sentence comprehension, spelling and maths computation. www.pearsonassessments.com

Woodcock Reading Mastery Tests Revised (1998) (Woodcock, R.W.) Pearson

Age Range: 5 – 7:5+ years

Comment:

This is a battery of tests to measure reading ability. Used to measure reading readiness skills, basic reading skills and reading comprehension skills. The Basic Skills Cluster has Word Identification (WID) and Word Attack (WA) tests. The Reading Comprehension Cluster has Word Comprehension (WC) and Passage Comprehension (PC) tests. www.pearsonassessments.com

Appendix 2

Programs

Orton–Gillingham
http://www.ortonacademy.org/approach.html
http://www.ogtutors.com/aboutog.php

Alphabetic Phonics
http://www.epsbooks.com/downloads/samplers/S-alphabetic_
phonics.pdf

Slingerland
http://www.slingerland.org/administration/testimonials.html

Alpha to Omega
http://www.amazon.co.uk/Alpha-Omega-Teaching-Reading-
Spelling/dp/0435104233

http://www.crossboweducation.com/Alpha_to_Omega_phonics%
20games.htm

Dyslexia: A Complete Guide for Parents and Those Who Help Them, Second Edition. Gavin Reid.
© 2011 John Wiley & Sons, Ltd. Published 2011 by John Wiley & Sons, Ltd.

Bangor Dyslexia Teaching System
http://eu.wiley.com/WileyCDA/WileyTitle/productCd-
1861560559.html

Hickey Language Course
http://www.amazon.co.uk/Hickey-Multisensory-Language-
Course/dp/1861561784

Reading Recovery
http://www.readingrecovery.org

Sound Linkage
http://eu.wiley.com/WileyCDA/WileyTitle/productCd-
1861561768.html

Toe by Toe
http://www.toebytoe.co.uk

Units of Sound
www.dyslexiaaction.org.uk

THRASS
http://www.thrass.co.uk

Letterland
http://www.letterland.com

Paired Reading – clear how to do it.

http://www.dyslexia.ie/paired.htm

Launch Into Reading Success – Test of Phonological Awareness

Lorna Bennett and Pamela Ottley
Phonological awareness program designed just for young children. Can prevent reading failure at an early stage if it is identified and intervention with the right program is used.

Launch Into Reading Success
A phonological skills-training program designed for use by teachers and other professionals in schools and for parents at home. Can provide effective first step for a child to take in the pursuit of literacy. For more information on programs see Reid, G. (2009) *Dyslexia: A Practitioners Handbook* (Wiley).

Appendix 3

DSM-IV and DSM-V: Criteria

ADHD

DSM-IV and DSM-V refer to the Diagnostic Statistical Manual published by the American Psychological Association and is generally regarded as the leading authority for professionals seeking advice on definitions and characteristics of learning difficulties. The term Learning Disabilities is currently used in DSM-IV in a broad manner and does not mention dyslexia but in the draft document for DSM-V which is expected to be implemented in 2013 it is proposed that the term dyslexia will be used alongside that of dyscalculia in order to reflect disabilities of reading and mathematics, comprising a new (for DSM) category of learning disabilities http://www.zimbio.com/Psychiatric+health/articles/tN5lOpkaSqR/Overview+Proposed+DSM+V+Changes

Dyslexia: A Complete Guide for Parents and Those Who Help Them, Second Edition. Gavin Reid.
© 2011 John Wiley & Sons, Ltd. Published 2011 by John Wiley & Sons, Ltd.

According to the DSM-IV (2001), a person with attention deficit/hyperactivity disorder must have either (1) or (2):

A1. Six (or more) of the following symptoms of inattention have persisted for at least 6 months to a degree that is maladaptive and inconsistent with developmental level:

Inattention
- often fails to give close attention to details or makes careless mistakes in school work, work, or other activities
- often has difficulty sustaining attention in tasks or play activities
- often does not seem to listen when spoken to directly
- often does not follow through on instructions and fails to finish schoolwork, chores, or duties in the workplace (not due to oppositional behaviour or failure to understand instructions)
- often has difficulty organizing tasks and activities
- often avoids, dislikes, or is reluctant to engage in tasks that require sustained mental effort (such as schoolwork or homework)
- often loses things necessary for tasks or activities (e.g., toys, school assignments, pencils, books, or tools)
- is often easily distracted by extraneous stimuli
- is often forgetful in daily activities

A2. Six (or more) of the following symptoms of hyperactivity-impulsivity have persisted for at least 6 months to a degree that is maladaptive and inconsistent with developmental level:

Hyperactivity
- often fidgets with hands or feet or squirms in seat
- often leaves seat in classroom or in other situations in which remaining seated is expected
- often runs about or climbs excessively in situations in which it is inappropriate (in adolescents or adults, may be limited to subjective feelings or restlessness)
- often has difficulty playing or engaging in leisure activities quietly
- is often 'on the go' or often acts as if 'driven by a motor'
- often talks excessively
- often blurts out answers before questions have been completed

- often has difficulty awaiting turn
- often interrupts or intrudes on others (e.g., butts into conversations or games)

Additionally DSM-IV indicates that the following should be present.

B. Some hyperactive-impulsive or inattentive symptoms that caused impairment were present before age 7 years.
C. Some impairment from the symptoms is present in two or more settings (e.g., at school [or work] and at home).
D. There must be clear evidence of clinically significant impairment in social, academic, or occupational functioning.
E. The symptoms do not occur exclusively during the course of a Pervasive Developmental Disorder, Schizophrenia, or other Psychotic Disorder and are not better accounted for by another mental disorder (e.g., Mood Disorder, Anxiety Disorder, Disassociative Disorder, or a Personality Disorder).

Attention Deficit/Hyperactivity Disorder, Combined Type: if both Criteria A1 and A2 are met for the past 6 months.

Attention Deficit/Hyperactivity Disorder, Predominantly Inattentive Type: if Criterion A1 is met but Criterion A2 is not met for the past 6 months.

Attention Deficit/Hyperactivity Disorder, Predominantly Hyperactive-Impulsive Type: if Criterion A2 is met but Criterion A1 is not met for the past 6 months.

The new DSM-V manual is due out in 2013 proposes to include some potentially important changes for ADHD and the category Predominantly Inattentive (ADHD-PI) may according to drafts receive more recognition. (http://ezinearticles.com/?Predominantly-Inattentive-ADHD,-a-DSM-V-Category-All-Their-Own&id=4049545)

Appendix 4

Information: Sources, resources and organizations

Each child with dyslexia is unique. This means that the needs, requirements and supports for parents may differ. It is for that reason that local contacts can be extremely valuable. These include local support groups and parents' associations, as well as the local school. The importance of the local school has been indicated many times throughout this book and the school should be the first line of information. It is very possible however that the school may not have the sources of information and support that are required by parents. The school may find out about recent developments in dyslexia from the parents. That varies, but the power and the influence of parents themselves as a source of information on dyslexia for the school, and other parents, should not be underestimated. The fact a number of teachers are also parents of children with dyslexia is also helpful and usually in cases like that the school will be more informed than usual on dyslexia. Teacher aides and teaching assistants can also be very well informed about dyslexia and some may also be parents of a dyslexic child.

Dyslexia: A Complete Guide for Parents and Those Who Help Them, Second Edition. Gavin Reid.
© 2011 John Wiley & Sons, Ltd. Published 2011 by John Wiley & Sons, Ltd.

Parents' association have a key role to play in pooling resources and disseminating information on dyslexia through open evenings, websites, leaflets and conferences. In fact, in some instances parents' groups have undertaken work that should be carried out in school. Dyslexia is a continuum and it can overlap with other conditions. This means that parents and parent support groups can link constructively with other organizations. Some of these are listed below. The list is by no means exhaustive. Although the internet provides a ready source of information on dyslexia for parents they have to be selective in what they access and always consult others before embarking on a program, especially a costly one, for their child. It is hoped this book has helped to prepare parents to do this and to be critical and selective of the sources of information they select.

There are also examples of contacts that can be useful for parents but it should be emphasized that these are only a sample and parents can access websites and materials that relate to their own geographical area and school system.

Resources

Crossbow Education, 41 Sawpit Lane, Brocton, Stafford ST17 0TE
www.crossboweducation.com

Crossbow Education specializes in games for children with dyslexia and produces activities on literacy, numeracy and study skills. These include Spingoes and onset and rime spinner bingo which comprises a total of 120 games using onset and rime; Funics, a practical handbook of activities to help children recognize and use rhyming words, blend and segment syllables, identify initial phonemes and link sounds to symbols. Funics is produced by Maggie Ford and Anne Tottman and is available from Crossbow Education. Crossbow also produce literacy games including Alphabet Lotto, which focusses on early phonics, Bing-Bang-Bong and CVC Spring, which help develop competence in short vowel sounds and 'Deebees' which is a stick and circle board game to deal with b/d confusion.

They also have a board games called Magic-E, Spinit and Hotwords - a five board set for teaching and reinforcing 'h' sounds such as 'wh', 'sh', 'ch', 'th', 'ph','gh' and silent 'h'. 'Oh No' a times table photocopiable game book, 'tens n' units' which consists of spinning board games which help children of all ages practice the basics of place value in addition and subtraction. Many of these activities are simple and fun to use and can be easily accessed by parents for home use.

The book *How to Write like a Writer* by Bob Hext from Crossbow Education (www.crossboweducation.com) is an excellent resource on supporting children with writing in sentences and paragraphs.

Multi-Sensory Learning (www.msl-online.net)
Provides a range of games and activities for reading, spelling and numeracy. They also have software and a number of kits and games called memory boosters. The memory boosters include pocketbook of reading and spelling reminders, signs and symbols, Lotto, line tracker, high frequency and key words, happy families for great spelling and wordsearch activities. These are all highly motivating colourful and have a high interest level. They also produce a structured reading and spelling program.

Smart Kids (www.smartkids.co.uk)
This company produce the eye-catching and highly colorful smart phonics series of activities. These include games and activities on developing consonants, vowels and digraph beginnings for kindergarten followed by a sequence of packs for different levels focussing on blend beginnings and endings, magic 'e' vowel digraphs and changeable vowel sounds. The activities have supplementary materials using poetry cards, magnetic whiteboards and whiteboard markers, foam magnetic letters in seven color groupings, picture sound magnets and spelling and sound cards. The company also have a branch in Auckland, New Zealand.

Thrass (www.thrass.com)
The Teaching of Handwriting, Reading and Spelling Program known as THRASS can be useful and has many different aspects that can be accessed by children and parents. Details of these can be found in the comprehensive THRASS web page (www.thrass.com).

TextHelp
The program known as TextHelp© is particularly useful for assisting with essay writing. TextHelp has a readback facility and has a

spellchecker which includes a dyslexic spellcheck option that searches for common dyslexic errors. Additionally TextHelp has a word prediction feature that can predict a word from the context of the sentence giving up to 10 options from a dropdown menu. Often dyslexic students have word finding difficulty and this feature can therefore be very useful. This software also has a Word Wizard that provides the user with a definition of any word; options regarding homophones; an outline of a phonic map and a talking help file.

Inspiration
Inspiration is a software program that can help in the development of ideas and to organize thinking. Through the use of diagrams it helps the student comprehend concepts and information. Essentially the use of diagrams can help to make creating and modifying concept maps and ideas easier. The user can also prioritize and rearrange ideas, helping with essay writing. Inspiration can therefore be used for brainstorming, organizing, pre-writing, concept mapping, planning and outlining. There are 35 inbuilt templates and these can be used for a range of subjects including English, History and Science. Dyslexic people often think in pictures rather than words. This technique can be used for note-taking, for remembering information and organizing ideas for written work. The Inspiration program converts this image into a linear outline.

www.r-e-m.co.uk
A comprehensive catalog of software for use with children with dyslexia. Programs include Starspell, Wordshark 3, Clicker 4 (this enables students to write with whole words and pictures), Text help read and write, Penfriend (able to predict words before they are typed), Wordswork (uses a learning styles approach), Inspiration (for creative planning and brainstorming), Numbershark, Times Tables and Parenting Snakes and Ladders.

iANSYST Ltd
Provide computers and technology for helping dyslexic people of all ages at college, school, work or home. Provide products such as TextHelp, Dragon Naturally Speaking, Inspiration and software on learning skills such as reading, spelling, grammar, comprehension and memory (www.iansyst.co.uk and www.dyslexic.com).

Crick Software (www.cricksoft.com)
Popular clicker programs can be used for sentence-building, word banks, writing frames and multimedia. Lively presentations, e.g., series on Find out and write about includes programs on explorers, castles and animals. Also provide Clicker books and Clicker animations.

An excellent review of software for children and adults with dyslexia can be found at http://www.dyslexia-teacher.com/t10e.html.

This international website comments on spellcheckers, electronic books, different kinds of calculators, wordshark and clicker4 (talking word processor), Kurzweil 3000 (scans and reads books), WordQ (writing tool that uses advanced word prediction), TextHelp, Co:Writer (provides vocabulary, spelling, composition and revision that supports that builds skills in writing), Write Outloud (talking word processor – very suitable for grades 3–12), PenFriend (supportive writing software featuring word prediction (predictive typing), on-screen keyboards, screen-reader speech feedback), Dragon 'Naturally Speaking' (a well-reviewed dictation program which allows you to speak to your word processing program and it will type what you say: 'An invaluable program which I use every day' (John Bradford, www.worldofdyslexia.org – another excellent resource).

100 Ideas for Supporting Children with Dyslexia (2nd edition, 2011) by Gavin Reid and Shannon Green, Continuum Publications, London.

Organizations/sources of information

Dyslexia

International Dyslexia Association 8600 LaSalle Road, Chester Building, Suite 382, Baltimore, MD 21286-2044, U.S.A. Tel.: (410) 296 0232. Fax: (410) 321 5069. Email.: info@interdys.org. Website: http//www.interdys.org IDA

British Dyslexia Association, 98 London Road, Reading, RG1 5AU Helpline: 0118 966 8217, Admin: 0118 966 2677, Fax: 0118 935 1927 e-mail: helpline@bda-dyslexia.demon.co.uk or admin@bda-dyslexia. demon.co.uk Website: http://www.bda-dyslexia.org.uk

Dyslexia in Scotland, Unit 3, Stirling Business Centre, Wellgreen Place, Stirling, Scotland, FK8 2DZ. Tel: 01786 446 650, Fax: 01786 471 235 www.dyslexia-in-scotland.org
Also Dyslexia Ayrshire www.dyslexiayrshire.org.uk

Northern Ireland Dyslexia Association, 7 Mount Pleasant, Stranmilis Road, Belfast, BT9 5DS www.nida.org.uk

Dyslexia Association of Ireland Suffolk Chambers, 1 Suffolk Street, Dublin 2. info@dyslexia.ie

Adult Dyslexia Organisation (ADO)
336 Brixton Road, London SW9 7AA. Helpline: 0171 924 9559.

SPELD Victoria: www.vicnet.net.au/~speld

SPELD South Australia: www.speld- sa.org.au/index.html SPELD New South

Wales: www.speldnsw.org.au SPELD (Tasmania): speldtasmania@ bigpond.com

SPELD Western Australia: speld@opera.iinet.net.au; www.dyslexia-speld.com

SPELD Queensland: www.speld.org.au

SPELD New Zealand: www.speld.org.nz/contact.html Learning and Behaviour

Charitable Trust: www.lbctnz.com

Learning Works Int: www.learning-works.org.uk

Oak Hill School, Chemin de Précossy, 31 1260 Nyon, Switzerland http://www.oakhill.ch/?page_id=126 Oak Hill School offers a unique half-day program to students with diagnosed learning disabilities or attention deficit disorders, who are experiencing difficulties in the mainstream classroom.

ALL Special Kids (ASK) Geneva: www.allspecialkids.org A Geneva-based organization, aiming to support the families of children with special needs and learning differences.

Fraser Academy in Vancouver, Canada: www.fraseracademy.ca

The Kenneth Gordon Maplewood School: http://www.kennethgordon. bc.ca

www.LDAlearning.com

DIBELS: http://dibels.uoregon.edu

PRO-ED Inc. A leading publisher of nationally standardized: tests. www.proedinc.com/index.html

Special Needs Assessment Profile: www.SNAPassessment.com
www.kuwaitdyslexia.com
Dyslexia Association (Hong Kong): www.dyslexia.org.hk
Dyslexia Association of Singapore: www.das.org.sg
Japan Dyslexia Society: info@npo- edge.jp
European Dyslexia Association (EDA): www.dyslexia.eu.com
Lindamood–Bell: www.Lindamoodbell.com
No to failure project: http://www.notofailure.com/ (accessed April
    2010)
Rose Report: http://search.publications.dcsf.gov.uk
Dr Loretta Giorcelli: www.doctorg.org. A well-known international
    consultant.
DysGuise http://dysguise.eu. Scottish based dyslexia consultancy and
    psychological assessments contact Dr. Jennie Guise jennieguise@
    dysguise.com

Institute of Child Education and Psychology Europe

ICEP Europe (Institute of Child Education and Psychology Europe)
is a leading provider of high quality online Continuing Professional
Development (CPD) and university-validated Diploma programs in
special educational needs for teachers, parents and allied professionals
who work with children and young people. http://www.icepe.ie/

Global Education Services (GES)

A top international provider of consultancy, professional development
    and projects worldwide (contact Dr. Gavin Reid gavinreid66@
    gmail.com)   www.globaleducationalconsultants.com   info@
    globaleducationalconsultants.com
The Lighthouse School, Cairo day school for students with dyslexia
    and other overlapping specific learning disabilities. The Lighthouse
    School offers the British National Curriculum and represents an aca-
    demic program dedicated to meeting the needs of students diagnosed
    as having a language-based learning disability, such as dyslexia. En-
    courages a broad and holistic concept of education and aims to

provide small classes, individualized and differentiated teaching.
http://www.lighthouseschoolonline.com

Arts Dyslexia Trust www.sniffout.net/home/adt

Council for the Registration of Schools Teaching Dyslexic Pupils (CReSTeD)

Dr. Gavin Reid's website www.drgavinreid.com

Red Rose School U.K. www.redroseschool.co.uk

Dyslexia Research Trust www.dyslexic.org.uk

Helen Arkell Dyslexia Centre, www.arkellcentre.org.uk

National Association of Special Educational Needs (NASEN) www.nasen.org.uk

Dyscovery Centre (multidisciplinary assessment centre for dyslexia, dyspraxia, attention deficit disorders, and autistic spectrum disorders www.dyscovery.co.uk

www.dyslexia-teacher.com contains a wealth of information for teachers and parents world wide. Information on materials, books and courses. Runs course on training for teachers and parents in the teaching of children with dyslexia. The course has students from 48 countries and is very practical based.

Canada Dyslexia Association (www.dyslexiaassociation.ca)

This association has produced an extremely interesting article titled 'Voices of Dyslexia' Tragedies and Triumphs which is available on their website. It provides illuminating accounts of the obstacles some individuals have had to overcome. For example one of the accounts from a computer expert, aged 50, who is a senior civil servant, reveals how he was told he could not learn when he took a second language course. He was tested for dyslexia only two years ago and has had to overcome many hurdles in life without realizing why he was experiencing difficulties. He said, 'the more you know yourself, the better you become at something, and that is the one thing that should be the centrepiece of your life's work'. There is also an account by a senior official of the Canadian government, aged 54, who hid her disability until three years ago when she told staff and actually received a lot of respect from colleagues and employees.

The article also contains advice for parents which encourages parents to accept dyslexia and suggests that the problem is 50% solved with your recognition and acceptance. There are also tips for employers of people with dyslexia.

Other specific learning difficulties

Attention deficit disorders

The National Attention Deficit Disorder Information Service www.addiss.co.uk
Attention Deficit Disorder Association www.chadd.org and www.add.org
ADHD behaviour management www.StressFreeADHD.com
ADHD books
www.adders.org and www.addwarehouse.com
ADHD diet – www.feingold.org
Dyscovery Centre (multidisciplinary assessment centre for dyslexia, dyspraxia, attention deficit disorders, and autistic spectrum disorders www.dyscovery.co.uk

Developmental coordination disorders/dyspraxia

Dyspraxia Foundation www.dyspraxiafoundation.org.uk
Dyspraxia Connexion (website offers support, information and practical help www.dysf.fsnet.co.uk
QuEST therapies www.questtherapies.com
www.hiddenhandicap.co.uk
www.dyspraxia.org.nz
Mindroom – a charity aimed at helping children and adults with learning difficulties www.mindroom.org

Autistic spectrum disorders; Asperger's syndrome

National Autistic Society www.nas.org.uk
www.futurehorizons-autism.com

Speech and language difficulties

Afasic www.afasic.org.uk
I CAN www.ican.org.uk
www.childspeech.net
www.talkingpoint.org.uk

This appendix has focused on the needs of parents by providing them with advice on the type of books that are available and websites where information can be accessed. There is a considerable range of resources available and this appendix has only highlighted a small section of these. Irrespective of the country, there are resources available, or certainly resources that can be ordered through the internet. The local needs of parents have the potential to be satisfied. Local support groups can also help, but what is very concerning is the wide disparity in provision for, and indeed acceptance of the needs of, children with dyslexia. This is a global concern. In time every country will provide in some way for dyslexia. It can be dangerous, costly and wasteful of any country's potential to ignore it.

Appendix 5

Selected glossary

ADHD – children with ADHD (attention difficulties with hyperactivity) will have a short attention span and tend to work on a number of different tasks at the same time. They will be easily distracted and may have difficulty settling in some classrooms, particularly if there is a number of competing distractions. It is also possible for some children to have attention difficulties without hyperactivity; this is referred to as ADD.

Auditory discrimination – many children with SpLD can have difficulties with auditory discrimination. It refers to the difficulties in identifying specific sounds and in distinguishing these sounds from other similar sounds. This can be associated with the phonological difficulties experienced by children with dyslexia (see phonological difficulties). Hearing loss or partial and intermittent hearing loss can also be associated with auditory discrimination.

Bottom-up reading approach – the method of reading using decoding skills. It means that the reader has to have a good grasp of the letters

Dyslexia: A Complete Guide for Parents and Those Who Help Them, Second Edition. Gavin Reid.
© 2011 John Wiley & Sons, Ltd. Published 2011 by John Wiley & Sons, Ltd.

and the sounds and be able to blend these to make words. Some readers with dyslexia may confuse words with similar sounds or those that look similar. It is common for beginning readers to learn to read this way. It is essential that children with SpLD are taught through the bottom-up process in order to ensure they can be familiar with the basic sounds and sound combinations (for comparison, see top-down method).

Cognition – the learning and thinking process. It is the process that describes how learners take in information and how they retain and understand the information.

Decoding – the reading processing, specifically the breaking down of words into individual sounds.

Differentiation – this is the process of adapting materials and teaching to suit a range of learners' abilities and level of attainments. Usually differentiation refers to the task, the teaching, the resources and the assessment. Each of these areas can be differentiated to suit the needs of individual or groups of learners.

Dyscalculia – this describes children and adults who have difficulties with numeracy. This could be due to difficulties in computation of numbers, remembering numbers or reading the instructions associated with number problems.

Dysgraphia – this is difficulties in handwriting. Some dyspraxic and dyslexic children may also show signs of dysgraphia. Children with dysgraphia benefit from lined paper as they have visual/spatial problems; they may also have an awkward pencil grip.

Dyslexia – refers to difficulties in accessing print, but also other factors such as memory, processing speed, sequencing, directions, syntax, spelling and written work can also be challenging. Children with dyslexia often have phonological difficulties which results in poor word attack skills. In many cases they require a dedicated, one-to-one intervention program.

Dyspraxia – this refers to children and adults with coordination difficulties. It is also called Developmental Coordination Disorder (DCD).

Eye tracking – the skill of being able to read a line and keep the eyes on track along the line. Children with poor eye tracking may omit lines or words on a page. Sometimes masking a part of a line or page or using a ruler can help with eye tracking.

Information processing – a process that describes how children and adults learn new information. It is usually described as a cycle – input, cognition and output. Often children with SpLD can have difficulties at all the stages of information processing.

Learning disabilities – a general term to describe the range of specific learning difficulties such as dyslexia, dyspraxia, dyscalculia and dysgraphia. Often referred to as LD, it is not equated with intelligence and children with LD are usually in the average to above average intelligence range. This term is used most widely in the US and Canada.

Learning style – this can describe the learner's preferences for learning using visual, auditory, kinesthetic or tactile stimuli; it can also relate to environmental preferences such as sound, the use of music when learning, preferences for time of day and working in pairs, groups or individually. There is a lot of literature on learning styles but it is still seen as quite controversial very likely because there are hundreds of different instruments, all of which claim to measure learning styles. Many learners are quite adaptable and can adjust to different types of learning situations and environments. Nevertheless it is a useful concept to apply in the classroom, particularly for children with learning disabilities, as using learning styles it is more possible to identify their strengths and use these in preparing materials and in teaching.

Long-term memory – this is used to recall information that has been learnt and needs to be recalled for a purpose. Many children with SpLD have difficulty with long-term memory as they have not organized the information they have learnt, so recalling it can be challenging as they may not have enough cues to assist with recall. Study skills programs can help with long-term memory.

Metacognition – the process of thinking about thinking, that is being aware of how one learns and how a problem was solved. It is a process-focussed approach and one that is necessary for effective and efficient learning. Many children with SpLD have poor metacognitive awareness because they are unsure of the process of learning. For that reason study skills programs can be useful.

Multiple intelligence – first developed by Howard Gardner in the early 1980s in his book *Frames of Mind* it turns the conventional view of intelligence on its head. Gardner provides insights into eight intelligences and shows how the educational and the social and emotional needs of all children can be catered for through the use of these intelligences. Traditionally, intelligence was equated with school success but often this focused predominantly on the verbal and language aspects of performance. Gardner's model is broader which indicates that the traditional view of intelligence may be restrictive.

Multisensory – the use of a range of modalities in learning. In this context multisensory usually refers to the use of visual, auditory, kinesthetic and tactile learning. It is generally accepted that children with SpLD need a multisensory approach that utilizes all of these modalities.

Neurological – this refers to brain-associated factors. This could be brain structure – that is the different components of the brain – or brain processing – how the components interact with each other. The research in SpLD shows that both brain structure and brain processing factors are implicated in SpLD.

Peer tutoring – this is when two or more children work together and try to learn from each other. It may also be the case that an older, more proficient learner works with a younger, less accomplished learner. i.e., the younger one is the tutee and the older the tutor.

Phonological awareness – the process of becoming familiar with the letter sounds and letter combinations that make the sounds in reading print. There are 44 sounds in the English language and some sounds are very similar. This can be confusing and challenging for children with SpLD and they often get the sounds confused or have difficulty in retaining and recognizing them when reading or in speech.

Specific learning difficulties (SpLD) – the range of difficulties experienced that can be of a specific nature such as reading, coordination, spelling, handwriting and number work. There are quite a number of specific learning difficulties and they can be seen as being distinct from general learning difficulties. Children with general learning difficulties usually find most areas of the curriculum challenging and they may have a lower level of comprehension than children with specific learning difficulties.

Top-down – this refers to the reading process and particularly the procedure and strategies used by young readers. The top-down method means that the reader begins with the context and the background of the text and uses contextual cues to help with the reading process. In the top-down model reading for meaning is more important than reading accuracy. Language experience is an important prerequisite for reading using the top-down method (for comparison see bottom-up method).

Working memory – this is the first stage in short-term memory. It involves the learner holding information in short-term store and carrying out a processing activity simultaneously. This can be solving a problem, reading instructions or merely walking around. Working memory is when one or more stimuli are held in memory for a short period of time. Children with SpLD often experience difficulties with working memory as they have difficulty in holding a number of different pieces of information at the same time.

References

Adamik-Jászò, A. (1995) Phonemic awareness and balanced reading instructions. In P. Owen & P. Pumfrey (Eds.), *Emergent and Developing Reading: Messages for Teachers*. London: Falmer Press.

Adams, M. J. (1990) *Beginning to Read: The New Phonics in Context*. Oxford: Heinemann.

American Psychiatric Association (2000) *Diagnostic and Statistical Manual*, 4th ed. Washington, DC: APA.

Anderson, O., Marsh, M. & Harvey, A. (1999) *Learn with the Classics, Using Music to Study Smart at Any Age*. San Francisco, CA: LIND Institute.

Arnold, L. E. (2001) Ingestive treatments for learning disorders. *Perspectives* 2(3): 18–20.

Association of Dyslexia Specialists in Higher Education Documents, http://www.adshe.org.uk.

Bath, J. B., Chinn, S. J. & Knox, D. E. (1986) *Test of Cognitive Style in Mathematics*. East Aurora, NY: Slosson Educational Publications.

Berryman, M. & Wearmouth, J. (2009) Responsive approaches to literacy learning within cultural contexts. In G. Reid (Ed.), *The Routledge Companion to Dyslexia*. London: Routledge.

Bishop, R. & Glynn, T. (1999) *Culture Counts: Changing Power Relations in Education*. Palmerston North: Dunmore.

Blyth, P. (1992) *A Physical Approach to Resolving Specific Learning Difficulties*. Chester: Institute for Neuro-Physiological Psychology.

Blythe, P. (2001) Personal communication.

Dyslexia: A Complete Guide for Parents and Those Who Help Them, Second Edition. Gavin Reid.
© 2011 John Wiley & Sons, Ltd. Published 2011 by John Wiley & Sons, Ltd.

Blythe, P. & Goddard, S. (2000) *Neuro-phsysiological Assessment Test Battery*. Chester: Institute for Neuro-Physiological Psychology.

Bradley, L. & Bryant, P. (1991) Phonological skills before and after learning to read. In S. A. Brady & D. P. Shankweiler (Eds.), *Phonological Processes in Literacy*. London: Lawrence Erlbaum.

British Dyslexia Association (2005) *The Employers' Guide to Dyslexia*. BDA, Sundial Events, Key 4 Learning, UK.

British Dyslexia Association Handbook (published annually) Reading: BDA.

Butterworth, B. (2003) *The Dyscalculia Screener*. London: NFER-Nelson.

Came, F. & Reid, G. (2007) *Cap It All Concern*. Marlborough: Assess and Provide Learning Works Intl.

Castles, A., Datta, H., Gayan, J. & Olson, R. K. (1999) Varieties of developmental reading disorder: Genetic and environmental influences. *Journal of Experimental Child Psychology*, *72*: 73.

Chall, J. S. & Popp, H. M. (1996) *Teaching and Assessing Phonics: Why, What, When, How, A Guide for Teachers*. Cambridge, MA: Educators Publishing Service.

Chinn, S. J. (2004) *The Trouble with Maths*. London: Routledge/Falmer.

Chinn, S. (2009) Dyscalculia and learning difficulties in maths. In G. Reid (Ed.), *The Routledge Companion Book of Dyslexia*. London: Routledge.

Chinn, S. J. & Everatt, J. M. (2009) *A Diagnostic Test Battery for MLD and Dyscalculia*. London: Pearson.

Cicci, R. (2001) *The Gift of Dyslexia* by Ronald D. Davis: A critique. *Perspectives*, *27*(3): 10–11.

Clark, K. (Ed.) (2004) *Count Me In, Responding to Dyslexia*. University of Strathclyde.

Coffield, M., Riddick, B., Barmby, P. & O'Neill, J. (2008) Dyslexia-friendly primary schools: What can we learn from asking the pupils? In G. Reid, A. Fawcett, F. Manis & L. Siegel, *The Sage Handbook of Dyslexia*. London: Sage.

Coventry, D., Pringle, M., Rifkind, H. & Weedon, C. (2001) Supporting students with dyslexia in the maths classroom. In L. Peer and G. Reid, *Dyslexia*. London: David Fulton.

CromaGen (CSD234) (2003) ChromaGen™ Report Issue One, March, Cantor and Nissel Ltd. www.cantor-nissel.co.uk.

Crombie, M. (2010) *The Assessment of Dyslexia: A Toolkit for Teachers*. Invited lecture to the Centre for Child Evaluation and Teaching (CCET) Kuwait, October (see also http://www.frameworkforinclusion.org/AssessingDyslexia).

Crombie, M., Knight, D. & Reid, G. (2004) Dyslexia: Early identification and early intervention. In G. Reid & A. Fawcett (Eds.), *Dyslexia in Context, Research, Policy and Practice*. London: Whurr.

Crombie, M. & McColl, H. (2001) Dyslexia and the teaching of modern foreign languages. In L. Peer & G. Reid (Eds.), *Dyslexia: Successful Inclusion in the Secondary School*. London: David Fulton.

Crombie, M. & Schneider, E. (2003) *Dyslexia and Modern Languages*. London: David Fulton.

Cyhlarova, E., Bell, J. G., Dick, J. R., Mackinlay, E. E., Stein, J. F. & Richardson, A. J. (2007) Membrane fatty acids, reading and spelling in dyslexic and non-dyslexic adults. *European Neuropsychopharmacology*, *17*: 116–121.

Dal, M, (2008) Dyslexia and foreign language learning. In G. Reid, A. Fawcett, F. Manis & L. Siegel, *The Sage Dyslexia Handbook*. London: Sage.

Dal, M., Arnbak, E. & Brandstätter, H. (2005) *Dyslexic Students and Foreign Language Learning*. Reykjavik: Iceland University of Education.

Dargie, R. (2001) Dyslexia and history. In L. Peer & G. Reid (Eds.), *Dyslexia – Successful Inclusion in the Secondary School*. London: David Fulton.

Davis, R. D. & Braun, E. M. (1994, revised 1997) *The Gift of Dyslexia. Why Some of the Smartest People Can't Read and How They Can Learn*. London: Souvenir Press.

Dennison, G. E. & Dennison, P. E. (1989) *Educational Kinesiology: Brain Organization Profiles*. Glendale, CA: Edu-Kinesthetics.

Dennison, G. E. & Dennison, P. E. (2000) *Educational Kinesiology: Brain Organization Profiles. Teachers' training manual*. 3rd ed. Glendale, CA: Edu-Kinesthetics.

Dennison, P. E. (1981) *Switching on: The Holistic Answer to Dyslexia*. Glendale, CA: Edu-Kinesthetics.

Dennison, P. E. & Hargrove, G. (1986) *Personalized Whole Brain Integration*. Glendale, CA: Educ-Kinesthetics.

Department for Education (1944) Education Act. London: HMSO.

DfES (1995) Disability Discrimination Act. London: Department for Education and Skills.

DfES (2001) *Special Educational Needs Code of Practice*. London: Department for Education and Skills.

DfES (1994, revised 2001) *Special Education Needs Code of Practice*. London: DfES.

Disability Discrimination Act (1995) London: HMSO.

DITT (2007) *Newsletter*, 27, Spring, p. 16.

Dobie, S. (1996) Perceptual motor and neurodevelopmental dimensions in identifying and remediating developmental delay in children with specific learning difficulties. In G. Reid (Ed.), *Dimensions of Dyslexia*. Edinburgh: Moray House.

Dore, W. & Rutherford, R. (2001) *Closing the Gap*. Paper presented at the BDA 6th International Conference on Dyslexia, York.

Dunn, R. & Dunn, K. (1992) *Teaching Elementary Students through Their Individual Learning Styles*. Boston, MA: Allyn & Bacon.

Dunn, R. & Dunn, K. (1993) *Teaching Secondary Students through Their Individual Learning Styles*. Boston, MA: Allyn & Bacon.

Dyspraxia Trust (1991) *Praxis Makes Perfect*. Hitchin: Dyspraxia Trust.

Dyspraxia Foundation (2008) www.dyspraxiafoundation.org.uk.

Dyslexia Scotland (2010) *Dyslexia Voice*.

Eames, F. H. (2002) Changing definitions and concepts of literacy: Implications for pedagogy and research. In G. Reid & J. Wearmouth (Eds.), *Dyslexia and Literacy: Theory and Practice*. Chichester: Wiley.

Ehri, L. (1995) The emergence of word reading in beginning reading. In P. Owen & P. Pumfrey (Eds.), *Emergent and Developing Reading: Messages for Teachers*. London: Falmer Press.

Ehri, L. C. (2002) Reading processes, acquisition, and instructional implications. In G. Reid & J. Wearmouth (Eds.), *Dyslexia and Literacy: Theory and Practice*. Chichester: Wiley.

Elbeheri, G. & Everatt, J. (2008) Dyslexia in different orthographies: Variability in transparency. In G. Reid, A. Fawcett, F. Manis & L. Siegel (Eds.), *The Sage Dyslexia Handbook*. London: Sage.

Equazen Nutraceuticals (2004) *Fatty Acids and Learning Conditions, The Facts. The Benefits. The Evidence*. London: Equazen Nutraceuticals. www.equazen.com.

Everatt, J. (2002) Visual processes. In G. Reid & J. Wearmouth (Eds.), *Dyslexia and Literacy: Theory and Practice*. Chichester: Wiley.

Everatt, J. & Brannan, P. (1996). The effects of a spelling task on the subsequent performance of dyslexics. *Dyslexia, 2*: 22–30.

Everatt, J., Smythe, I., Ocampo, D. & Gyarmathy, E. (2004) Issues in the assessment of literacy-related difficulties across language backgrounds: A cross-linguistic comparison. *Journal of Research in Reading, 27*: 141–151.

Farquhar, S.-E. (2003) *Parents as Teachers First: A Study of the New Zealand PAFT programme*. Wellington, NZ: Child Forum Research, www.childforum.com.

Fawcett, A. (2001) A parents' perspective. In L. Peer & G. Reid, *Dyslexia and Good Practice in the Secondary School*. London: David Fulton.

Fawcett, A. J. & Nicolson, R. I. (1996) *The Dyslexia Screening Test*. London: Psychological Corporation.

Fawcett, A. J. & Nicolson, R. I. (1997) *The Dyslexia Early Screening Test.* London: Psychological Corporation.

Fawcett, A. & Nicolson, R. (2004) Dyslexia: The role of the cerebellum. In G. Reid & A. Fawcett (Eds.), *Dyslexia in Context, Research, Policy and Practice.* London: Whurr.

Fawcett, A. & Nicolson, R. (2008) Dyslexia and the cerebellum. In G. Reid, A. Fawcett, F. Manis & L. Siegel (Eds.), *The Sage Dyslexia Handbook.* London: Sage.

Fawcett, A. Nicolson, R. & Lee, R. (2001) *The Pre-school Screening Test (PREST).* Kent: Psychological Corporation.

Fawcett, A. & Reid, G. (2009) Dyslexia and alternative interventions. In G. Reid (Ed.), *The Routledge Companion Book of Dyslexia.* London: Routledge.

Fife Education Authority (1996) *Partnership: Professionals, Parents and Pupils.* Fife.

Fisher, S. E., Marlow, A. J., Lamb, J., Maestrini, E., Williams, D. F., Richardson, A. J., Weeks, D. E., Stein, J. F. & Monaco, A. P. (1999) A quantitative-trait locus on chromosome 6p influences different aspects of developmental dyslexia. *American Journal of Human Genetics, 64*: 146–156.

Fox, A. (1999) *Brain Gym.* Unpublished MEd dissertation. University of Edinburgh.

Frith, U. (2002) Resolving the paradoxes of dyslexia. In G. Reid & J. Wearmouth, *Dyslexia and Literacy, Theory and Practice.* Chichester: Wiley

Galaburda A. (1993a) *Cortical and Sub-cortical Mechanisms in Dyslexia.* Paper presented at 44th Annual Conference, Orton Dyslexia Society, New Orleans, LA.

Galaburda, A. (Ed.) (1993b) *Dyslexia and Development: Neurobiological Aspects of Extraordinary Brains.* Cambridge, MA: Harvard University Press.

Galaburda, A. M. & Rosen, G. D. (2001) Neural plasticity in dyslexia: A window to mechanisms of learning disabilities. In J. L. McClelland & R. S. Siegler (Eds.), *Mechanisms of Cognitive Development: Behavioral and Neural Perspectives.* Mahwah, NJ: Lawrence Erlbaum.

Geschwind, N. & Galaburda, A. (1985) Cerebral lateralisation biological mechanisms associations and pathology: a hypothesis and a programme for research. *Archives of Neurology, 42*: 428–459.

Gilger, J. W. (2008) Some special issues concerning the genetics of dyslexia: Revisiting multivariate profiles, comorbidities, and genetic correlations. In G. Reid, A. Fawcett, F. Manis & L. Siegel, *The Sage Dyslexia Handbook.* London: Sage.

Goddard Blythe, S. (2005) Releasing educational potential through movement. *Child Care in Practice, 11*(4): 415–432.

Goldberg, R., Higgins, E., Raskind, M. & Herman, K. (2003) Predictors of success in individuals with learning disabilities: A qualitative analysis of a 20 year longitudinal study. *Learning Disabilities Research and Practice*, *18*: 222–236.

Goodman, K. (1976) Reading – A psycholinguistic guessing game. In H. Singer & R. B. Ruddell (Eds.), *Theoretical Models and Processes of Reading*. International Reading Association.

Government of Ireland (2001) *Report of the Task Force on Dyslexia*, July, Dublin.

Guyer, R. L. (2010) *Dyslexia Leaves its Mark: Research in the News*. National Institute of Health, Office of Science Education. http://science.education. nih.gov.

Hales, G. (2009) Self-esteem and counselling. In G. Reid (Ed.), *The Routledge Companion Book of Dyslexia*. London: Routledge.

Hannaford, C. (1995) *Smart Moves. Why Learning Is Not All in Your Head*. Arlington, VA: Great Ocean.

Hannaford, C. (1997) *The Dominance Factor. How Knowing Your Dominant Eye, Ear, Brain, Hand and Foot Can Improve Your Learning*. Arlington, VA: Great Ocean.

Harris, D. A. & MacRow-Hill, S. L. (1998) A comparative study with the intuitive colorimeter. *Optometry Today*, *38*: 15, 31 July.

Hatcher, P. (1994) *Sound Linkage: Integrated Programme for Overcoming Reading Difficulties*. London: Whurr.

Healy, J. M. (1994) *Your Child's Growing Mind*. New York: Doubleday Dell.

Healy, J. M. (1991) *Endangered Minds*. New York: Touchstone, Simon & Schuster.

Heaton, P. (1996) *Dyslexia – Parents in Need*. London: Wiley.

Helveston, E. M. (2001) Tinted lenses – A critique in perspectives. *International Dyslexia Association*, *27*(3): 12–13.

Henderson, A., Came, F. & Brough, M. (2003) *Working with Dyscalculia*. Marlborough: Learning Works Intl.

Henderson, A. & Sugden, D. A. (1992) *Movement Assessment Battery for Children*. London: Psychological Corporation.

Henry, M. (1996) The Orton–Gillingham approach. In G. Reid (Ed.), *Dimensions of Dyslexia. Vol. 1: Assessment, Teaching and the Curriculum*. Edinburgh: Moray House.

Henry, M. K. (2003) *Unlocking Literacy: Effective Decoding and Spelling Instruction*. Baltimore, MD: Paul Brookes.

Henry, G., Rickman, D., Ponder, B., Henderson, L., Mashburn, A. & Gordon, C. (2004) *The Georgia Early Childhood Study: 2001–2004 Final Report*, Georgia State University, Andrew Young School of Policy Studies.

Hunter, V. (2009) Dyslexia: overcoming the barriers of transition. In G. Reid (Ed.), *The Routledge Companion Book of Dyslexia*. London: Routledge.

Irons, P. (2004) Scientific and non-technical papers. Tinta Vision, www.tintavisionj.com/sci papers.htm.

Johanson, K. (1997) *Left Hemisphere Stimulation with Music and Sounds in Dyslexia Remediation*. Paper presented at the 48th annual conference the International Dyslexia Association (formerly Orton Dyslexia Association), Baltimore, MD.

Johnston, R., Connelly, V. D. & Watson, J. (1995) Some effects of phonics teaching on early reading development. In P. Owen & P. Pumfrey (Eds.), *Emergent and Developing Reading: Messages for Teachers*. London: Falmer Press.

Jones, N. (Ed.) (2005) *Developing School Provision for Children with Dyspraxia*. London: Sage.

Jordan, I. (2002) *Visual Dyslexia, Signs, Symptoms and Assessment*. Scunthorpe: Desktop Publications. www.desktoppublications.co.uk.

Kaplan, B. J., Dewey, D. M., Crawford, S. G. & Wilson, B. N. (2001) The term comorbidity is of questionable value in reference to developmental disorders: data and theory. *Journal of Learning Disabilities, 34*(6): 555–565, November/December.

Keene, E. & Zimmerman, S. (2007) *Mosaic of Thought: The Power of Comprehension Strategy Instruction*. Portsmouth, NH: Heinemann.

Killick, S. (2005) *Emotional Literacy – At the Heart of the School Ethos*. London: Paul Chapman.

Knight, D. F., Day, K. & Patton-Terry, N. (2009) Preventing and identifying reading difficulties in young children. In G. Reid, G. Elbeheri, J. Everatt, J. Wearmouth, D. & Knight (Eds.), *The Routledge Dyslexia Companion*. London: Routledge.

Knight, D. K. & Hynd, G. W. (2002) The neurobiology of dyslexia. In G. Reid & J. Wearmouth (Eds.) *Dyslexia and Literacy*. Chichester: Wiley.

Kriss, I. & Evans, B. J. W. (2005) The relationship between dyslexia and Meares-Irlen syndrome. *Journal of Research in Reading, 28*: 350–364.

Lawrence, D. (1987) *Enhancing Self-Esteem in the Classroom*. London: Paul Chapman.

Longdon, A. B. (2004) Brain Gym® in schools: An update. *The Mag*, The Magazine of Dyslexia Scotland, May.

Longdon, W. A. (2001) Brain Gym training. *News and Views*, Scottish Dyslexia Trust newsletter, Spring.

Lynch, R. (2007) *Enriching Children, Enriching the Nation: Public Investment in High-quality Prekindergarten*. Economic Policy Institute (Executive Summary), http://www.epi.org.

Lyon Reid, G. (1998) Statement of Dr. G. Lyon Reid, Chief Child Development and Behavior Branch, National Institute of Child Health and Human Development, National Institutes of Health to the Committee on Labor and Human Resources Room 430 Senate Dirkson Building Washington, DC, 28 April. http://www.readbygrade3.com/readbygrade3co/lyon.htm.

Lyon Reid, G., Shaywitz, S. E., Chhabra, V. & Sweet, R. (2004) Evidence-based reading policy in the U.S. In G. Reid & A. Fawcett (Eds.), *Dyslexia in Context, Research, Policy and Practice.* London: Whurr.

Macintyre, C. (2009) *Dyspraxia* (2nd ed.). London & New York: Routledge.

Mackay, N. (2004) The case for dyslexia-friendly schools. In G. Reid & A. Fawcett (Eds.), *Dyslexia in Context, Research, Policy and Practice.* London: Whurr.

Mahfoudi, A. & Haynes, C. (2008) Phonological awareness in reading disabilities remediation: Some general issues. In G. Reid, G. Elbeheri, J. Everatt, J. Wearmouth, & D. Knight (Eds.), *The Routledge Dyslexia Companion,* London: Routledge.

Marolda, M. R. & Davidson, P. S. (2000) Mathematical learning styles and differentiated learning strategies. *Perspectives, 26*(3): 10–15.

Marshall, A. (2003) *Brain Scans show Dyslexics Read Better with Alternative Strategies.* Kent: Davis® Dyslexia Association, UK. davisUK@ dyslexia.com.

Mathews, M. (1993) *Can Children be Helped by Applied Kinesiology?* Paper presented at 5th European Conference in Neuro-Developmental Delay in Children with Specific Learning Difficulties, Chester.

McIntyre, C. (2001) *Dyspraxia 5-11.* London: David Fulton.

McLoughlin, D., Fitzgibbon, G. & Young, V. (1994) *Adult Dyslexia, Assessment, Counselling and Training.* London: Whurr.

McLoughlin, D., Leather, C. & Stringer, P. (2002) *The Adult Dyslexic Interventions and Outcomes.* London: Whurr.

McPhillips, M., Hepper, P. G. & Mulhern, G. (2000) Effects of replicating primary – Reflex movements on specific reading difficulties in children: a randomised double-blind, controlled trial. *The Lancet, 355,* 537–541.

Miles, T. R. (2003) Commentary on the Reynolds et al. article. *Dyslexia, 9*(2): 112–123.

Miles, T. R. (2004) *Dyslexia and Stress.* London: Whurr.

Mueller, J. H. (1976). Anxiety and cue utilization in human learning and memory. In M. Zuckerman & C. D. Speilberger (Eds.), *Emotion and Anxiety: New Concepts, Methods and Application.* Hillsdale, NJ: Lawrence Erlbaum Associates.

National Institute of Child Health and Human Development (2000). Report of the National Reading Panel. *Teaching Children to Read: An*

Evidence-based Assessment of the Scientific Research Literature on Reading and its Implications for Instruction. Reports of the subgroup. Washington, DC: U.S. Government Printing Office.

New Zealand Government (2010) *Dyslexia*. Ministry of Education NZ, Wellington.

Nicolson, R. I. & Fawcett, A. J. (1990) Automaticity: a new framework for dyslexia research? *Cognition, 35*, 159–182.

Nicolson, R. I., Fawcett, A. J. & Dean, P. (2001) Developmental dyslexia. The cerebellar deficit hypothesis. *Trends in Neurosciences, 24*(9): 508–511.

Nicolson, R. I. & Reynolds, D. (2003) Sound findings and appropriate statistics: Response to Snowling and Hulme. *Dyslexia, 9*(2): 134–135, May.

Northern Ireland Education Department (2002) *Task Group Report on Dyslexia*. Belfast.

Palmer, S. (2006) *Toxic Childhood: How Modern Life is Damaging Our Children . . . and What We Can Do About It*. London: Orion.

Peel, H. A. & Foster, E. S. (1993) Inviting parents to the middle: A proactive stance for improving student performance. *Journal of Invitational Theory and Practice, 2*(1). http://www.invitationaleducation.net/journal/v21p43.htm.

Peer, L. (2009) Dyslexia and glue ear: A sticky educational problem. In G. Reid (Ed.), *The Routledge Companion Book of Dyslexia*, London: Routledge.

Portwood, M. (2001) *Developmental Dyspraxia A Practical Manual for Parents and Professional*. Durham: Durham County Council Educational Psychology Service County Hall.

Pugh, N. (2003) Managing the system – How parents can make it happen. In M. Johnson & L. Peer (Eds.), *The Dyslexia Handbook*. London: BDA.

Reid, G. (2001) Specialist Teacher Training in the U.K.: Issues, considerations and future directions. In M. Hunter-Carsch (Ed.), *Dyslexia, A Psychosocial Perspective*. London: Whurr.

Reid, G. (2003) *Dyslexia: A Practitioner's Handbook*. Chichester: Wiley.

Reid, G. (2004) *Dyslexia: A Complete Guide for Parents*. Chichester: Wiley.

Reid, G. (2007) *Motivating Learners in the Classroom*. London: Sage.

Reid, G. (2009) *Dyslexia: A Practitioners Handbook* (4th ed.). Chichester: Wiley.

Reid, G., Deponio, P. & Davidson-Petch, L. (2004) *Scotland-wide Audit of Education Authority Early Years Policies and Provision Regarding Specific Learning Difficulties (SpLD) and Dyslexia*. Edinburgh: SEED.

Reid, G. & Kirk, J. (2001) *Dyslexia in Adults*. Chichester: Wiley.

Reid, G. and Green, S. (2011) *100 Ideas for Supporting Children with Dyslexia* (2nd edition). Continuum Publications, London

Reynolds, D., Nicolson, R. I. & Hambly, H. (2003) Evaluation of an exercise-based treatment for children with reading difficulties. *Dyslexia, 9*(1): 48–71.

Richardson, A. J. (2001) *Dyslexia, Dyspraxia and ADHD – Can Nutrition Help?* Paper presented at 4th Cambridge Conference, Helen Arkell Dyslexia Association, March.

Richardson, A. J. & Puri, B. K. (2000) The potential role of fatty acids in attention deficit/hyperactivity disorder (ADHD). *Prostaglandins Leukotr Essent Fatty Acids, 63*: 79–87.

Riddick, B. (1995) Dyslexia: Dispelling the myths. *Disability and Society, 10*(4): 457–473.

Riddick, B., Farmer, M. & Sterling, C. (1997) *Students and Dyslexia: Growing up with a Specific Learning Difficulty*. London: Whurr.

Riddick, B., Wolfe, J. & Lumsdon, D. (2002) *Dyslexia: A Practical Guide for Teachers and Parents*. London: David Fulton.

Robertson, J. & Bakker, D. J. (2002) The balance model of reading and dyslexia. In G. Reid & J. Wearmouth (Eds.), *Dyslexia and Literacy: Theory and Practice*. Chichester: Wiley.

Rose, J. (2006) *Independent Review of the Teaching of Early Reading: Final Report*. http://www.standards.dfes.gov.uk/phonics/report.pdf.

Rose, J. (2009) *Identifying and Teaching Children and Young People with Dyslexia and Literacy Difficulties*. London: Department for Children, Schools and Families.

Scott, L, McWinnie, H. Taylor, L., Stevenson, N., Irons, P., Lewis, E., Evans, M., Evans, B. & Wilkins, A. (2002) Coloured overlays in schools: Orthoptic and optometric findings. *Ophthal. Physiol. Opt., 22*: 156–165.

Scottish Executive (2004) Education (Additional Support for Learning) (Scotland) Act, Edinburgh: HMSO.

Shankweiler, D. & Fowler, A. E. (2004) Questions people ask about the role of phonological processes in learning to reading. *Reading and Writing, 17*, 483–515.

Sharma, M. (1989) *How Children Learn Mathematics*. Interview. London.

Silver, L. (2001) Controversial therapies. *Perspectives*, Summer.

Singleton, C. H. (1996) *COPS 1 Cognitive Profiling System*. Nottingham: Chameleon Educational Ltd (now Beverley, East Yorkshire: U.K. Lucid Creative Ltd).

Singleton, C. H. (2002) Dyslexia: Cognitive factors and implications for literacy. In G. Reid & J. Wearmouth (Eds.) *Dyslexia and Literacy: Theory and Practice*. London: Wiley.

Singleton, C. H. (2003) Cognitive factors and implications for literacy. In G. Reid & J. Wearmouth (Eds.), *Dyslexia and Literacy Theory and Practice*. Chichester: Wiley.

Singleton, C. H., Horne, J. K. & Thomas, K. V. (2002) *Lucid Adult Dyslexia Screening (LADS)*. Beverley, East Yorkshire: U.K. Lucid Creative Ltd.

Smith, F. (1973) *Psycholinguistics and Reading*. New York: Holt, Rinehart & Winston.

Smith, F. (1985) *Reading*. Cambridge: Cambridge University Press.

Smits-Engelsman, B. C. M. & Van Galen, G. P. (1997) Dysgraphia in children: Lasting psychomotor deficiency of transient developmental delay? *Journal of Experimental Child Psychology*, *67*: 164–184.

Smythe, I., Everatt, J. & Salter, R. (Eds.) (2004) *The International Book of Dyslexia* (2nd ed.). London: Wiley.

Snow, C. E. & Juel, C. (2005) Teaching children to read: What do we know about how to do it? In M. J. Snowling & C. Hulme (Eds.), *The Science of Reading: A Handbook*. Oxford: Blackwell.

Snowling, M. J. (2000) *Dyslexia*. (2nd ed.). Oxford: Blackwell.

Snowling, M. J. & Hulme, C. (2003) A critique of claims that DDAT is an effective treatment for children with reading difficulties – 'Lies, damned lies and (inappropriate) statistics?' *Dyslexia*, *9*(2): 127–133.

The Southern Education Foundation (2007) *Pre-Kindergarten in the South: The Region's Comparative Advantage in Education*. Atlanta, GA.

The Southern Education Foundation (2008) *Time to Lead Again: The Promise of Georgia Pre-K*. Atlanta, GA.

Special Educational Needs and Disability Act (2001) London: HMSO.

Stainthorp, R. (1995) Some effects of context on reading. In P. Owen & P. Pumfrey (Eds.), *Emergent and Developing Reading: Messages for Teachers*. London: Falmer Press.

Stein, J. (2002) *The Sensorimotor Basis of Learning Disabilities*. Paper presented at New Developments in Research and Practice Conference, County Hall, Durham, 14 June.

Stein, J. (2003) Evaluation of an exercise based treatment for children with reading difficulties. *Dyslexia*. *9*(2): 124–126.

Stein, J. (2004) Dyslexia genetics. In G. Reid & A. Fawcett (Eds.), *Dyslexia in Context, Research, Policy and Practice*. London: Whurr.

Stein, J. (2008) The neurobiological basis of dyslexia. In G. Reid, A. Fawcett, F. Manis & L. Siegel, *The Sage Dyslexia Handbook*. London: Sage.

Tannock, R (1976) Doman-Delacato method for treating brain injured children. *Physiotherapy*, *28*(4).

Task Force on Dyslexia in the Republic of Ireland (2001) Dublin: Government Publications. http://www.irlgov.ie/educ/pub.htm.

Taylor, M. F. (2002) *Stress-induced Atypical Brain Lateralization in Boys with Attention-Deficit/Hyperactivity Disorder. Implications for Scholastic*

Performance. Unpublished PhD thesis. Perth: University of Western Australia.

Taylor, M. F. (1998) *An Evaluation of the Effects of Educational Kinesiology (Brain Gym©) on Children Manifesting ADHD in a South African Context.* Unpublished M.Phil dissertation, University of Exeter.

Terras, M., Minnis, H., Mackenzie, E. & Thomson, L. (2004) *'I feel very, very small': Reflections on Living with Dyslexia.* Poster presentation. 6th International BDA Conference, Warwick, March.

TES (2010) Framework for Inclusion Assessment toolkit. *Times Education Supplement, 27* August.

Tunmer, W. E. & Chapman, J. (1996) A developmental model of dyslexia. Can the construct be saved? *Dyslexia, 2*(3): 179–189.

Tunmer, W. E. & Chapman, J. W. (2006) Metalinguistic abilities, phonological recoding skills, and the use of sentence context in beginning reading development: A longitudinal study. In R. M. Joshi & P. G. Aaron (Eds.), *Handbook of Orthography and Literacy.* Mahwah, NJ: Lawrence Erlbaum.

Tunmer W. E. & Greaney, K. T. (2008) Reading intervention research: An integrative framework. In G. Reid, A. Fawcett, F. Manis & L. Siegel (Eds.), *The Sage Dyslexia Handbook.* London: Sage.

Turner, M. (1991) Finding out. *Support for Learning, 6*(3): 99–102.

UNESCO (1994) Salamanca Statement, Spain.

US Department of Education (2000) Office of Vocational and Adult Education, Division of Adult Education and Literacy, *Learning Disabilities and Spanish-Speaking Adult Populations: The Beginning of a Process.* Washington, DC.

US Department of Education (2003) Office of Special Education and Rehabilitative Services (OSERS) *Longitudinal Study of the Vocational Rehabilitation Services Program Final Report 2: VR Services and Outcomes Rehabilitation Services Administration,* Chapter IV: pp. 4–7. Washington, DC (May), Contract No. HR92022001.

US Government (2001) Full Funding of the Individuals with Disabilities Education Act.

US Government (2001) Reauthorization of the Elementary and Secondary Education Act.

US Government (2001) No Child Left Behind Act, Washington, DC.

Vellutino, F. R., Fletcher, J. D., Snowling, M. & Scanlon, D. M. (2004) Specific reading disability (dyslexia): What have we learned from the last four decades? *Journal of Child Psychology and Psychiatry 45*(1): 2–40.

Weedon, C. & Reid, G. (2003) *Special Needs Assessment Profile.* London: Hodder & Stoughton.

Welch, A. R. & Freebody, P. (2002) Explanations of the current international literacy crises. In J. Soler, J. Wearmouth & G. Reid (Eds.), *Contextualising Difficulties in Literacy Development-Exploring Politics, Culture, Ethnicity and Ethics*. London: Routledge/Falmer.

West, T. G. (1991, second edition 1997) *In the Mind's Eye. Visual Thinkers, Gifted People with Learning Difficulties, Computer Images and the Ironies of Creativity*. Buffalo, NY: Prometheus Books.

Wilkins, A. J., Jeanes, J. R., Pumfrey, P. D. & Laskier, M. (1996) *Rate of Reading Test R: Its Reliability, and its Validity in the Assessment of the Effects of Coloured Overlays*. MRC Applied Psychology Unit, 15 Chaucer Road, Cambridge.

Wilkins, A. (2003) *Reading Through Colour. How Colour Filters Can Reduce Reading Difficulty, Eye Strain and Headaches*. Chichester: Wiley.

Wise, B., W., Ring, J. & Olson, R. (1999) Training phonological awareness with and without explicit attention to articulation. *Journal of Experimental Child Psychology, 72*: 271–304.

Wolf, M. (1996) *The Double-Deficit Hypothesis for the Developmental Dyslexics*. Paper read at the 47th Annual Conference of the Orton Dyslexia Society, November, Boston, MA.

Wray, D. (2006) Developing critical literacy: A priority for the 21st century. *The Journal of Reading, Writing and Literacy, 1*(1), April: 19–34.

Wray, D. (2009) Extending literacy skills – Issues for practice. In G. Reid, G. Elbeheri, J. Everatt, J. Wearmouth & D. Knight (Eds.), *The Routledge Dyslexia Companion*. London: Routledge.

Wright, H. C. & Sugden, D. A. (1996) The nature of developmental disorder. *Adapted Physical Activity Quarterly, 13*(4): 357–371.

Young, G. & Browning, J. (2004) Learning disability/dyslexia and employment. In G. Reid & A. Fawcett (Eds.), *Dyslexia in Context, Research, Policy and Practice*. London: Whurr.

Zeigler, J. C. & Goswami, U. (2005) Reading acquisition, developmental dyslexia, and skilled reading across languages: A psycholinguistic grain size theory. *Psychological Bulletin, 131*: 3–29.

Index

Dyslexia: A Complete Guide for Parents and Those Who Help Them, Second Edition. Gavin Reid.
© 2011 John Wiley & Sons, Ltd. Published 2011 by John Wiley & Sons, Ltd.